A GIFT FOR

_____

FROM

_____

DATE

_____

JESUS LISTENS

JESUS LISTENS

365 PRAYERS FOR KIDS

SARAH YOUNG

Adapted by Tama Fortner

Edited by Kris Bearss

Tommy
NELSON

An imprint of Thomas Nelson

Jesus Listens: 365 Prayers for Kids

© 2022 Sarah Young

Tommy Nelson, PO Box 141000, Nashville, TN 37214

Published in Nashville, Tennessee, by Tommy Nelson. Tommy Nelson is an imprint of Thomas Nelson. Thomas Nelson is a registered trademark of HarperCollins Christian Publishing, Inc.

Tommy Nelson titles may be purchased in bulk for educational, business, fund-raising, or sales promotional use. For information, please email SpecialMarkets@ThomasNelson.com.

Unless otherwise noted, Scripture quotations are taken from the International Children's Bible®. Copyright © 1986, 1988, 1999, 2015 by Thomas Nelson. Used by permission. All rights reserved.

Scripture quotations marked AMPC are taken from the Amplified ® Bible (AMPC). Copyright © 1954, 1958, 1962, 1964, 1965, 1987 by The Lockman Foundation. Used by permission. www.Lockman.org

Scripture quotations marked CEB are taken from the Common English Bible. Copyright © 2011 by Common English Bible.

Scripture quotations marked ERV are taken from the Easy-to-Read Version. Copyright © 2006 by Bible League International.

Scripture quotations marked ESV are taken from the ESV ® Bible (The Holy Bible, English Standard Version ®). Copyright © 2001 by Crossway, a publishing ministry of Good News Publishers. All rights reserved.

Scripture quotations marked GNT are taken from the Good News Translation in Today's English Version—Second Edition. Copyright © 1992 by American Bible Society. Used by permission.

Scripture quotations marked HCSB are taken from the Holman Christian Standard Bible® Copyright © 1999, 2000, 2002, 2003, 2009 by Holman Bible Publishers. Used with permission by Holman Bible Publishers. Used by permission. HCSB® is a federally registered trademark of Holman Bible Publishers.

Scripture quotations marked THE MESSAGE are taken from The Message. Copyright © 1993, 2002, 2018 by Eugene H. Peterson. Used by permission of NavPress. All rights reserved. Represented by Tyndale House Publishers, a Division of Tyndale House Ministries.

Scripture quotations marked NASB are taken from the New American Standard Bible®, Copyright © 1960, 1962, 1963, 1968, 1971, 1973, 1975, 1977, 1985 by The Lockman Foundation. Used by permission. www.Lockman.org

Scripture quotations marked NCV are taken from the New Century Version®. Copyright © 2005 by Thomas Nelson. Used by permission. All rights reserved.

Scripture quotations marked NET are taken from the Net Bible® copyright ©1996–2017 by Biblical Studies Press, L.L.C. http://netbible.com. All rights reserved.

Scripture quotations marked NIRV are taken from the Holy Bible, New International Reader's Version®, NIrV®. Copyright © 1995, 1996, 1998, 2014 by Biblica, Inc.® Used by permission of Zondervan. All rights reserved worldwide. www.zondervan.com. The "NIrV" and "New International Reader's Version" are trademarks registered in the United States Patent and Trademark Office by Biblica, Inc.®

Scripture quotations marked NIV are taken from the Holy Bible, New International Version®, NIV® Copyright © 1973, 1978, 1984 by Biblica, Inc.® Used by permission of Zondervan. All rights reserved worldwide. www.zondervan.com. The "NIV" and "New International Version" are trademarks registered in the United States Patent and Trademark Office by Biblica, Inc.®

Scripture quotations marked NKJV are taken from the New King James Version®. Copyright © 1982 by Thomas Nelson. Used by permission. All rights reserved.

Scripture quotations marked NLT are taken from the Holy Bible, New Living Translation. Copyright © 1996, 2004, 2015 by Tyndale House Foundation. Used by permission of Tyndale House Ministries, Carol Stream, Illinois 60188. All rights reserved.

Scripture quotations marked TLB are taken from The Living Bible. Copyright © 1971. Used by permission of Tyndale House Publishers, a Division of Tyndale House Ministries, Carol Stream, Illinois 60188. All rights reserved.

ISBN 978-1-4002-3665-7 (audiobook)
ISBN 978-1-4002-3664-0 (eBook)
ISBN 978-1-4002-3663-3 (HC)

Library of Congress Cataloging-in-Publication Data

Names: Young, Sarah, 1946- author. | Fortner, Tama, 1969- author. | Bearss, Kris, editor.

Title: Jesus listens : 365 prayers for kids / Sarah Young ; adapted by Tama Fortner edited by Kris Bearss.

Description: Nashville, Tennese : Thomas Nelson, 2022. | Audience: Ages 8-12 | Summary: "The newest 365-day devotional from Sarah Young, author of Jesus Calling, is now available for children. This brand-new daily devotional includes a prayer for every day of the year. Take your children on a journey to develop a meaningful prayer life and a closer relationship with God"-- Provided by publisher.

Identifiers: LCCN 2022011188 (print) | LCCN 2022011189 (ebook) | ISBN 9781400236633 (hardcover) | ISBN 9781400236640 (epub)

Subjects: LCSH: Children--Prayers and devotions--Juvenile literature. | Devotional calendars--Juvenile literature.

Classification: LCC BV265 .Y67 2022 (print) | LCC BV265 (ebook) | DDC 242/.82--dc23/eng/20220414

LC record available at https://lccn.loc.gov/2022011188

LC ebook record available at https://lccn.loc.gov/2022011189

Printed in China

22 23 24 25 DSC 6 5 4 3 2 1

Mfr: RRD / Dongguan / October 2022 / PO # 12149118

I dedicate Jesus Listens: 365 Prayers for Kids to every kid who reads this book. I'm praying that God will use the daily prayers in this book to help you know Him better.

If you have not yet asked Jesus to forgive all your sins and be your Savior, I hope you will do that very soon. That's the most important decision you will ever make!

I'll be praying that you will trust Jesus as your Savior and as your very best Friend. Jesus is the Friend who will never let you down. Best friends like to talk to each other, and Jesus wants you to talk to Him. That's what praying is all about!

INTRODUCTION

Jesus invites us to pour out our hearts to Him—telling Him everything we're thinking and feeling and all that's happening in our lives. We can ask Him any question, trust Him with any secret, and share with Him any joy. All because Jesus listens to every word we say. That's why I have called this book *Jesus Listens*. Because that is what He does.

In my other books, I wrote as if Jesus were talking to you. But in this book, each devotion is a prayer—written as if *you* are talking to *Him*. There are prayers about peace, joy, hope, and most of all, about the never-ending Love that Jesus has for you. My hope is that you'll use these prayers as the beginning of your own conversations with Him.

When you pour out your heart to Jesus, you can trust that He will always answer you. Sometimes His answers will be exactly what you hoped. Other times, they won't be. But His answers will always lead you closer to Him.

Jesus Listens has prayers for every day of the year. As you pray through these prayers each day, remember that I'm praying for you. But the most important thing to remember is that Jesus is with you, listening to all your prayers!

Sarah Young

JANUARY

"I know what I have planned for you,"
says the Lord. "I have good plans for
you. I don't plan to hurt you. I plan to
give you hope and a good future."

—Jeremiah 29:11

A BRAND-NEW BEGINNING

This is the day that the Lord has made.
Let us rejoice and be glad today!
—Psalm 118:24

Dear Jesus,

It's a brand-new year, and I'm so thankful I get to live it with You. I know You'll be working on me and making me more like You. You are *going to do new things* in my life, and I can't wait to see what they are! I *don't have to think about the past.* I don't have to worry about mistakes I've made or things I wish had done or said. Today is a fresh start!

There is no end to Your creativity. After all, You paint a different sunset every single day. So I wonder what creative surprises You have planned for me.

This is the day that You have made. You have carefully filled it with so many good and wonderful things—both big and small. My heart is full of reasons to *rejoice and be glad!*

As I walk through this day, I will be looking for all the blessings You've hidden for me. Every time I find one, I will say, "Thank You, God!" Praising You helps me stay close to You. It also reminds me that *You fill my life with joy.*

In Your amazing Name, Jesus, *Amen*

READ ON YOUR OWN

ISAIAH 43:18–19; PSALM 118:24; PSALM 16:11

ALL YOURS!

The everlasting God is your place of safety.
His arms will hold you up forever.
—Deuteronomy 33:27

Dear Jesus,

I want to be all Yours! I really do. But it's not easy for me to depend on You for everything I need. Sometimes it feels like I'm trying to walk across a tightrope. When I do things my way without talking to You, or when I try to take care of things by myself, I feel all wobbly. It's like I'm about to fall right off that tightrope! But even if that happens, I know *Your arms* will catch me like a safety net.

Please teach me to keep looking to You for help—not to myself or the world around me. You have this amazing ability to be with me both right now and in the future, showing me which way to go. When I close my eyes and listen, I can almost hear You whispering, "Follow Me."

Lord, *I know that nothing—not death, not life, not angels, not ruling spirits, nothing now, nothing in the future, no powers, nothing above us, nothing below us, or anything else in the whole world will ever be able to separate me from Your Love and Presence.*

In Your precious Name, Jesus, *Amen*

READ ON YOUR OWN

DEUTERONOMY 33:27; PROVERBS 16:9; ROMANS 8:38–39

YOUR LOVE NEVER FAILS

Long ago the Lord said to Israel: "I have loved you, my people, with an everlasting love. With unfailing love I have drawn you to myself."
—Jeremiah 31:3 NLT

Dear Jesus,

In the Bible, You remind me, *"I have loved you with an everlasting Love. I have drawn you to Myself with unfailing Love."* That means You knew me and loved me before I was born—even before the beginning of the earth and time! Those are Your words, Lord, so I know they are true.

There will still be some tough days. I might feel alone and lost. I might wonder what I'm supposed to do and why. But You are always with me, ready to help. And when the time is just right, You show me that You are by my side.

Your Presence is a light that chases away the darkness. Sometimes You use a Bible verse or a song. Sometimes it's a friend who says just what I need to hear. Sometimes You simply *wrap me up in a coat of Your goodness* and sing a song of Love to me that never ends. I want to sing with You, Jesus. Teach me to use my voice to help other people *come out of the darkness and step into Your wonderful Light.*

In Your bright, shining Name, Jesus, *Amen*

READ ON YOUR OWN

JEREMIAH 31:3 NLT; ISAIAH 61:10; 1 PETER 2:9

YOU KNOW ME!

The Lord's delight is in those who fear him,
those who put their hope in his unfailing love.
—Psalm 147:11 NLT

Dear Jesus,

You know me! Not just my name or what I look like, but absolutely everything about me. You know what I'm thinking and feeling—and You understand. You even see the things I try to hide. Yet You still love me with a perfect *Love that never, ever fails.* The closer I get to You, the more I become the person You made me to be.

Help me be real with You, Jesus. I don't have to pretend to have all the answers when I'm talking to You—because You already know all my questions! I don't have to pretend to be perfect either, because You know all my mistakes. Even the mistakes I don't know I've made!

Lord, *search through everything in my heart and my thoughts. Point out anything in me that displeases You.* I know there are things I need to change, but I also know You'll help me. So I'm going to open up my heart to You and soak up Your never-ending Love. I'm going to let this Love fill me up until I'm so full that it spills out of me in joy-filled praise. Thank You for knowing me and loving me forever!

In Your loving Name, Jesus, *Amen*

READ ON YOUR OWN

1 CORINTHIANS 13:12; PSALM 147:11 NLT; PSALM 139:23–24 NLT

SOMETHING GOOD OUT OF MY TROUBLES

You will have many kinds of troubles. But when these things happen, you should be very happy.
—James 1:2

Dear Jesus,

The Bible tells me *You are able to make everything work together for the good of those who love You.* You can even bring something good out of my troubles! Every problem can teach me something if I trust You to take care of it. But I'm learning that if I try to fix my problems without You, they grow bigger and tougher and harder to handle.

Help me not to see my problems as bad things. Help me instead to see them as friends—friends that You'll use to make me more like You. The best way to make friends with my troubles is to thank You for them. It's not easy, but that's when I can see the blessings hiding behind the problems—like meeting new friends when I have to change schools.

Lord, please keep training me to trust You with my problems. As I tell You about them, I imagine putting them in Your hands. Once I leave them with You, I *don't have to worry about them* anymore. You have everything under control! And the *peace You give me is so big and great that I can't understand it. Thank You!*

In Your wonderful Name, Jesus, *Amen*

READ ON YOUR OWN

JAMES 1:2; ROMANS 8:28 NLT; PHILIPPIANS 4:6–7

SHOW ME YOUR WAYS

Lord, tell me your ways. Show me how to live. Guide me in your truth.
—Psalm 25:4–5

Dear Jesus,

I want to learn to *thank You for everything*—including my problems. As soon as I see trouble coming, that's the time to start talking to You about it. I'll start by *thanking You* for listening to my prayers. Thanking You helps me shake off worry and fear. Problems don't seem nearly as big when I remember how powerful You are! Then I'll ask You to show me what to do. Help me trust that *Your* way is the best way to deal with my problem. Show me whether You want me to face it head-on or to set it aside for a while and keep praying about it.

I have to admit that most of the things I worry about aren't even problems I have to deal with today. They're things that *might* happen tomorrow, next week, next month, or even next year. Or they might not ever happen at all! When I worry like that, Jesus, please take those thoughts from my mind and put them in the future, where they belong. Then show me what You want me to do today so I can live close to You and enjoy *Your Peace*.

In Your perfect Name, Jesus, *Amen*

READ ON YOUR OWN

EPHESIANS 5:20; PHILIPPIANS 4:6; PSALM 25:4–5; JOHN 14:27

I *CAN* BE HAPPY

I have learned the secret of being happy at
any time in everything that happens.
—Philippians 4:12

Dear Jesus,

I love to *worship You*. I *worship You because You are holy* and good. You made this amazing world that's all around me, and it shows me how wonderful You are. Just seeing the clouds in the sky and feeling the wind on my face makes me smile. You're the Great Artist! And You are working in me, making me lovely inside too. You're clearing out all the selfishness and pride to make more room for Your Spirit. Help me cooperate with You as You're working to change me. I want to get rid of the things that make You sad.

I know You're training me to trust in You—not in the *stuff* I have. Those things can get lost. Or somebody can steal them or break them. Whether I have a lot of stuff or just a little, You know exactly what I need, and You have promised to give it to me. Sometimes You give me even more than I hoped for!

I shouldn't trust in what I can do on my own either. That doesn't always work out for the best. No matter what's happening in my life, *I can be happy* because You are with me and You do what is best for me.

In Your beautiful Name, Jesus, *Amen*

READ ON YOUR OWN

PSALM 29:2; PSALM 27:4; PHILIPPIANS 4:19; PHILIPPIANS 4:12

NOTHING IS IMPOSSIBLE FOR YOU

Jesus looked at them and said, "For men this is impossible. But for God all things are possible."
—Matthew 19:26

Dear Jesus,

I messed up, and now I can't stop thinking about it. Please help me to let it go—*forget what happened and not think about it anymore.* I can learn from the past but I can't change it, no matter how hard I try. So I'll spend time with You and *tell You all my problems.* I know *You watch over me and protect me.* I can trust You *all the time.*

Simply saying, "I trust You, Lord," helps me remember that You are taking care of me. I can say it when I wake up in the morning and before I go to bed at night. I can say it every time something starts to worry or upset me. Just saying that I trust You blows away the dark clouds of fear and brightens up my day.

You are always doing *new things* in my life, so I'm going to be on the lookout today, watching for You. Please open my eyes to see what You're up to. And show me all the chances I have to serve You.

I'm learning that You can shine Your Light into even the darkest day. *With You all things are possible!*

In Your awesome Name, Jesus, *Amen*

READ ON YOUR OWN

ISAIAH 43:18–19; PSALM 62:8; MATTHEW 19:26

YOU MAKE ME STRONG

He is the God who makes me strong,
who makes my pathway safe.
—Psalm 18:32 GNT

Dear Jesus,

You are the One who makes me strong. That means I can come to You just the way I am: When I'm feeling weak. When I've made mistakes. When I've messed up. I don't have to pretend to be perfect. I can tell You all about the things I've done wrong and ask You to forgive me. Then You take away my sins and send them *as far from me as the east is from the west.*

I am like a *clay jar* full of worries and mistakes and fears. But You use all those things that make me feel weak to teach me to depend on You. When I give You my weaknesses and struggles, You fill me up with *Your power* instead.

You also travel with me all through my day, *making my path safe.* You protect me from dangers and remind me not to worry about the future. You are right beside me, every step I take. Help me to keep talking to You and trusting You to show me the very best way to live. I want to live for You, Jesus!

In Your strong Name, Jesus, *Amen*

READ ON YOUR OWN

PSALM 18:32 GNT; PSALM 103:12;
2 CORINTHIANS 4:7; 2 CORINTHIANS 12:9

TOGETHER WITH YOU

"Don't worry, because I am with you.
Don't be afraid, because I am your God."
—Isaiah 41:10

Dear Jesus,

Please help me learn to be thankful for the hard days. Because when everything is going my way, I may not learn as much about myself or about You. But on tough days, when I'm facing a challenge, I can learn to trust You more as You help me tackle my troubles. There's nothing that we can't handle *together*! I know this because the Bible promises this is true. You are always with me, and You've never let me down.

When I think about the tough days I've had in the past, I can see that You helped me through each and every one. When a new problem pops up, though, I sometimes wonder if You'll help me *this* time. I need to toss those kinds of thoughts and doubts out the window. Things in my life may always be changing, but *You never change*. It's by *Your power that I live and move and exist*. Because of You, I can laugh and play, help and love. I am Your child. And because You are always close to me, always loving and watching over me, I can get through the toughest days.

In Your powerful Name, Jesus, *Amen*

READ ON YOUR OWN

ISAIAH 41:10; PSALM 102:27; PHILIPPIANS 4:13; ACTS 17:27–28

I LOVE TALKING TO YOU

Continue praying and keep alert. And when
you pray, always thank God.
—Colossians 4:2

Dear Jesus,

You are training me to talk to You—not just once a day or once in a while, but all the time. Sometimes it's with words, sometimes it's with thoughts, and sometimes it's just in my heart. The more I talk to You, the more I *love* talking to You.

When everything is still and quiet, it's easy to find You and tell You what's on my mind. But other times it's not so easy—when homework piles up, or when I have practices and chores to do. Even fun things, like hanging out with friends and taking trips to my grandparents' house, can make it harder to find a quiet place and talk with You. Teach me to *search for You* in the busy times. You promise that *when I really, really search for You, I will find You!*

Thank You, Jesus, that You want to be found! And thank You for listening when I tell You all about my day and my feelings. You're never too busy, and You never have other things You need to do. Even if my troubles don't completely go away, I feel better just knowing I've told You about them. I know You'll take care of me.

In Your great Name, Jesus, *Amen*

READ ON YOUR OWN

COLOSSIANS 4:2; JEREMIAH 29:13; PROVERBS 3:6; GALATIANS 5:25

THE GREATEST ADVENTURE

A person may think up plans.
But the Lord decides what he will do.
—Proverbs 16:9

Dear Jesus,

I'm on an exciting adventure with You! Some days are easy and fun. Other days are filled with challenges and troubles to get through. But each step is good because I'm with You. Help me learn everything You want to teach me as we travel together. And help me be open to trying new things when You ask me to.

I know *You will give me everything I need* to face any challenge that might pop up. So I don't want to waste one minute worrying about what *might* happen. That would be like saying I don't believe that You'll give me what I need when I need it.

I'll *never stop praying* and asking You to guide me, Jesus! That's how much I want to make the best choices on our adventure together. You know everything—You see the blessings and the troubles that are coming. Sometimes I get busy *thinking up plans* about what I want to do, but *You are the One who really decides what I will do*. And I trust that Your plan will always be the best.

In Your wise Name, Jesus, *Amen*

READ ON YOUR OWN

PHILIPPIANS 4:19; DEUTERONOMY 29:29;
1 THESSALONIANS 5:17; PROVERBS 16:9

A NEW ME

If anyone belongs to Christ, then he is made new. The
old things have gone; everything is made new!
—2 Corinthians 5:17

Dear Jesus,

Thank You for coming to earth! *Because You rose from the dead, I have the hope of a new life with You—a living hope.* And that's not all! When I decide to follow You, trusting You as my Savior and my God, *You make me into a new person.* You make me more like You. You even adopt me into Your royal family. That makes *me* royal too! And if that wasn't enough, You have *blessings in heaven that You are keeping safe for me. They will never be destroyed or spoiled. They will never lose their beauty.*

But being made into a new person doesn't happen right away. You're going to be working on my heart for a long time—my whole life! Sometimes it will be hard, but I know You're helping me get ready to spend forever with You.

Please give me the courage I need to follow You, even when others are not. And please open my eyes to see all the wonderful things You're doing in my life.

In Your magnificent Name, Jesus, *Amen*

READ ON YOUR OWN

1 PETER 1:3–4; 2 CORINTHIANS 5:17; EPHESIANS 4:22–24; ROMANS 6:4

UNDER YOUR WINGS

Protect me as a bird protects its young under its wings.

—Psalm 61:4

Dear Jesus,

Help me to *trust You and not be afraid*. There are so many things that are out of my control—so many things that are mixed-up and a little crazy. I like it better when I know what's going to happen. Whenever my life feels out of control, I just want to run to You. And that's the very best thing I can do! So please *protect me and hide me under Your wings—just like a mama bird protects her babies.* I know I am safe with You.

The crazier things get in my life, the tighter I need to hold on to You. You promise in the Bible that You will use these times to help me *change and grow to be more like You.* Just show me what I need to do, Lord. And help me not to make the tough times worse by *worrying about what might happen tomorrow.* Because it might not happen at all! Remind me to take a deep breath and relax. As I calm down, it's easier to trust that You'll help me deal with any troubles that come my way—*when* they come my way.

In Your sheltering Name, Jesus, *Amen*

READ ON YOUR OWN

ISAIAH 12:2 NLT; PSALM 61:2–4; MATTHEW 6:34; 2 CORINTHIANS 3:18

THANKFUL PRAYERS

Pray at all times.
—1 Thessalonians 5:17 GNT

Dear Jesus,

As You and I walk through this day together, please teach me to thank You all day long. This is one way I can learn to *pray at all times,* just like You ask me to. I do want to talk to You more and more, but I admit that sometimes I forget. That's why I need to keep learning to be thankful for everything. Even my troubles can help me pray more if I thank You for them.

When I remember to say thank You, it reminds me to pray about other things. Thanking You for my breakfast reminds me to thank You for my parents, who made it, and for our house, where I eat it. The more I thank You, the easier it is to keep talking to You. And if I'm busy thanking You, I don't have time to worry or complain!

With a heart full of gratitude and thanksgiving, *I can live closer to You.* Please fill me up with so much *joy and peace* that they spill out in my smile—and in praise to You. I love being with You, Jesus!

In Your joyful Name, Jesus, *Amen*

READ ON YOUR OWN

1 THESSALONIANS 5:16–18; JAMES 4:8; ROMANS 15:13

I WILL SING TO YOU!

Come into his city with songs of thanksgiving.
Come into his courtyards with songs of praise.
Thank him, and praise his name.

—Psalm 100:4–5

Dear Jesus,

Please help me live with Your Joy in my heart, even when I'm struggling. Help me see that there is always something to sing about—like the fact that You are by my side every minute of every day, guiding me and loving me.

Sometimes I pray and pray for the things I think I need. Then I wait for You to answer. But when You don't answer the way I want, I admit that I get a little sad and discouraged. It's easy to think that maybe I've done something wrong and that's why You're not answering my prayers the way I'd hoped. Anytime I start to think like that, help me remember that You always do what's best for me and You're always taking care of me. I'm so thankful that I can count on You!

Nothing chases away my sadness faster than thanking You and singing praises to You. Your Word tells me to *come to You with songs of thanksgiving and praise*—and that's exactly what I will do!

In Your dependable Name, Jesus, *Amen*

READ ON YOUR OWN

ISAIAH 40:10; 1 PETER 5:7; PSALM 100:4–5

THE MOST WONDERFUL HUG

The Lord, the Lord, gives me strength and makes me sing.
He has saved me.
—Isaiah 12:2

Dear Jesus,

You make me strong, and You make me want to sing. But today I'm not feeling so great. I'm looking at the big things coming my way in the future, and they look a little scary. I'm afraid I won't be able to handle them. Help me, Lord, to focus on *this* day and the fact that You are right here with me. If those big things do come my way, I trust You to give me the strength to handle them.

When my thoughts wander into the future, please pull me back to right now. *Worrying about tomorrow* is a sign that I'm not trusting You enough. I'm sorry for that. Open my eyes to the joy You're pouring into my life today. I want to be so busy singing Your praises that I don't have time to worry or be upset.

As I fill up my mind with thoughts about You and heaven, the Light of Your Presence wraps around me like the most wonderful hug. *You are the One who saves me*—and that's the best reason to *trust You and not be afraid.*

In Your heavenly Name, Jesus, *Amen*

READ ON YOUR OWN

ISAIAH 12:2; 2 CORINTHIANS 10:5; MATTHEW 6:34; 1 PETER 1:3–4

YOU WILL MAKE EVERYTHING NEW

The One who was sitting on the throne said,
"Look! I am making everything new!"
—Revelation 21:5

Dear Jesus,

I know that I can always talk to You and that You hear my prayers. But I think it's just so amazing that You talk to me too! You use Your Word to tell me things like, *"Look! I am making everything new!"*

Today, I pray that You would open my eyes and show me all the good, new things You are doing in this world. Because honestly, it sometimes seems like I'm surrounded by bad, broken things. The news is filled with terrible stories, people I love get sick, and some kids are just not nice. That's why I can't wait to see how You will keep Your promise to make everything new.

I try to follow You and make things better the way You ask me to—by being kind and helpful and telling people about You. But it doesn't always work. Help me not to get discouraged or to give up when that happens. Instead, please encourage me to keep trying to do my best. Remind me that I still have a great reason to be happy. Because someday You will come again and make everything perfect and new—including me!

In Your glorious Name, Jesus, *Amen*

READ ON YOUR OWN

REVELATION 21:5; PHILIPPIANS 1:21; ROMANS 8:22–23

A SHIELD OF PEACE

Do not worry about anything. But pray and ask God for everything you need. And when you pray, always give thanks.

—Philippians 4:6

Dear Jesus,

Help me to be *full of joy always*, simply because *You are near*. The more time I spend with You, the more I believe that *I can ask You for everything I need*. Thank You, Lord, for meeting my needs and blessing me with *Your Peace*. Your *amazing Peace is so great and powerful that I can't begin to understand it*. It wraps around me like a shield, protecting my heart and my mind from evil.

You promise that Your children are never alone. But the devil likes to make me think I'm all by myself. He tries to stand between You and me like a cloud between the earth and the sun. But just as the sun is still shining on a cloudy day, You are with me even when I feel alone. Help me not to forget that. Remind me that I can fight the devil with Your Word, the Bible. It's like *a living sword, sharp and powerful and always working*. I can read Your Word, think about it, memorize it, even shout it out loud—and that sends the devil running!

Teach me to pray when I'm feeling lonely, trusting that *You are with me always*. Knowing that I can talk with You anytime, in any situation, fills me with joy and peace.

In Your beloved Name, Jesus, *Amen*

READ ON YOUR OWN

PHILIPPIANS 4:4–7; HEBREWS 4:12; MATTHEW 28:20

MY GUIDE

The path of life of the people who are right with God is level.
Lord, you make the way of life smooth for those people.
—Isaiah 26:7

Dear Jesus,

As we walk through this day together, help me keep my eyes on You and trust You to guide me. *Teach me the way You want me to live.*

At times I feel stuck—like there's a gigantic rock in the middle of my path that I can't get around. It might be a problem, a friend who has hurt my feelings, or a really bad day. The thing is, if I just stare at that rock, then all I see is the rock. But if I keep my eyes on You, my Guide, You lead me over the rock or show me how to go around it. Or You might move it out of the way before I get to it.

That's what I have to remember. When I come to a big rock in the road, I need to look at You instead of staring at the problem. Because no matter what is happening—no matter what kind of "rock" drops into my day—You are with me. You are big enough, strong enough, and wise enough to take care of any problems that come my way.

In Your encouraging Name, Jesus, *Amen*

READ ON YOUR OWN

PSALM 16:11; JOHN 10:14–15; ISAIAH 26:7; PROVERBS 3:26

RIGHT HERE
AND RIGHT NOW

Guide me in your truth.
Teach me, my God, my Savior.
I trust you all day long.
—Psalm 25:5

Dear Jesus,

Today is stretching out in front of me like a long, twisting path. As I stare at the path, I start thinking about all the things I have to do, need to do, and want to do. It makes me wonder how I'm ever going to get it all done. My chest feels tight, and it's even a little hard to breathe. But then I remember: *You are always with me.* And even though I can't feel it, *You are holding my hand* and gently *guiding me* through the day. When I remember that, I can relax and breathe more easily.

The next time I think about the day ahead, it's like a soft fog has drifted across my path. I can only see a few steps in front of me. That "fog" is Your way of keeping me from worrying about the future.

Because You are God, You can be in all times—past, present, and future—all at the same time. But here and now is where I am, and it's where I can talk with You. Teach me to keep my thoughts on You and on what is happening in this moment. Thank You for always walking with me.

In Your comforting Name, Jesus, *Amen*

READ ON YOUR OWN

PSALM 73:23–24; PSALM 25:4–5;
1 CORINTHIANS 13:12; 2 CORINTHIANS 5:7 NKJV

WHEN THINGS DON'T GO MY WAY

Be humble under God's powerful hand. Then he
will lift you up when the right time comes.

—1 Peter 5:6

Dear Jesus,

I want to keep remembering—all day long—that You are right beside me. I *want* to see the way You are working and hear Your whispers to me. I *want* to do what You want me to do.

I know Your plans are perfect, and I'm thankful You're in control. This world is a big and scary place, so I need Someone big and powerful to help me through it. But when Your plans aren't the same as mine, I sometimes wish a little bit that I was the one in control.

Instead of trying to pretend that I'm not upset, I can come and talk to You about what I'm feeling. Help me remember that every good thing I have is a gift from You—and that if I *don't* have something, You must have a good reason.

The Bible tells me to praise You even when You take away something I like: *The LORD gave me what I have, and the Lord can take it away. Praise the name of the LORD!* Teach me to be grateful for the blessings You give me. And help me to let go of anything You take away—without ever letting go of Your hand!

In Your precious Name, Jesus, *Amen*

READ ON YOUR OWN

PSALM 139:24; 1 PETER 5:6; JOB 1:21 NLT

NO MATTER WHAT

"Now you are sad. But I will see you again and you will
be happy. And no one will take away your joy."
—John 16:22

Dear Jesus,

Your Word shows me that it's possible to be *afraid and also filled with joy*—all at the same time. That's what the women felt when they visited Your tomb after You died on the cross. They were afraid because the tomb was empty and because an angel suddenly appeared before them. But they were also filled with joy because that angel told them You are alive! You had risen from the grave!

So I know I can be filled with Your Joy even when I'm worried, upset, or afraid—because You are alive and with me at all times! No matter what's happening around me, Your Love and Presence are mine to enjoy today, tomorrow, and forever.

Help me not to let troubles or worries about what *might* happen steal my joy. I need to remember that *nothing in the whole world will ever be able to separate me from Your Love.*

Thank You for always listening to my thoughts and feelings. Talking to You reminds me that I can trust You to take care of me. As I sit here with You, please bless me with Your Joy—something that *no one can take away from me.*

In Your delightful Name, Jesus, *Amen*

READ ON YOUR OWN

MATTHEW 28:8 NIV; ROMANS 8:38–39; JOHN 16:22

A COAT OF GOODNESS

The Lord has covered me with clothes of salvation.
He has covered me with a coat of goodness.

—Isaiah 61:10

Dear Jesus,

When I trust You as my Savior, You wrap me up in Your salvation—like a *coat of goodness* covering me from head to toe. I could never be perfectly good on my own, no matter how hard I try. But You love me so much that You bought clothes of goodness for me with Your own blood on the cross. And then You just give them to me to wear! A completely free gift! I can never say thank You enough, Jesus.

Your coat of goodness is the *clothing of salvation*. Your goodness saves me and lets me be part of Your royal family. That means I need to *act* like I'm part of Your family. And that's where I need You to help me so much. Please teach me to be more like You and to do the things You want me to do.

Sometimes that's hard for me. Sometimes I think about throwing off Your coat so I can do whatever I want—even things I know are wrong. Help me throw off that wrong thinking instead! Then I can feel so comfortable in Your coat of goodness that I never, ever want to take it off!

In Your royal Name, Jesus, *Amen*

READ ON YOUR OWN

ISAIAH 61:10; 2 CORINTHIANS 5:21; EPHESIANS 4:22–24

WHEREVER YOU LEAD ME

We live by believing and not by seeing.
—2 Corinthians 5:7 NLT

Dear Jesus,

I want to follow You wherever You lead. Help me chase after You with all my heart, as fast as I can. I don't know what's going to happen next year, or next week, or even tomorrow. But *You* do! So I will trust You to take care of me. I believe some of Your biggest blessings are just around the corner—out of sight, but still very real. I can't see those good gifts right now, but I know You have them waiting. I just need to keep *believing—even though I can't see* those blessings yet.

Sometimes I feel like You're leading me up a tall, tall mountain. Your hand is guiding me away from all the troubles of this world so I can spend time alone with You. The higher up the mountain I climb, the happier I am just to be in Your Presence. I love being with You! Then, when You lead me back down the mountain and back to all the troubles, I feel ready to face them.

The Light of Your Presence keeps shining on me and helps me bless others with Your Joy.

In Your majestic Name, Jesus, *Amen*

READ ON YOUR OWN

2 CORINTHIANS 5:7 NLT; PSALM 96:6; JOHN 8:12; PSALM 36:9

A LIGHT IN THE DARK

You light a lamp for me.
The LORD, my God, lights up my darkness.
—Psalm 18:28 NLT

Dear Jesus,

You light up the darkness around me—like turning on a lamp in a dark room. Sometimes *when I'm tired and carrying a heavy load* of worry or fear, I feel like my lamp is burning out. It's flickering and sputtering. When this happens, help me remember to call out to You. I can rest in Your Presence while You watch over me. I know You can keep my lamp burning brightly. *You make me strong.*

You are also my Light. Whenever I turn to You, the Light of Your Presence shines on me. Your beauty brightens my life and helps me see all the ways You are working. If I turn away from You and look at the darkness of this world, it's easy to get upset and worried. But even with so much trouble in the world, I can be full of joy because I have You. *You are the Light that shines in the darkness.* I don't have to be afraid.

Instead of thinking about my troubles, I want to trust You with all my heart. I know You are going to change my dark times into bright joy—and I can't wait to see how You do it.

In Your beautiful Name, Jesus, *Amen*

READ ON YOUR OWN

PSALM 18:28 NLT; MATTHEW 11:28; PSALM 18:1; JOHN 1:5

SO MANY BLESSINGS

God, your love is so precious!
—Psalm 36:7

Dear Jesus,

You are the God who created all the little things, like snowflakes and butterfly wings. You are the God who made a universe so huge we can't count all its stars. *And* You are the God who cares so much about every detail of my life that You answer my prayers very carefully! You even care if I stub my toe or I'm feeling thirsty.

The Bible tells me to *never stop praying*. I'm happy that You listen to all my prayers. I'm learning that the more I pray, the more I see Your answers. This helps me trust You more.

I praise You for Your unlimited Love, Power, and Strength. I don't ever have to worry about You running out of anything. I can ask You for whatever I need and then wait joyfully for You to help me. You often give me even more than I ask for!

I'm starting to see how the hard times in my life can be blessings. They teach me to keep going and to keep trusting You. So I open up my heart and my hands to You—ready for all the blessings You have to give me. Thank You, Lord!

In Your great Name, Jesus, *Amen*

READ ON YOUR OWN

1 THESSALONIANS 5:17; PSALM 36:7–8; PSALM 132:15

SAFE WITH YOU

*"My Father gave my sheep to me. He is greater than all, and
no person can steal my sheep out of my Father's hand."*
—John 10:29

Dear Jesus,

Help me remember how safe I am with You. The Bible tells me that You are always with me. Whether I'm happy or sad or even angry, You never leave me. And when I trust You as my Savior, You take away all my sins. That's why You came and died on the cross and then rose to life—so that I could have a way to get to heaven. When I believe in You, *nothing* can stop me from getting there. In heaven, I will see You *face to Face*, and I'll be much, much happier than I've ever been before!

Even in this world, I never have to be apart from You. I can't see You with my eyes, but—by faith—I know and believe that You are right here with me. You promise to walk beside me all through my life, all the way to heaven. That gives me so much peace. Yet I sometimes feel afraid, worried, or lonely. In those times, please remind me that You haven't gone anywhere; You're still by my side. Just remembering Your nearness to me helps chase away those feelings that upset me. Teach me to keep looking for all the ways You show me that You're taking care of me.

In Your wonderful Name, Jesus, *Amen*

READ ON YOUR OWN

JOHN 10:28–29; 2 CORINTHIANS 5:1;
1 CORINTHIANS 13:12 NIV; PSALM 29:11

I WILL TRUST YOU

"If you will be calm and trust me, you will be strong."
—Isaiah 30:15

Dear Jesus,

I'm tired already, and the day has barely started! I keep thinking about the problems I *might* have. And I'm trying to figure out how to escape from trouble that hasn't even happened yet. It's exhausting! Help me to stop doing that, Lord. Help me *find rest* by trusting in You. When I think too much about the future, I forget that *You are with me wherever I go.* And no matter what happens, *You will never leave me.*

I have to admit that I rehearse my problems sometimes. It's almost like practicing for a part in a play. I just keeping running the same troubles through my thoughts, living them over and over again. That's silly! I'm only supposed to experience a problem one time—when it actually happens. Please help me to stop rehearsing my troubles.

Instead of thinking so much about problems, I want to come to You and relax in Your loving Presence. I ask You to give me strength to do whatever I need to do this day. You've promised to *make me strong* as I calmly follow You, so I'm going to *trust You* to do exactly that.

In Your trustworthy Name, Jesus, *Amen*

READ ON YOUR OWN

MATTHEW 11:28–30; JOSHUA 1:5, 9; ISAIAH 30:15

EVERYTHING IS POSSIBLE

Jesus looked straight at them and said, "For people this is impossible. But for God all things are possible."
—Mark 10:27

Dear Jesus,

All things are possible with You! This powerful promise encourages me when I feel stuck in a problem. You are teaching me to *live by what I believe about You and Your power, not just by what I can see with my own eyes.* So even though it might look like the bad guys are winning sometimes, or a problem is too big to be fixed, I'm going to watch and wait for the way You make things right.

Waiting for You is something I need to get better at. I'm thankful I can see so many wonderful things with my eyes. But it's easy for me to get caught up in what I'm seeing and forget about You. I'm sorry, Lord. Help me focus on You and Your promises. Teach me to look at this world and other people the way You do.

When You lived on earth as a man, *Your miracles proved that You are the Son of God.* I'm thankful that You're still doing miracles today! Please fill me up with Your Joy as I watch to see the wonderful ways You are working in this world.

In Your powerful Name, Jesus, *Amen*

READ ON YOUR OWN

MARK 10:27; 2 CORINTHIANS 5:7; MICAH 7:7; JOHN 2:11

YOUR PLANS

People can make many different plans.
But only the Lord's plan will happen.
—Proverbs 19:21

Dear Jesus,

It makes me so happy to know that You're my Friend and You love me. Yet I know You are also *Lord of lords and King of kings*. You are the Ruler of everything!

I already have some plans for my day, but please help me be ready to change them to match *Your* plans. I trust that Your ideas are better than mine. Please show me what You want me to do right now.

I can waste a lot of time thinking about what might happen or what I might need to do sometime in the future. Instead, help me focus on the task in front of me, and on You—the One who is right here with me. Sweep all those other thoughts out of my mind. With them out of the way, there is more room in my mind for thinking about You.

When I finish this task I'm working on right now, then I'll ask You to show me what to do next. I'll trust You to guide me down the perfect path for my life—*a path filled with Your Peace*. Thank You, Lord, for *giving me strength and for blessing me with peace*.

In Your exalted Name, Jesus, *Amen*

READ ON YOUR OWN

REVELATION 17:14; PROVERBS 19:21; LUKE 1:79 NLT; PSALM 29:11

FEBRUARY

Later, Jesus talked to the people again. He said, "I am the light of the world. The person who follows me will never live in darkness. He will have the light that gives life."

—John 8:12

IN THIS PLACE

"I am with you, and I will protect you everywhere you go."
—Genesis 28:15

Dear Jesus,

Your Presence is like a light, and I want it to shine on every part of my life so I can see things the way You see them. Help me remember that You are with me in every situation I face.

I think about Jacob from the Bible. He ran away because his brother, Esau, was angry with him for stealing their father's blessing. Alone in the wilderness, he lay down to sleep with a stone as his only pillow. But he dreamed of heaven and angels and Your promise to be with him always. When he woke up, Jacob said, *"Surely the Lord is in this place. But I did not know it."* Thank You that Jacob's discovery wasn't just for him. It's true for me too! You are in every place I'll ever go.

Help me discover all the ways You're with me—no matter where I am or what's happening. If I ever start to feel far away from You, open my eyes to see that You are with me in this place. I praise You, Jesus, because *nothing in the whole wide world will ever be able to separate me from Your Love and Presence.*

In Your magnificent Name, Jesus, *Amen*

READ ON YOUR OWN
GENESIS 28:11–16; ROMANS 8:39

AWAKE OR ASLEEP

You are my help.
Because of your protection, I sing.
—Psalm 63:7

Dear Jesus,

I know You are alive and working in my life. *You pour out Your Love on me every day, and each night I sing Your songs.* I'm so thankful that You're in charge of everything!

Your Love blesses me in so many ways that I can't count them all. But I'm going to be on the lookout for them, just to see how many I can find during the day. And I'll thank You for each and every one. Help me not to be discouraged or to *give up* when I run into tough situations. Instead, help me see that they are part of living in this world—and what this world needs most is more of *You.*

Your songs fill me with joy all through the night too. I know You are watching over me. If I have trouble sleeping, I can *talk to You* and enjoy simply being with You. I feel wonderfully safe and close to You as *I remember You while I'm lying in bed.*

When I'm awake, You are with me. When I'm asleep, You are with me. You are the God of my whole life!

In Your blessed Name, Jesus, *Amen*

READ ON YOUR OWN

PSALM 42:8 NLT; 2 CORINTHIANS 4:16–17; PSALM 27:8 NLT; PSALM 63:6–7

YOU GIVE ME PEACE

The Lord gives strength to his people.
The Lord blesses his people with peace.
—Psalm 29:11

Dear Jesus,

There are things I can't do, and there are times when I don't know what to do. Whenever I'm weak, please give me Your Peace. Don't let my imagination make things worse. Help me to see my life just as it is. Remind me that You are Lord over everything—including whatever is worrying me today. Instead of wearing myself out by trying to plan my whole day, I can thank You for this day and trust You to guide me through it.

The Bible tells me that You are not only with me but also *for me*, cheering me on. That means I never have to face anything alone! When I feel worried, it's because I'm looking at my problems and forgetting about You. The answer is to *stop looking at the troubles I can see and instead look at what I can't see—You!* I know You can bring me safely through this day and every day.

As I live in the Light of Your Presence, Your Peace shines on me and I stop thinking about all the things I can't do. You've promised that this path we're walking on together is headed for heaven. That wonderful promise helps me be strong today.

In Your comforting Name, Jesus, *Amen*

READ ON YOUR OWN

ROMANS 8:31; 2 CORINTHIANS 4:18 NLT; NUMBERS 6:24–26; PSALM 29:11

SHINING ARMOR

Remove your dark deeds like dirty clothes, and
put on the shining armor of right living.
—Romans 13:12 NLT

Dear Jesus,

Help me to toss away the wrong things I do—as if I'm *taking off dirty clothes*—and *put on the shining armor of living right*. When I turn away from doing wrong and do what is right, it's like I'm wearing Your bright armor. Wrapping myself in Your Light protects my heart from the darkness of this world.

You are the Light that shines on my path and helps me see where to go. I love walking by Your side—living close to You and knowing You are with me. Just as I put on my clothes every morning, I need to *clothe myself with You* each day. That means asking You to protect me, guide me, and help me make good choices. Sometimes I still make bad choices. Please forgive me, Lord. Remind me that You can forgive every one of my sins because You died on the cross for me. Your forgiveness keeps me walking in Your Light.

The Bible promises that *if I confess my sins*—if I tell You all about them—*You will forgive me*. I know *I can trust You to keep that promise and clean away all the wrong things I have done*. Thank You, my Savior!

In Your good and kind Name, Jesus, *Amen*

READ ON YOUR OWN

ROMANS 13:12 NLT; 1 JOHN 1:7; ROMANS 13:14; 1 JOHN 1:9

LIVING IN YOUR LIGHT

I am always with you.
You hold my hand.
—Psalm 73:23 ERV

Dear Jesus,

Some of the things on this earth make me happy for a while. But it's only with You that I can find the kind of joy that lasts forever. You pour so many blessings into my life that they're like raindrops—I can't even count them all. The closer I get to You, the more I see Your blessings and the more thankful I am. This gives me even more joy!

Some days are so filled with sadness, though, that it's hard to remember what joy feels like. That's when I need to *search for You* more than ever. Instead of letting my troubles or my feelings drag me down, I can encourage myself with this truth from the Bible: *You are always with me. You hold my hand. You lead me and give me good advice. And later You will lead me to heaven.* These words of truth guide me as I travel through this world. Help me remember that You are *the Truth*. You are also *the Way*, so I need to follow You. *The Light of Your Presence* is with me always—lighting up the path that's right in front of me.

In Your bright Name, Jesus, *Amen*

READ ON YOUR OWN

PSALM 105:4 NLT; PSALM 73:23–24 ERV; JOHN 14:6; PSALM 89:15

EVERY MORNING

I am overwhelmed with joy in the Lord my God!
—Isaiah 61:10 NLT

Dear Jesus,

Your Love never ends. Your mercies never stop. They are new every morning. I want to believe these comforting words, but I'm having a hard time right now. So much is going wrong! It's like there's no end to the troubles. But I do believe You are here and You are ready to guide me through this day. Your Love and Presence help me keep going.

When everything is going my way, it's easy to trust You. But when problems pop up, trusting You is harder. Help me remember that Your power is always bigger than my problem. You are taking care of me, and You have promised You will never leave me.

As I get dressed, I like to remember that You give me the most wonderful clothes—*clothes of salvation.* You wrap a *robe of goodness* around me that shows I belong to You and I'm on my way to heaven.

You don't have to do these things, Lord. But You choose to because You love me. The greatest gift I could ever receive is the one You give me—the amazing gift of *eternal life* in heaven with You.

In Your glorious Name, Jesus, *Amen*

READ ON YOUR OWN

LAMENTATIONS 3:22–23; ISAIAH 61:10 NLT; JOHN 3:16

JESUS, MY JOY!

The Lord himself will go before you. He will be with you. He will not leave you or forget you. Don't be afraid. Don't worry.
—Deuteronomy 31:8

Dear Jesus,

You are my Joy! I like to say these words and let them bounce around in my brain and then sink deep into my heart. You are the Friend who *will never leave me*. That promise is an endless source of joy for me. Thinking about this wonderful truth helps me see each day as a good day.

No day is truly and completely bad since You are in it. Sure, I have some rough days and plenty of troubles, but I know *You are always with me and You're holding on to my hand*. There is something good in this day—and in every day. And that something is *You!*

Your Love is so precious, I can always rely on it. Your Love promises to protect me just the way a mama bird protects the babies *under her wings*. When my world isn't looking very happy, lead me to *the river of Your Joy*. I want to take a great, big, long drink! No matter what's happening around me—in good times *and* hard times—You are my Joy!

In Your joyful Name, Jesus, *Amen*

READ ON YOUR OWN

DEUTERONOMY 31:8; PSALM 73:23; PSALM 36:7–8

RESCUED!

In the past you were full of darkness, but now you are full of light in the Lord. So live like children who belong to the light.

—Ephesians 5:8

Dear Jesus,

You rescued me because You delight in me. You pour out Your Love on me simply because I am Yours—not because of any great thing I've done. You rescued me from being *a slave to sin* and *led me to Your wide-open, safe place* of salvation.

Even when I'm trying my hardest to be good, I can't be perfect. So You saved me and wrapped me up in Your own perfect goodness. Help me to wear this *clothing of salvation* with joy. Because of Your Love, I can *live as a child who is full of Your Light*—safe and secure in Your goodness.

Salvation is the most wonderful, most precious gift I could ever get, and I'll never stop thanking You for it! When I wake up, I'll say, "Thank You for adopting me into Your royal family!" And before I go to sleep, I'll say, "Thank You for forgiving my sins!"

Lord, I want to live in a way that helps others see You as the loving God who gives wonderful, never-ending Life!

In Your saving Name, Jesus, *Amen*

READ ON YOUR OWN

PSALM 18:19 NLT; JOHN 8:34; ISAIAH 61:10 NLT; EPHESIANS 5:8

YOU ARE MY STRENGTH

My God will use his wonderful riches in Christ
Jesus to give you everything you need.
—Philippians 4:19

Dear Jesus,

You are the One who *gives me my strength*! You know I'm not strong enough to handle every problem. But You use my weakness to teach me to trust You. When I can't do something on my own, I remember that I need You—and then I hold on even tighter to Your promise to *give me everything I need*.

On the days I'm really tired and running out of energy, help me to reach out to You. Sometimes You give me a big boost of energy to finish what I'm doing quickly and easily. At other times, You give me just enough strength to take the next step and then the next. I have to keep coming back to You for more strength. You're teaching me that this is Your way of keeping me close to You. And the whole time, You're whispering to me, "I love you."

I want to keep hearing Your whispers, so I need to trust that You're doing the best things for my life. I believe You are filling this day—and all my days—with Your blessings. I do, Lord! But help me trust You more and more!

In Your powerful Name, Jesus, *Amen*

READ ON YOUR OWN

HABAKKUK 3:19; PHILIPPIANS 4:19; PSALM 96:6–7

FILLED WITH JOY

You will teach me God's way to live.
Being with you will fill me with joy.
—Psalm 16:11

Dear Jesus,

Your Word promises that *being with You will fill me with joy.* So, as I sit here with You now, I think about who You are—about how powerful and wonderful You are. And I praise You for the way You never stop loving me. *Nothing in all creation will ever be able to separate me from Your Love!* Our relationship will last forever, and it starts as soon as I decide to trust You to be my Savior. Help me to always know and remember that I am Your beloved child. That's who I really am!

Even with all the troubles in this world, You've shown me that I can find joy because *You are with me always.* As I spend time with You every day, I learn to *delight in who You are.* When I'm with You, I can completely relax.

As my love for You grows stronger, I want to help others learn to love You too. Please let Your Love shine so brightly through me that it lights up other people's lives. Lord, *teach me Your way to live* so I can show Your Love to others.

In Your cherished Name, Jesus, *Amen*

READ ON YOUR OWN

PSALM 16:11; ROMANS 8:39 NLT; MATTHEW 28:20; PSALM 37:4 NLT

THE GREATEST PEACE

The peace that God gives is so great that we cannot understand it.
—Philippians 4:7

Dear Jesus,

I really want to rest in Your Peace. As I sit here with You, I can feel Your Light shining on me and blessing me with *a peace that's so great I cannot understand it*. Instead of trying to figure everything out for myself, I'm going to stay here with You for a little while. You already know and understand all that's happening in my life. So I'm going to count on You to take care of me. I love this time we spend together. This is how You created me to live: close to You.

When I'm around other people, I often try to be who they want me to be. Sometimes that means pretending to be someone I'm not. The more I try to please others, the more tired I get—and the farther away You seem to be. It's like my heart dries up inside of me, instead of flowing with the *living water* of Your Spirit. That's not how You want me to be.

Help me to keep talking to You no matter how busy I may be. And please give me the right words to say so that others will live close to You too.

In Your peaceful Name, Jesus, *Amen*

READ ON YOUR OWN

PHILIPPIANS 4:6–7; JOHN 7:38; EPHESIANS 5:18–20

CREATED BY YOU

*God created human beings in his image. In the image of God
he created them. He created them male and female.*
—Genesis 1:27

Dear Jesus,

The Bible tells me that You *created me in Your own image. You made
me a little lower than the angels, and You crowned me with glory.* So please
help me remember how precious I am to You!

You made me with an amazing brain. I can use it to talk to You, to
think, to create things, to make choices, and so much more. You made
people *to rule over the fish in the sea and over the birds in the sky and every
living thing that moves on the earth.* But out of all those living things, only
people are made in Your image. That makes every moment of my life
important.

My greatest purpose is to praise You and enjoy being with You—now
and forever. When I choose to follow You, *You crown me with glory* so that
I can *shine with Your Glory.* You help me light up this dark world and point
others to You.

Thank You for creating me with the ability to love You. The joy You
give me here on earth is just a tiny sample of how amazing heaven will be!

In Your awesome Name, Jesus, *Amen*

READ ON YOUR OWN

GENESIS 1:27–28; PSALM 8:5; 2 CORINTHIANS 3:18

YOUR TRUE PEACE

You, Lord, give true peace.
You give peace to those who depend on you.
You give peace to those who trust you.
—Isaiah 26:3

Dear Jesus,

You are the *Lord of Peace*. Whenever something worries or frightens me—even just a little bit—I need to *come to You* and talk to You about it. So today, I'm stepping boldly into Your Presence with this prayer, just like Your Word invites me to do. I'm *asking You for everything I need*, and *I'm thanking You* for all the ways You take care of me.

So many times, it's the troubles in my life that teach me to trust You more. And even though troubles aren't my favorite thing, I'm grateful for the lessons I learn from them.

Trusting You gives me many blessings, and one of the greatest is Your Peace. Your Word tells me that *You give true Peace to those who depend on You and trust You.*

The world has it all wrong. It says that peace comes from being famous or rich or popular. But Your Peace doesn't depend on any of those things. No matter what I have or don't have, I am rich when I have Your Peace. Thank You for this wonderful gift!

In Your trustworthy Name, Jesus, *Amen*

READ ON YOUR OWN

2 THESSALONIANS 3:16; MATTHEW 11:28; PHILIPPIANS 4:6; ISAIAH 26:3

YOU HOLD MY HAND

He will not let you stumble;
the one who watches over you will not slumber.
—Psalm 121:3 NLT

Dear Jesus,

Whenever I'm feeling lonely, You are the perfect answer! Because *You are the Lord my God. You are holding my right hand. And You tell me, "Don't be afraid. I will help you."* Sometimes I like to close my right hand— just as if I were holding *Your* hand. It helps me feel connected to You. When I'm sad or lonely or afraid, I need to feel that closeness to You more than ever.

Thank You for listening when I tell You about my feelings and my problems. You already know all about them, but it feels really good to talk with You about my troubles. While I'm spending time with You, I soak up the Light of Your Presence—and I realize how safe I am with You. *You are with me* every second of my life. I am never alone!

The more time I spend with You, the more I can see my life the way You see it. Sometimes it helps me to write out my prayers. I love being able to look back and see how You answer them. Writing down prayers also helps me give my troubles to You, leaving them in Your strong hands. Thank You for *always watching over me*.

In Your mighty Name, Jesus, *Amen*

READ ON YOUR OWN

ISAIAH 41:13; MATTHEW 28:20; PSALM 27:4; PSALM 121:3 NLT

NO NEED TO BE AFRAID

Even if I walk through a very dark valley,
I will not be afraid because you are with me.
—Psalm 23:4

Dear Jesus,

I love hearing You whisper in my heart, "I am taking care of you." Sometimes I feel all alone and afraid that something bad is just waiting to happen. When I feel this way, I need to stop and remember that *You care for me*—You are taking care of me! That's Your promise to me. It comforts me and helps me feel closer to You. As I sit and rest in Your Presence, I stop trying to figure out all the answers.

Help me remember that You're always watching over me—even when my life leaves me wondering what to do. I'm thankful that You understand everything about me and what I'm going through. I can trust You to have the perfect answers for today *and* for all my tomorrows. This makes me smile and gives me hope.

Whenever I start to feel afraid, please remind me that *You are with me*. You promise that *You will never leave me or forget about me*. And more than that, *You will go ahead of me wherever I go*.

Even if *I'm walking through a very dark valley* of trouble, I'll keep saying Your words to myself: *I will not be afraid because You are with me*.

In Your watchful Name, Jesus, *Amen*

READ ON YOUR OWN

1 PETER 5:7; PSALM 23:4; DEUTERONOMY 31:8

WORKING WITH YOU

In all the work you are doing, work the best you can. Work
as if you were working for the Lord, not for men.
—Colossians 3:23

Dear Jesus,

You are teaching me that each moment of my life has a purpose. *Here* and *Now* are where I live. Not in the past and not in the future. Because I live in the present, this moment is also where I meet You, my forever Savior. Every minute of every day is alive with Your wonderful Presence! Help me to keep You in the center of my thoughts—enjoying Your Presence with me here and now.

I'm sorry for letting time slip away from me. Sometimes I've wasted hours because I wasn't really paying attention. Or because I was worrying about what might happen in the future. Or because I was too busy wishing I was somewhere else, doing something else. Please open up my eyes to the wonders of *this* day! I need to start seeing everything I do—from homework, to hanging out with friends, to helping my family—as a way to *work for You*. Working side by side with You will make the work easier and help me enjoy what I do.

The more I talk to You, Jesus, the less I worry. And that gives me more time to follow You as *You guide me* along *the path of peace*.

In Your guiding Name, Jesus, *Amen*

READ ON YOUR OWN

LUKE 12:25–26; COLOSSIANS 3:23; JOHN 10:10; LUKE 1:79 NLT

YOU ARE THE ONE, JESUS

I wait patiently for God to save me.
Only he gives me hope.
—Psalm 62:5

Dear Jesus,

You're the answer to everything I want and need. The Bible says that *You are the Alpha and the Omega—the beginning and the end. You are the Almighty One who is, who always was, and who is still to come.* You're the One my heart is searching for. There is so much evil and badness in this world, but You *call me out of the darkness* and *into Your wonderful Light.* You are like a shield all around me. You take care of me and keep me safe.

You bless me with so many things, Jesus—my pets, my family, my church, my friends. Thank You for each and every one. I want to enjoy Your blessings, but I also want to remember that You are the greatest blessing of all. Help me not to hold on to things so tightly that I forget about You.

You're the Giver of *every good and perfect gift*, but the best gift I could ever get is *You*. Your Presence with me is the one thing I need more than anything else—and it's the one thing I can never, ever lose. That makes me so happy that I want to sing and shout!

In Your perfect Name, Jesus, *Amen*

READ ON YOUR OWN

PSALM 62:5; REVELATION 1:8 NLT; 1 PETER 2:9; JAMES 1:17

A HANDFUL OF BLESSINGS

You have made me very happy.

—Psalm 4:7

Dear Jesus,

As I sit here quietly with You, please fill my heart and mind with thankfulness. I love spending time with You, thanking You for all that You do in my life. Thinking about You and Your endless Love makes me happy and settles me down. Especially when I remember that *nothing above me, nothing below me, or anything else in the whole world will ever be able to separate me from Your Love*. By remembering this, I'm building a foundation beneath me—a foundation of gratitude. And *like the wise man's house that was built on the rock*, this foundation will stand strong through *any* storm.

You go ahead of me and plant treasures for me to find all through the day, just because You want to add joy to my day. I'll search for these treasures and gather them up like wildflowers. Then, at the end of the day, I'll have a whole handful of Your blessings. And I'll offer them up to You, Lord, praising You for each one.

When it's time for me to *lie down in my bed to sleep*, help me relax in Your loving Presence. Please fill me with Your Peace—and let thankful thoughts play like a lullaby in my mind.

In Your comforting Name, Jesus, *Amen*

READ ON YOUR OWN

ROMANS 8:38–39; MATTHEW 7:24–25; 1 CORINTHIANS 3:11; PSALM 4:7–8

I AM FREE!

Those who are in Christ Jesus are not judged guilty.

—Romans 8:1

Dear Jesus,

I will never be able to thank You enough for dying on the cross for me. When I decided to follow You, You paid for all my sins—the ones in the past and the ones in the future. *I am not found guilty because I belong to You!* And that gives me a reason for joy every day of my life.

Ever since Adam and Eve disobeyed You in the garden of Eden, the world has been full of sin. But You came to offer us a way out of this terrible problem. The gospel—Your good news—is the best news a person could ever imagine! You did more than pay the price for all my sins. You took my sin—*You became sin for me*—and You gave me Your own perfect righteousness.

You *set me free from sin and death.* That doesn't mean I can do whatever I want and then just say, "It doesn't matter. Jesus will forgive me." But it does mean that I'm a loved and precious *child of God* forever. That's who I really am! And it means that every moment of my life matters to You. Thank You for loving me so much!

In Your precious Name, Jesus, *Amen*

READ ON YOUR OWN

ROMANS 8:1–2; GENESIS 3:6; 2 CORINTHIANS 5:21; JOHN 1:11–12

LOVE LIKE AN OCEAN

I pray that you and all God's holy people will have the
power to understand the greatness of Christ's love.
—Ephesians 3:18

Dear Jesus,

Fill me with Your Love in the morning. Then I will sing and rejoice all my life. It's easy to look for happiness in the world, in friendships, or in the things I own. But even good things are nothing compared to *You*. So I come to You and ask You to fill up all the empty places inside me with Your unending Love.

It's wonderful to think about *how wide and how long and how high and how deep* Your love is. It's like an ocean—so deep that I could never reach the bottom of it!

The people and things of this world change, but I know I can always be sure of You. Being sure of You makes me happy and helps me get through my day without worrying. I know there will be problems, and things won't always be easy. That's just the way life is in this broken world. But I can count on You to *guide me* and help me do the right thing. Lord, I trust You to lead me through each day of my life—all the way to heaven!

In Your wonderful Name, Jesus, *Amen*

READ ON YOUR OWN

PSALM 90:14; EPHESIANS 3:17–18; PHILIPPIANS 4:13; PSALM 73:24

THE LORD OF PEACE

"I leave you peace. My peace I give you."
—John 14:27

Dear Jesus,

You are *the Lord of Peace. You give me Peace in all times and in every way.* There's a giant hole inside of me that only You can fill. It can't be filled with friends, games, clothes, or even family. I've tried! And the hole is too big to pretend it isn't there. I need Your Peace and Your Presence in every moment and every situation. But remembering that I need You is only half the battle. The other half is believing that You can—and will—*give me everything I need.*

Before You went to the cross, You promised Your Peace to everyone who chooses to follow You. You made it clear that this Peace is a gift. And You give it to everyone who trusts in You. I can receive this gift by admitting that I really want and need Your Peace in my life.

Help me wait patiently for You to bless me with Your Peace. To show You that I am waiting, I lift up my hands to You—open and ready to receive Your gift. And I say to You, "Jesus, I receive Your Peace."

In Your comforting Name, Jesus, *Amen*

READ ON YOUR OWN

2 THESSALONIANS 3:16; PHILIPPIANS 4:19; JOHN 14:27

LIKE COINS OF FAITH

When I am afraid,
I will trust you.
—Psalm 56:3

Dear Jesus,

Please guide me through this day, one step at a time. I will hold Your hand and trust You to show me the way to go. I don't know what might happen in the future, but You do. And *even though I can't see You, I will believe* that You are clearing out the path ahead of me.

Every time I decide to trust You, it's like putting a coin of faith into my piggy bank. As those coins add up, my faith grows. Then, when trouble comes, I can look at all those faith coins and see the ways You've taken care of me in the past. This helps me know that You will take care of me through this trouble too. In fact, I'm learning that when I trust You like this, You help me trust You even more!

I need to practice *telling* You how much I trust You. Because whether I tell You silently in my heart, whisper it to You, shout it out, or sing it in a song, saying "I trust You, Jesus" helps me not to be afraid. It also keeps me close to You, where I can relax and enjoy Your peaceful Presence.

In Your guiding Name, Jesus, *Amen*

READ ON YOUR OWN

2 CORINTHIANS 5:7; PSALM 56:3–4; MATTHEW 6:20; ISAIAH 26:3

A NEW WAY OF THINKING

Be changed within by a new way of thinking. Then you will
be able to decide what God wants for you. And you will
be able to know what is good and pleasing to God.

—Romans 12:2

Dear Jesus,

Help me follow wherever You lead—cheerfully, not with a complaining heart or a bossy attitude. I don't want to push so hard to get my own way that I miss the good things You have planned for me. Instead, I want to relax with You while You *change me and give me a new way of thinking*.

Teach me to *be still* in Your Presence. Help me trust You enough to let go of what *I* want, Jesus, so I can choose the things *You* have for me.

Sometimes I don't get what I'm hoping for because I'm trying too hard to make it happen *right now*. Help me to believe and know that Your timing is best. Instead of pushing for things to happen when and how I want them to, I need to take a break from all my trying—and spend time talking with You. After resting in Your Presence, I can ask You to show me the next step to take.

You give me this promise: *"I will make you wise. I will show you where to go. I will guide you and watch over you."* I'm happy to be able to count on Your help!

In Your loving Name, Jesus, *Amen*

READ ON YOUR OWN

ROMANS 12:2; PSALM 46:10; 1 CHRONICLES 16:11; PSALM 32:8

GREATER THAN I COULD EVER KNOW

If we love each other, God lives in us. If we love each other,
God's love has reached its goal. It is made perfect in us.

—1 John 4:12

Dear Jesus,

Your love is *greater than I could ever know*! I'm learning that there's a big difference between just knowing about You and actually knowing *You*. I want to know more than facts such as "You were born in Bethlehem" and "Mary was Your mother." I want to really get to know You and experience what it's like to enjoy Your Presence. That's one big way Your Holy Spirit helps me. He comes to live inside of me when I trust You as my Savior. *The Spirit can give me the power to understand how wide and how long and how high and how deep Your Love is.*

I'm seeing that the more room I make for You in my heart, the more Love You pour into me. I can make extra space in my heart by spending time with You and soaking up Your Word. I also need to keep talking to You—this keeps me close to You and gives me joy.

Lord, please pour so much of Your Love into me that it overflows and spills out on the people around me. Loving others is what *makes Your Love complete in me.*

In Your loving Name, Jesus, *Amen*

READ ON YOUR OWN

EPHESIANS 3:16–19; 1 THESSALONIANS 5:17; 1 JOHN 4:12

I'LL START THE DAY WITH YOU

Remember the Lord in everything you do.
And he will give you success.
—Proverbs 3:6

Dear Jesus,

Please wrap me up in Your Presence and Your Peace. Help me relax with You and forget about my worries. Remind me that You are *Immanuel—God with us.* You are with me! It seems like everything in this world is changing all the time. That's why it's so comforting to know that *You are the same yesterday, today, and forever.*

Sometimes I get so focused on the stuff that's right in front of me—like the next test, lunch with my friends, or what people are doing online—that I forget about You. But I'm learning that the best way to live is to live every moment of the day with You.

To do that, I need to spend time alone with You each morning. This helps me remember that You really are here with me. I like to begin the day reading Your Word and asking You to lead me—step by step—through my day. Then, as I get busy with the day's activities, I'll know I'm ready because I've spent time with You.

I will hold Your hand and depend on You all day long—and all through the night. I know You'll go ahead of me and prepare the path You want me to take. Thank You, Jesus!

In Your dependable Name, Jesus, *Amen*

READ ON YOUR OWN

MATTHEW 1:23; HEBREWS 13:8; PROVERBS 3:6

WITH ALL MY HEART

I trust God's love forever and ever.

—Psalm 52:8

Dear Jesus,

Help me trust You so much that I can forget about my troubles and relax in Your Presence. To be honest, that's not so easy for me to do. Sometimes I feel like a firefighter—always ready to jump up and run to the next emergency. Your Word tells me that my body is *made in an amazing and wonderful way*. It can leap into action when I need it to. It's also made to slow down and rest when the emergency is over. But because there's so much craziness in this world, it's hard for me to slow down and really rest.

Please help me remember that You are always with me. I know I can depend on You, Jesus. I can *tell You all my troubles*—and trust You to help me get through every one of them.

You're teaching me to *trust You with all my heart*. Thank You for that! As I learn to relax in the Light of Your Love, You shine Peace into my heart and mind. I begin to see all the ways You are taking care of me. And *Your never-ending Love* soaks deep into my heart.

In Your healing Name, Jesus, *Amen*

READ ON YOUR OWN

PSALM 139:14; PSALM 62:8; PROVERBS 3:5; PSALM 52:8

JESUS, MY FRIEND

*"Now I call you friends because I have made known
to you everything I heard from my Father."*
—John 15:15

Dear Jesus,

You are not only my Lord and King, but also my best Friend. I want to walk hand in hand with You every day of my life. Help me face whatever comes my way today—the good things, the not-so-great things, the problems, and the adventures. I'll need to keep trusting You and leaning on You every step of the way.

Not one second is wasted when it's shared with You. You can create something good out of even the worst day. You can bring joy when I am sad and give me peace in times of trouble. There's no one like You, Lord!

Your friendship with me is very down-to-earth and real—You help me and You are always with me. At the same time, this friendship is full of Your heavenly Glory. Living with You by my side means that I'm living in two worlds at once. One is the world I can see. The other one is the heavenly world; I can't see this one yet, but I know it's just as real. Thank You for helping me to be aware of *You* even while I'm walking around the lunchroom, playing on the playground—anywhere I go. As Your Word tells me, *I am made in an amazing and wonderful way!*

In Your awesome Name, Jesus, *Amen*

READ ON YOUR OWN

JOHN 15:15; ISAIAH 61:3; 2 CORINTHIANS 6:10; PSALM 139:14

I WILL PRAISE YOU

Happy are the people who know how to praise you.
Lord, let them live in the light of your presence.
—Psalm 89:15

Dear Jesus,

Help me *live in the Light of Your Presence—praising Your goodness and joyfully singing Your name.* I don't want to keep my praises quiet. I want to share them with the world, shouting and cheering and clapping. I'm full of joy because You are my Savior and Shepherd, my Lord and my God, my King and my Friend forever. You love me with *a Love that will never fail* and that never gives up on me.

When I decide to follow You, You take away my sins and give me Your perfect holiness. Thank You, Jesus! I still have to fight against sin, and I still have to try to do what's right. But You're here to help me and to forgive me when I mess up.

As soon as I become Your child, *Your blood makes me clean from every sin.* The closer I get to You, the more I can see how much I need Your forgiveness. The Light of Your Presence helps me see the ways I need to change. It also helps me be able to love others.

Lord, I love walking with You. Your Presence is like a bright and shining Light that chases away the dark.

In Your shining Name, Jesus, *Amen*

READ ON YOUR OWN

PSALM 89:15–16; PSALM 31:16 NIV; ROMANS 3:22; 1 JOHN 1:7

TEACH ME TO REMEMBER

Remember the wonderful things he has done.
Remember his miracles and his decisions.
—1 Chronicles 16:12

Dear Jesus,

I pray so hard for things, and then I wait with excitement for Your answer. If You give me what I ask for, I'm really happy and I'm quick to say thank You. But instead of staying grateful, I move right on and start asking for the next thing I want. I know it's not good to be grateful for only a minute or two, Lord. Help me learn to *stay* grateful and to *stay* joyful.

Help me also to form the habit of remembering Your wonderful answers to my prayers. One way I can do this is to tell others about the blessings You give me. Another way is to write down Your answers in a place where I'll see them every day—like on my bathroom mirror or on a note by my bed.

Please teach me to *remember all the wonderful things You have done* and to thank You for them. You've shown me that being thankful blesses me twice—once when I look back on how You answered my prayer and then again when I tell You how happy I am!

In Your joyful Name, Jesus, *Amen*

READ ON YOUR OWN

PSALM 95:2; 1 CORINTHIANS 15:57; 1 CHRONICLES 16:12

MARCH

Jesus answered, "I am the way. And I am the truth and the life. The only way to the Father is through me."

—John 14:6

A FOREVER KIND OF JOY

You have not seen Christ, but still you love him. You cannot see him now, but you believe in him. You are filled with a joy that cannot be explained. And that joy is full of glory.

—1 Peter 1:8

Dear Jesus,

Your Word tells me that *all the treasures of wisdom and knowledge are safely kept in You.* That means You know everything. There is no end to Your wisdom. It also means there is no end to the treasures I can find in loving You.

Joy is one of those treasures. Your Joy is like a waterfall. It washes over me and spills out over my whole life. So I'm opening my heart, mind, and spirit as wide as I can—to receive all the joy You have for me!

Your Joy doesn't depend on everything going right. I can be joyful in good times *and* bad times. No matter what's happening, *the Light of Your Presence* keeps shining on me. As I trust You and look to You for answers, Your Light shines through even the darkest clouds of trouble. This wonderful Light helps me see my blessings and fills me with joy.

Thank You, Jesus, for *the blessings you are keeping for me in heaven. These blessings cannot be destroyed or spoiled. They'll never lose their beauty.* Because *I believe in You, I am filled with a great, glorious joy that cannot be explained.* It's mine to have—now and forever!

In Your joyful Name, Jesus, *Amen*

READ ON YOUR OWN

COLOSSIANS 2:3; PSALM 89:15; 1 PETER 1:3–4, 8

AS I WAKE UP

When I wake up,
I am still with you.
—Psalm 139:18

Dear Jesus,

Every morning You wake me and teach me to listen to You. Thank You for always remembering me. At night, I can go right to sleep—without any worries—because I know You never sleep. You watch over me all through the night. Then, *when I wake up, You are still with me.* As I stretch and yawn, I become more and more aware of Your Presence. Like combing the tangles out of my hair, You untangle my sleepy thoughts. I feel Your Love and *I come nearer to You.* I feed my soul a breakfast of Your Word.

Our mornings together make me smile and give me the strength I need for the day ahead. Every time I read the Bible, You teach me what it means and how to use it in my life. Please show me what You want me to do today. As I walk with You, trying to do Your will, I know You'll give me everything I need to handle whatever happens today.

Teach me, Lord, how to *trust You all the time*—no matter what.

In Your trustworthy Name, Jesus, *Amen*

READ ON YOUR OWN

ISAIAH 50:4; PSALM 139:17–18; JAMES 4:8; PSALM 62:8

YOU CALL MY NAME

*This is what the Lord says. . . . "Don't be afraid, because I have
saved you. I have called you by name, and you are mine."*
—Isaiah 43:1

Dear Jesus,

I love to hear You saying to me, *"I have called you by name, and you
are mine."* I belong to You—no matter how alone I might sometimes feel.
Thank You for saving me by dying for my sins. And thank You for the
thoughtful, caring way You work in my life. You work through my expe-
riences, You know my thoughts, and You guide my steps. You speak Your
words into my heart and mind.

There are millions and millions of people who follow You, but I'm
never just one of the crowd to You. You know my name. The Bible says I
am so precious to You that *You have written my name on Your hand. Nothing
will ever be able to separate me from Your loving Presence!*

When troubles are swirling all around me, and I'm feeling shaky and
scared, help me not to focus on the things that are going wrong. Instead,
help me focus on You. I can do this by simply whispering, "You are with
me, Jesus." These words comfort me and remind me of what is true.
Even though this world is full of trouble, I know You are with me and You
are in control!

In Your strong Name, Jesus, *Amen*

READ ON YOUR OWN

ISAIAH 43:1; ISAIAH 49:16; ROMANS 8:38–39

PROTECTED

God is our protection and our strength.
He always helps in times of trouble.
—Psalm 46:1

Dear Jesus,

I know You are with me. Please help me not to worry or be afraid. When I'm upset, I love hearing Your words, *"Peace! Be still!"* You have promised that no matter what happens, *You will not leave me or forget about me.* When I let this promise soak into my mind and heart, it fills me with peace and hope.

There is so much bad news in the world. It seems like it's everywhere—and the news is always changing from one terrible thing to the next. But instead of paying attention to all that is wrong, I'm going to pay attention to *You.* You are always good, and this is a truth that never changes.

I want to fill my mind and heart with Your Word, because it's Your truth that will help me stay on the right path. The Bible tells me that *I don't have to be afraid—not even if the earth shakes or the mountains fall into the sea.* I don't know what will happen tomorrow, but I know I will be with You. *You hold my hand, and You guide me* every step of the way. Thank You, Lord!

In Your wonderful Name, Jesus, *Amen*

READ ON YOUR OWN

MARK 4:39 ESV; DEUTERONOMY 31:6; PSALM 46:1–2; PSALM 73:23–24

IN CONTROL

You have shown me the way of life,
and you will fill me with the joy of your presence.
—Acts 2:28 NLT

Dear Jesus,

I want to learn how to be joyful even when things don't go my way. Sometimes I try to force things to happen the way I want, but that doesn't work very well. No matter how hard I try, at least one thing every day will go wrong. It might be something little, like a crazy hair day. Or it might be something big, like a friend getting really sick.

I know You aren't a magic genie who goes around granting my wishes. You are the Lord! And You always do what's best for me. Please help me trust You all the time, whether or not things go my way.

When I try to control everything, I usually end up frustrated and upset. It's just a waste of time. Teach me instead to be grateful for all the ways You help me—and to trust that You'll keep on helping me.

I want to relax and remember that You are in control. I'm so thankful that You're always near. Your Word tells me that *You will fill me with joy in Your Presence.* And that's not all! *Your Face shines with Joy because of me*—and You shine Your Joy on me!

In Your bright, shining Name, Jesus, *Amen*

READ ON YOUR OWN

PSALM 62:8; PROVERBS 23:18 NLT; ACTS 2:28 NLT; NUMBERS 6:25 TLB

YOU COME TO MEET ME

Fill us with your love every morning.
Then we will sing and rejoice all our lives.
—Psalm 90:14

Dear Jesus,

Please *fill me with Your Love*. The best time for me to start praying is in the morning, right after I wake up. Talking with You gets me ready to face the day. Your endless Love tells me that I am precious and important to You—and I believe that's true! Knowing that I am forever loved makes me strong and gives me the courage to do hard things.

Being with You makes me want to *sing and rejoice*. You are the *King of all kings and the Lord of all lords*—and yet You come here, to my room, to meet me! And that's not all! When I trust You as my Savior, my name is *written in the Lamb's Book of Life*. That means I get to spend forever with You!

So I want to take time to enjoy being in Your Presence—reading the Bible, praying, and praising You with my words and songs. I'm so thankful that *nothing in the whole wide world will ever separate me from Your Love*!

In Your glorious Name, Jesus, *Amen*

READ ON YOUR OWN

PSALM 90:14; REVELATION 19:16 NLT; REVELATION 21:27; ROMANS 8:39

I NEED TO TELL YOU

Why am I so sad?
Why am I so upset?
I should put my hope in God.
I should keep praising him.
—Psalm 42:5

Dear Jesus,

I need to tell You about some things that have been upsetting me. I realize that You already know all about them, but telling You helps me feel better.

Whenever I'm discouraged and almost ready to give up, that's when it's extra-important to spend time *remembering You*. You are *my Lord and my God*, my Savior and Shepherd, and the Friend who *will never leave me*. Just thinking about these wonderful things cheers me up and brightens my day.

I'm so grateful that You know all about me and my life—right down to every thought and feeling. Everything about me is important to You! As I sit with You in Your loving Presence, help me to remember all the ways You take care of me, giving me exactly what I need. I'll try to thank You for each blessing I remember.

Talking to You helps me see things more clearly—so I can figure out what's important and what is not. As I spend time with You, Jesus, You bless me, encourage me, and comfort me. I'll *keep on praising You* for all the ways You help me.

In Your mighty Name, Jesus, *Amen*

READ ON YOUR OWN

PSALM 42:6; JOHN 20:28; DEUTERONOMY 31:8; PSALM 42:5

YOUR PERFECT WAY

God's way is perfect.
All the Lord's promises prove true.
—Psalm 18:30 NLT

Dear Jesus,

Things are not working out the way I hoped. I'm trying to trust You and remember that You only want good things for me. Please help me, Lord.

You are Light, and in You there is no darkness at all. Not one speck. So I will look for Your Light in this dark situation. I want to follow You wherever You lead. But I'm learning that sometimes this means letting go of plans or dreams that are really important to me. When that happens, I need to remember and believe that *Your way is perfect.* Even when it's so hard for me.

You are a shield to all who look to You for protection. When I'm feeling disappointed or afraid, please remind me to come closer to You. Help me remember that You are my safe place. I know You don't take away every problem from my life, but You are preparing me to handle them.

Please help me *live the way You want me to live*—joyfully trusting in You. Then *I will be as content as if I had eaten the very best foods. My lips will sing, and my mouth will praise You*!

In Your perfect Name, Jesus, *Amen*

READ ON YOUR OWN

1 JOHN 1:5; PSALM 18:30 NLT; 1 CORINTHIANS 7:17; PSALM 63:5

YOU COMFORT ME

Comfort me with your love,
as you promised me.
—Psalm 119:76

Dear Jesus,

I've been thinking about the future—about all the things I don't know. And it's starting to upset me. Fear and discouragement will sneak in and walk with me all day if I let them. Please keep reminding me that *You go before me* wherever I go. And *You are always with me, holding my hand.*

You don't live in time the way I do. I can only be right here, in this moment. But You can be here *and* in the future. You're on the path up ahead of me—waving and encouraging me to keep my eyes on You. Help me to hold tight to Your hand and walk right past those dark troubles and fears. The Light of *Your never-ending Love* shines out into the dark—comforting me and guiding me.

I can be confident because *You are with me* now and You are already getting things ready for me in the future. If I listen carefully, I can hear You calling to me from the path ahead. You whisper words of courage, hope, and encouragement: *"Don't worry, because I am with you. Don't be afraid, because I am your God. I will make you strong and will help you."*

In Your powerful Name, Jesus, *Amen*

READ ON YOUR OWN

DEUTERONOMY 31:8; PSALM 73:23; PSALM 119:76; ISAIAH 41:10

THE STRENGTH I NEED

Depend on the Lord and his strength.
Always go to him for help.
—Psalm 105:4

Dear Jesus,

Some pretty hard things are happening in the world—and sometimes in *my* world. I don't want to let those things frighten me. Please keep reminding me that the tougher my day is, the more power and strength You send my way.

I used to think that You give me the same amount of strength and power each day. But that's not true. When I need more help than usual, You give me the extra help. Sometimes, though, I still wake up and wonder if I'm strong enough to face all my problems. Then I remember that You are with me and I don't have to face my troubles alone.

You already know what will happen every day of my life. So You know exactly how much strength and power I'll need. The amount of strength You give me depends on two things: how tough my day is, and how much I'm trusting You to get me through the day. Help me, Lord, to trust You more!

Teach me to see tough days as a chance to receive more of Your power than usual. Instead of worrying or panicking, I can look to You for everything I need. The Bible tells me You will help me *be strong as long as I live.*

In Your strong Name, Jesus, *Amen*

READ ON YOUR OWN

2 CORINTHIANS 12:9; PSALM 105:4; DEUTERONOMY 33:25

TRUE HOPE

"Accept my work and learn from me. I am gentle and humble in spirit. And you will find rest for your souls."
—Matthew 11:29

Dear Jesus,

My thoughts are jumping around from one thing to another. It's so hard to keep them still. But Your Word tells me to *be still and know that You are God.* When I sit quietly in Your Presence, my heart can hear You saying, *"Come to Me, and I will give you rest."*

I need to take time to focus my thoughts on You. One way I can do this is by whispering Your Name and then waiting in Your Presence. You help me *find rest in You,* and *You give me hope.*

True hope only comes from You, Jesus. It's found in all Your promises—promises to be with me, to listen, to help me, and to give me Your Joy and Peace. There are plenty of places to find false hope, though. The ads I see and hear are the worst. They're always telling me I need this thing or that thing to be happy. Help me to see through those lies. Please protect me from believing things that aren't true. I'm learning that the best way to escape the lies is to spend time thinking about You. It's only in Your peaceful Presence that I find true hope and rest.

In Your comforting Name, Jesus, *Amen*

READ ON YOUR OWN

PSALM 62:5 NCV; PSALM 46:10; MATTHEW 11:28–29; PSALM 42:5

EVERY ANSWER I NEED

I want you to know fully God's secret truth. That
truth is Christ himself. And in him all the treasures
of wisdom and knowledge are safely kept.
—Colossians 2:2–3

Dear Jesus,

Sometimes I feel like I'm being pulled in ten different directions, all at the same time. Friends want this, my family wants that, and I really want to do something else. I run from one thing to the next, trying to make everybody happy. But even though I try so hard, no one ends up happy.

When everyone is tugging at me, please remind me to stop, take a deep breath, and turn to You. Help me to focus on this truth: *All the treasures of wisdom and knowledge are safely kept in You.* That means I can find every answer I need in *You.*

When I make You the most important thing in my life—*my First Love*—You protect me from being pulled in all those different directions. You're teaching me to bring my wandering thoughts back to You. I still need to work on that. Thank You for never giving up on me, Lord!

I'm trying to obey Your commands so I can live closer to You. But I still mess up a lot. Thank You for covering my sins with *Your clothes of salvation* and *Your coat of goodness*!

In Your holy Name, Jesus, Amen

READ ON YOUR OWN

COLOSSIANS 2:2–3; REVELATION 2:4 NKJV; ISAIAH 61:10

BETTER THAN ANY MAP

The Lord answered, "I myself will go with
you. And I will give you victory."
—Exodus 33:14

Dear Jesus,

Please help me to be ready for everything that will happen today. I think I know some of the things that are going to happen, but You know every single detail. I wish I could see a map that showed each twist and turn in my path through this day. I'd feel better if I could see what's around the corner—and around all the other turns too. But You're teaching me that the best way to prepare for whatever I will face is to spend time with You.

Even though I don't know what's waiting for me on today's path, I trust that *You* do. You will give me everything I need for this journey. And best of all, You promise to walk with me each step of the way! I'm learning to keep talking to You all day long. I can just whisper Your Name and it brings my thoughts right back to You.

Thank You, Lord, for always staying right by my side. You're better than any map could ever be!

In Your delightful Name, Jesus, *Amen*

READ ON YOUR OWN

EXODUS 33:14; PHILIPPIANS 4:4; JOHN 15:4–5

A CORD OF HOPE

I pray that the God who gives hope will fill you with
much joy and peace while you trust in him.
—Romans 15:13

Dear Jesus,

You are teaching me that Your hope is so much more than a wish or a dream. Your hope is a promise. It's like a golden cord—a kind of safety rope—that connects me to heaven. This cord helps me hold my head up high even when I'm facing troubles and even when others are laughing at my faith. I know that You never leave my side, and You never let go of my hand. But without that cord of hope, my head sometimes slumps over and my feet start to drag. It's Your hope that lifts up my head so that I can see You and all the blessings You've placed around me.

Thank You, Lord, for always being with me. I'm excited that this road we're traveling together is leading me all the way to heaven! When I think about how wonderful heaven will be, I stop worrying about today's troubles. And I stop wondering about the bumps in the road that I might have to face tomorrow. Please teach me to keep these two thoughts in my mind: You are always with me, and You give me the hope—the promise—of heaven.

In Your wonderful Name, Jesus, *Amen*

READ ON YOUR OWN

ROMANS 12:12; 1 THESSALONIANS 5:8;
HEBREWS 6:19–20; ROMANS 15:13 HCSB

IN YOUR LIGHT

God is in the light. We should live in the light, too.
—1 John 1:7

Dear Jesus,

Your Word promises that *if I live in the Light with You*—living close to You and trying to follow You—then *Your blood will clean away my every sin*. So I bring my sins to You. I confess them to You, Lord. And I ask You to forgive me and help me not to do those things again.

I know I'm not perfect. But when I trust You as my Savior, You cover me with Your perfect goodness. It's Your gift to me. You died on the cross so that You could wrap me up in Your beautiful *coat of goodness*. It lets me step right up to You and be in Your holy Presence without feeling afraid.

I'm learning that *living in the Light of Your Presence* blesses me in so many ways. Good things are better and hard things are easier to handle when I share them with You. I'm able to love others more and to *share in fellowship* and friendship with them. It's easier to make good choices too, because Your Light shows me the way.

Lord, teach me to *rejoice in Your Name all the time*. Help me learn to enjoy Your Presence and *praise Your goodness* more and more!

In Your great Name, Jesus, *Amen*

READ ON YOUR OWN

1 JOHN 1:7; ISAIAH 61:10; PSALM 89:15–16

SAFE IN THE STORMS

Trust God all the time.
Tell him all your problems.
—Psalm 62:8

Dear Jesus,

When everything is going my way, it's easy for me to start thinking that I'm the one in control of my life. I need to stop thinking that way. Because the more I believe I'm in control, the more I try to actually *be* in control. And I forget that You're the One who is Lord over all.

You want me to enjoy the good days in my life—the days when there isn't a problem in sight. Those are a gift from You. But I shouldn't expect every day to be like that. There are problems in this world. Sometimes they're small, but sometimes they're big storms with lots of problems. If I try to take control and fix everything myself, then I'm probably going to make things worse.

Help me *trust You, Lord—all the time. I want to tell You all my troubles and trust You to protect me.* Thank You for using the hard times to remind me that I'm not in control—*You* are. When troubles come my way, I can turn to You for help. *Knowing You* and trusting You to be in control keeps me safe in the storms of life.

In Your trustworthy Name, Jesus, *Amen*

READ ON YOUR OWN

JAMES 4:13–14; PSALM 62:8; JOHN 17:3

MORE AND MORE

Jesus told her, "I am the resurrection and the life. Anyone who believes in me will live, even after dying."
—John 11:25 NLT

Dear Jesus,

You said, *"I am the resurrection and the life. Anyone who believes in Me will live, even after dying."* That's what you told Martha. She was Lazarus's sister, and he had been dead for four days when You said this to her. And she believed You. *Then You shouted, "Lazarus, come out!"* and he came out of his grave!

The Bible tells me that *You are the Way. And You are the Truth and the Life.* I like to think about what this means. You're everything I could ever need—for my life on earth and my life in heaven with You. *All the treasures of wisdom and knowledge are hidden in You.* Believing that truth makes my life so much simpler. It means that *You* are my Treasure and the answer to all my troubles!

You give me joy on good days and tough days. You make hard times easier to get through, and You make good times even better. So I *come to You*, Jesus, just as I am. I want to learn to share more and more of my life with You. I'm so thankful that we walk through each day together. You are *the Way*—the One who guides me step by step, all the way to heaven!

In Your majestic Name, Jesus, *Amen*

READ ON YOUR OWN

JOHN 11:25, 43–44 NLT; JOHN 14:6;
COLOSSIANS 2:2–3 NLT; MATTHEW 11:28

ALWAYS WORKING

Surely I talked about things I did not understand.
I spoke of things too wonderful for me to know.
—Job 42:3

Dear Jesus,

I love knowing that You take care of me! When I spend time with You, I can feel the warmth of Your Love, and I feel safe in Your Presence. This makes it so much easier to trust that You're in control of all the details of my life. The Bible tells me that *You cause everything to work together for the good of those who love You and who are called according to Your purpose for them.*

Sometimes this world seems so mixed-up. Bad things happen to nice people, and that doesn't make any sense to me. Good things happen to not-so-nice people—even bad people—and that doesn't seem fair either. But when I look at the world this way, I'm forgetting a wonderful truth: You are always working for good. I may not see it or understand it, but I can trust that You know what You're doing.

If I could actually *see* how close You are to me, and all the things You do for me, I would be amazed. I would never doubt how much You take care of me. Your Word teaches me to *live by what I believe, not just what I can see with my eyes.* Please help me do that, Jesus.

In Your wonderful Name, Jesus, *Amen*

READ ON YOUR OWN

ROMANS 8:28 NLT; JOB 42:3; 1 PETER 5:7; 2 CORINTHIANS 5:7

ONE STEP AT A TIME

He has put his angels in charge of you.
They will watch over you wherever you go.
—Psalm 91:11

Dear Jesus,

Help me to follow You one step at a time. That's all You really ask of me. In fact, I'm learning that one step at a time is the only way to walk through this world. But I get into trouble when I start looking at the future. The things that *might* happen begin to look as big as mountains, and I wonder how I'll ever climb over them. Then, because I'm busy looking at those "might-be" mountains, I trip on a tiny "pebble-problem" today.

As You help me get back on my feet, I tell You about those big, scary mountains up ahead. That's when You remind that You're my Guide and You love me. You might lead me on a path that takes me away from those huge mountains—or there might be an easier way to get over the mountains that I can't see yet. Even if You do lead me up a steep path, You promise to give me everything I need for that difficult climb. You even *tell Your angels to watch over me wherever I go.*

Teach me to *live by what I believe, not just what I can see.* Help me trust You to open up the way ahead and show me the right path to take.

In Your loving Name, Jesus, *Amen*

READ ON YOUR OWN

PSALM 18:29; PSALM 91:11–12; 2 CORINTHIANS 5:7

STAND STRONG

You need to get God's full armor. Then on the day of evil you will be able to stand strong. And when you have finished the whole fight, you will still be standing.
—Ephesians 6:13

Dear Jesus,

Your Word tells me that *You make my feet like the feet of a deer, which does not stumble. You help me stand on the steep mountains.* Lord, You created deer to be able to climb steep mountains easily and to stand fearlessly on top of them. When I choose to follow You—to trust You as my Savior—You make it possible for me to stand fearlessly too. My "mountains" might be a huge problem, a worry, or a fear. But whenever I face one of those mountains, I know I can turn to You for strength and courage.

I have to remember that I live in a world where the devil never stops fighting. He likes to throw all kinds of trouble and temptation at me. Help me to *stay alert* and be ready for battle at all times—day or night. Remind me to *put on the full armor* of Your Love, which protects me. No matter what happens, I want to *be able to stand strong and to still be standing when I have finished fighting.*

Help me never forget that You're always in the battle with me, fighting right beside me and giving me the strength I need. My assignment is to trust You and *stand strong*—stay on my feet. You will lead me to victory!

In Your powerful Name, Jesus, *Amen*

READ ON YOUR OWN

2 SAMUEL 22:34; HABAKKUK 3:19; 1 PETER 5:8 NLT; EPHESIANS 6:13

YOU LIFT ME UP

When Peter saw the wind and the waves, he became afraid
and began to sink. He shouted, "Lord, save me!"
—Matthew 14:30

Dear Jesus,

Your Face is shining on me, and I feel *a peace so great that I cannot understand it*. There are problems all around me. Some are mine and some belong to others. But when I'm face to Face with You in prayer, You give me Peace.

As long as I focus on You, Your Peace stays with me. But if I look at my problems too long, I get worried and even afraid. Sometimes I feel like Peter when he was walking on the water. He could stay on top of the water until he stopped looking at You and he looked at the waves instead. That's when *he became afraid and started to sink*. Anytime I feel like I'm sinking in my problems, I can call out, *"Lord, save me!"*—just like Peter did—and You will lift me up!

Everything in this world changes, and some of those changes look scary. Help me *keep my eyes on You* because You never change. You're always good and always ready to help me. There's no trouble that You can't handle.

You've been showing me that the future likes to jump into my thoughts and say, "Boo!" It tries to scare me. But I can laugh at the future because I'm staying close to You.

In Your mighty Name, Jesus, *Amen*

READ ON YOUR OWN

PHILIPPIANS 4:7; MATTHEW 14:29–30; HEBREWS 12:2; HEBREWS 13:8

SO AMAZING

The Lord's loved ones will lie down in safety.
The Lord protects them all day long.
—Deuteronomy 33:12

Dear Jesus,

Sometimes I get so scared and upset about the things happening in my life. Then I hear You whisper to my heart, "Relax, My child. I'm taking care of you. I've got this." I like to think about those words over and over again. They wash away the worry and fear, assuring me that Your Love for me never ends.

I waste a lot of time trying to figure out the future. But You're already there, preparing the way for me. You're also sprinkling blessings for me to find along my path today. Open my eyes, Lord, to see all Your wonderful surprises—the things that only *You* could have planned for me. Please keep reminding me that I am Yours, that You love me, and that You always want what is best for me.

Your Love makes me so happy! You're the King of the universe, and You are *planning good things for me*. That's so amazing! I may not know what's going to happen in the future, but I do know who I am—*I am the one You love*. And when I walk with You, *You fill my heart with joy* and my mind with peace.

In Your beautiful Name, Jesus, *Amen*

READ ON YOUR OWN

JEREMIAH 29:11; DEUTERONOMY 33:12; PSALM 16:11

MORE LIKE YOU

I can do all things through Christ because he gives me strength.
—Philippians 4:13

Dear Jesus,

Your Word tells me that *I can have joy with my troubles*. That's because *troubles produce patience. And patience produces character, and character produces hope.* So my problems and my hurts can actually become blessings—because of the way they change me and help me grow. This doesn't happen by itself, though. It's only when I let You help me through those problems and hurts that I can find the blessings and the joy.

It doesn't happen right away, either. Sometimes it takes a long time. But You're using the stories and promises in the Bible to teach me to wait for You and Your perfect timing. As I trust You, I learn to be patient. I love watching the way You work through the troubles in my life, using those tough times to make me more like You. I know You're getting me ready to live with You forever in heaven—where everything will be perfect!

The more I become like You, the more I *know* that I belong to You! Just being close to You helps me handle the problems that come along—because I trust that You and I can handle them together!

In Your wonderful Name, Jesus, *Amen*

READ ON YOUR OWN

ROMANS 5:3–4; JOHN 14:16–17; PHILIPPIANS 4:13

THE MIGHTY ONE

Lord, even when I have trouble all around me. . . .
you will reach down and save me by your power.
—Psalm 138:7

Dear Jesus,

Even when I have trouble all around me, You will protect me. So I won't let that trouble scare me. Instead, I'll remember that You are *the Mighty One. You are with me*, and You are greater than all the trouble in the world! The Bible promises that *You will save me by Your power*. If I hold tight to Your hand, I can bravely walk through even the toughest times.

Thank You, Lord, for helping me get through the hard times. And more than that, thank You for using them to make me stronger. Sometimes I still get tired, even with You helping me. On those tiring days, please remind me that You're still with me.

Hard times are just part of living in this world, and everyone has struggles. The best way to remember that You are with me is to keep talking to You. I like to tell You all about my thoughts and feelings and what's happening in my life. Every time I come to You, *You give me strength and bless me with Your Peace*.

In Your strong Name, Jesus, *Amen*

READ ON YOUR OWN

PSALM 138:7; ZEPHANIAH 3:17; 1 PETER 5:9; PSALM 29:11

YOU WON'T LET GO

"I am the Lord your God.
I am holding your right hand."
—Isaiah 41:13

Dear Jesus,

I'm feeling so worn-out! My troubles and struggles seem to be more than I can handle. But You already know all about them, and that comforts me. Because it means You already know how to help me.

Even though You know everything, it feels good to *tell You all about my problems*. I don't have to pretend that I'm not worried or upset. I can be honest and real with You—*and* with myself. Telling You about my troubles brings me closer to You. Help me rest with You for a little while. I know I'm safe here, in Your Presence. I can trust You to understand me completely and to love me *with a Love that will last forever*.

While I spend time with You, You make me stronger and You show me what to do next. Thank You for never leaving me. Thank You for holding me tight. Knowing You won't let go of my hand gives me the courage I need to keep going. As I walk along this rocky trail with You, I can hear *You telling me, "Don't be afraid. I will help you."*

In Your faithful Name, Jesus, *Amen*

READ ON YOUR OWN

PSALM 62:8; JEREMIAH 31:3; PSALM 46:10; ISAIAH 41:13

DON'T WASTE A MINUTE

"Don't worry about tomorrow. Each day has enough trouble of its own. Tomorrow will have its own worries."
—Matthew 6:34

Dear Jesus,

The most important fact in my life is that You are always with me—and always taking care of me. My parents, my friends, and the people who love me are often with me. But they can't be here every second of the day and night. *You* can, though, because You are bigger than time and space. You can be everywhere and in every moment—all at the same time!

That means I don't have to *worry about tomorrow* since You're already there! My future is safe in Your hands. So whenever a little bit of worry starts to sneak in, help me hear You saying, "My child, *don't worry.*"

Lord, I want to live this day abundantly. That means I want to see all there is to see and do all there is to do. Instead of wasting time thinking about tomorrow, I can trust You to take care of the future.

Today is a gift from You. Help me to live it joyfully—*in all its fullness*—forgetting about yesterday and not rushing ahead to tomorrow. When I focus on Your Presence with me, I can walk happily through my whole day!

In Your treasured Name, Jesus, *Amen*

READ ON YOUR OWN

PROVERBS 3:5–6; MATTHEW 6:34; JOHN 10:10

FIXING PROBLEMS

The Lord says, "I will make you wise. I will show you where to go.
I will guide you and watch over you."
—Psalm 32:8

Dear Jesus,

I'm learning that I will always have some problems. It's impossible to escape them because troubles are just a part of living in this broken world. I admit, though, that every time a problem pops up, I start trying to fix it. This is a habit that frustrates me and pulls me away from You.

Sure, there are some problems I can take care of, like studying more to bring up my grades or cleaning up the mess I made in my room. But there are other problems that I need Your help with—and some that I just need to trust You to take care of.

Remind me to talk to You about every trouble, asking You to show me what You want me to do. It might be something I can fix on my own, like cleaning up that big mess in my room. Or it might be something I can fix with Your help, like saying, "I'm sorry" when I've hurt a friend's feelings. Or it might be a bigger problem that You tell me not to worry about because You'll fix it Yourself in Your own perfect way.

When I focus on You, every problem—no matter how big—fades in the Light of Your wonderful Presence.

In Your bright Name, Jesus, *Amen*

READ ON YOUR OWN

PSALM 32:8; LUKE 10:41–42; PHILIPPIANS 3:20; JOHN 14:2–3

SEEING WITH MY HEART

*We are hoping for something that we do not
have yet. We are waiting for it patiently.*
—Romans 8:25

Dear Jesus,

You have given me five amazing senses: seeing, hearing, tasting, touching, and smelling. I use all these senses to experience the world around me. But seeing is the sense that I enjoy most of all. This world You've made is so beautiful! I love seeing it all, from the bright-yellow butterflies to the tall trees and the clouds in the sky. But the greatest gifts You've given me are things I can't see with my eyes. I can only see them with the "eyes" of my heart—with hope. These are amazing things like Your Face and the hope of heaven.

Even though I can't see Your Face with my eyes, I know that You are with me because You promised to be. I can't see heaven either—*not yet*. But one day I will because that's what You've promised to everyone who *believes in You*. It's why You died on the cross and were raised to life again—so that we could live forever with You and share in Your Glory. And You always keep Your promises.

Teach me to see all the blessings You give me in this world. And teach me to "see" with my heart and *wait patiently* for all the blessings You'll give me in heaven.

In Your great Name, Jesus, *Amen*

READ ON YOUR OWN

ROMANS 8:25; JOHN 3:16; JOHN 17:22; HEBREWS 11:1

PRAISE AND PROBLEMS

I will give an offering to show thanks to you.
And I will worship the Lord.
—Psalm 116:17

Dear Jesus,

Some things are bothering me, Lord. Some troubles. And if I'm honest, what I really feel like doing is whining and complaining about them. I just want to grumble about my troubles and ask, "Jesus, why are You letting all these things happen to me?" But I've learned that when I start complaining about the way You're treating me, I don't feel any better. I get more upset—and I feel sorry for myself. So I ask You to help me thank You and praise You, even though I'm still having these troubles. I know it sounds a little crazy. Who praises in the middle of their problems? But I'm noticing that when I'm busy praising You, it's impossible for me to whine or complain or get upset with You.

It's hard for me to get started with praise when I'm thinking about my troubles so much. But once I *do* start thanking You and worshiping You for all the blessings in my life, my heart begins to change. I remember that You are with me, that You're always helping me, and that You are bigger than any trouble I could ever face. Lord, *being with You fills me with joy!*

In Your joyful Name, Jesus, *Amen*

READ ON YOUR OWN

PSALM 116:17; PHILIPPIANS 4:4–7; PSALM 16:11

COMFORT WHEN I NEED IT

He comforts us every time we have trouble, so that we can comfort others when they have trouble. We can comfort them with the same comfort that God gives us.

—2 Corinthians 1:4

Dear Jesus,

Your Love never fails. It always comforts me. Because *this world* is broken, I often face *some kind of trouble.* I have lots of people and things to comfort me—my family and friends, my pet, my favorite toys. They can comfort me *some* of the time. But there is only one thing that is with me *all* of the time and never, ever fails: Your Love!

Your Love for me is perfect, even though I'm not at all perfect. You have an endless supply of Love for me—it will never run out or run low. But Your Love isn't just a *thing* that helps me feel better. It's You! You are Love! So *nothing in the whole world will ever be able to separate me from Your loving Presence.*

Help me remember who I really am. I'm Your beloved child. Because You love me so much, I know I can come to You for comfort anytime I need to. Your wonderful Love isn't just for me, though; it's for others too. Help me show my friends and family how much You love them by *comforting them when they have troubles—the same way You comfort me.*

In Your comforting Name, Jesus, *Amen*

READ ON YOUR OWN

PSALM 119:76; JOHN 16:33; ROMANS 8:38–39; 2 CORINTHIANS 1:3–4

MY JOY

"You should be happy because your names are written in heaven."
—Luke 10:20

Dear Jesus,

Because I trust You as my Savior, I know that *my name is written in heaven—in Your Book of Life*. That means I can have joy no matter what is happening around me. When I believe that You are God's own Son, who died and was raised to life again, then *I am made right with You*. All my sins are washed away, and You share *Your Glory* with me. But that's not all! *I am raised up with You and seated with You in the heavens.*

Anyone who is Your child can have Your Joy in good times, in hard times, and in every time between. So I come to You this morning with my heart and my hands wide open, saying, "Jesus, please give me Your Joy." While I wait here with You, the Light of Your Presence shines on me. It soaks all the way down into my heart and soul. This gives me the strength I need and gets me ready for today.

If my joy ever starts to run out, I can always come to You for more. You have an endless supply—there's always more than enough for me!

In Your joyful Name, Jesus, *Amen*

READ ON YOUR OWN

LUKE 10:20; REVELATION 21:27; ROMANS 8:30; EPHESIANS 2:6

APRIL

You have been saved by grace because you believe. You did not save yourselves. It was a gift from God.

—Ephesians 2:8

HAPPY TO NEED YOU

I praise you, O L<small>ORD</small>;
teach me your decrees.
—Psalm 119:12 <small>NLT</small>

Dear Jesus,

I'm growing up and learning to do things on my own. For some things, that's great—like tying my shoes, riding a bike, and doing my homework. But finding my own joy? Or finding my way to heaven? I won't ever be able to do those things without You, Lord. No one can! I need *You*.

The truth is, You created me to need You all the time—and to be happy about needing You. Help me to have this attitude so I can come closer to You in my heart, my thoughts, and my prayers. As I come close to You and You draw near to me, our friendship grows stronger and stronger. The Bible tells me to *always be joyful*. That can only happen when I'm living close to You.

Your Word also tells me to *never stop praying*. You hear my prayers, and You care about everything I say. Praying is the way I tell You how much I need You. I can also ask You to use the Bible to teach me and change me. These things keep me close to You and Your Joy. As I learn to find my *delight in You*, my joy becomes a way I praise You.

In Your wonderful Name, Jesus, *Amen*

READ ON YOUR OWN

1 THESSALONIANS 5:16–17 <small>NLT</small>;
DEUTERONOMY 31:8; PSALM 119:11–12 <small>NLT</small>; PSALM 37:4

BUILDING TRUST-MUSCLES

Stand against the devil, and the devil will run away from you.
—James 4:7

Dear Jesus,

Help me to *trust You and not be afraid.* You're teaching me that my troubles are like exercises. Just as doing jumping jacks over and over makes my heart and leg muscles stronger, trusting You with my troubles over and over makes my trust-muscles stronger.

Fierce battles are going on all around me—invisible battles between good and evil. And fear is one of the devil's favorite ways to attack me. Anytime I start to feel afraid, the best way to fight back is to tell You that I trust You. I can say it in my thoughts or in a whisper, or yell it out loud, but I really need to say it: "I trust You, Jesus."

The Bible tells me that if I *stand up against the devil, he will run away from me.* I can stand up to him by running to You. As I praise You and sing to You, *Your Face shines on me and You give me Your Peace.*

Help me remember that when I trust You as my Savior, You wash away my sins. Because You died on the cross, *I am not judged guilty.* So *I will trust in You and not be afraid. You are my strength and my song.*

In Your saving Name, Jesus, *Amen*

READ ON YOUR OWN

ISAIAH 12:2 NLT; JAMES 4:7; NUMBERS 6:24–26 NIV; ROMANS 8:1 NLT

I CAN GIVE MY WORRIES TO YOU

Give all your worries to him, because he cares for you.
—1 Peter 5:7

Dear Jesus,

Carrying around all my worries is wearing me out! They're so heavy that I feel like I'm carrying around a backpack full of rocks. But my back and shoulders aren't strong enough to handle this much weight. My heart and soul aren't strong enough to carry around a bunch of worries either. That's why You tell me to *give my worries to You*—and You promise to *take care of me*. What a relief! It feels so good to put these worries in Your hands.

Sometimes I don't realize I'm carrying them with me until they get so heavy I almost can't move. That's when I really need to talk to You! Help me to see my worries the way You see them. Show me if it's a problem I need to fix, like saying I'm sorry for a hurtful thing I said. If it's not my problem at all, please show me that too. Maybe it's something I just need to let go of, like worrying about whether my game will get rained out.

I'm happy that You promise *to use Your wonderful riches to give me everything I need*. Thank You for taking such good care of me, Jesus.

In Your precious Name, Jesus, *Amen*

READ ON YOUR OWN

PSALM 55:22; ISAIAH 9:6; 1 PETER 5:7; PHILIPPIANS 4:19

YOUR BRIGHT AND SHINING LIGHT

There will never be night again. They will not need the light of a lamp or the light of the sun. The Lord God will give them light.

—Revelation 22:5

Dear Jesus,

There's a lot of darkness—a lot of evil and meanness—in this world. But once I choose to follow You, I *never have to live in darkness.* Because You are with me, *I have the Light that gives Life.* And Your Light chases away the darkness.

I'm not sure what might happen tomorrow or the day after that. Sometimes I wish I knew so I could get ready for it. But the truth is, knowing *You* is enough! You have promised to take care of me today, tomorrow, and every day. You are God, so You can be in the future *and* be here with me—all at the same time. I just need to trust You and follow You one step at a time, as You shine Your Light on my path.

Someday I'll be with You in heaven, and Your Light will have chased away every speck of darkness. I'll be able to see everything clearly—including You! *There will never be night again. I won't need the light of a lamp or the light of the sun. You will give me Light*—brighter and better than anything I could ever imagine!

In Your bright and shining Name, Jesus, *Amen*

READ ON YOUR OWN

JOHN 8:12; PROVERBS 4:18; REVELATION 22:5

LOOK TO JESUS

*Let us look only to Jesus. He is the one who began
our faith, and he makes our faith perfect.*
—Hebrews 12:2

Dear Jesus,

Help me *not to get tired or stop trying* to do what is right and good. When I'm wrestling with problems that won't go away, it's easy to get tired and want to give up. Those kinds of problems wear me out. But it's not good to just sit around and think about my troubles. That can turn into a pity party *fast*!

Everything looks worse when I'm tired. That's when I'm most likely to quit trying. But then You remind me that You are near and I can *look to You* for help. I know You paid a terrible price so that You could be my Savior. *You suffered death on the cross.* When I think about how You went through so much pain and misery for me, I find new strength to face my troubles.

I'm learning that praising You is a wonderful way to feel stronger. As I worship You, Your Light shines on me even when I have a lot of problems. Please help me live close to You so I can be like a mirror and reflect Your Light to others. Thank You, Lord, for *changing me to be more and more like You.*

In Your beautiful Name, Jesus, *Amen*

READ ON YOUR OWN

HEBREWS 12:2–3; 2 CORINTHIANS 5:7; 2 CORINTHIANS 3:18

IN EVERY SITUATION

Depend on the Lord.
Trust him, and he will take care of you.
—Psalm 37:5

Dear Jesus,

I want to trust You so much that I don't try to force things to go my way. Sometimes I need to take a break from making plans and just rest in the Light of Your never-ending Love.

Your Light never fades or grows dim, but I don't always see it. Usually that's because I'm too busy thinking about the future. I'm planning who to see, and what to say and do next. Instead of all this planning, I should be trusting You and asking what *Your* plans are. Help me learn to live in the present, not the future. I want to depend on You to guide me through *this* moment to the next, and the next, and the next. Because You're with me, I don't have to be afraid of my weaknesses and the things I can't do. *You* can do anything!

You are training me to *always go to You for help*, even when I think I can handle it by myself. I don't want to divide my life into two parts: things I can do and things I need Your help for. You're teaching me to depend on You in *every* situation. When I'm trusting You, I can forget about my worries and just enjoy the day with You!

In Your loving Name, Jesus, *Amen*

READ ON YOUR OWN

PSALM 37:5; PHILIPPIANS 4:19; PSALM 105:4; PHILIPPIANS 4:13

NOT A PROBLEM

If God is for us, then no one can defeat us.
—Romans 8:31

Dear Jesus,

I wish I didn't have a single problem in my life. But I know that's not going to happen. In fact, before You went to the cross, You told Your followers, *"In this world you will have trouble."* In heaven, though, there won't be any more problems—not ever again! And when I trust You as my Savior, You save a spot in heaven just for me. That's a joy no one can ever take away. Help me wait patiently for the perfection of heaven. Because trying to make everything perfect here on earth just doesn't work.

Lord, please remind me to begin each day by talking to You. I ask You to give me the strength and wisdom I need to face what's ahead of me on my path. That's the best way to face any day: with *You* by my side. If I keep turning to You all through the day as problems pop up, You'll show me they aren't really just *my* problems. They're troubles that You and I will handle *together*. Help me remember that You are on my side, and *You have already defeated the world*!

In Your mighty Name, Jesus, *Amen*

READ ON YOUR OWN

JOHN 16:33; PSALM 73:23; PHILIPPIANS 4:13; ROMANS 8:31

KEEP SHINING

You shine like stars in the dark world.

—Philippians 2:15

Dear Jesus,

You are the Light that shines in the darkness. The darkness has not overpowered Your Light—and it never will! But when problems pile up around me, sometimes it's hard to see Your Light. I begin to forget that You're always close to me. Whenever I'm feeling like the darkness is surrounding me, remind to stop everything and *tell You all my problems.* As I talk to You, please show me what to do.

No matter how much evil I see in the world around me, Your Light *keeps shining*—strong and bright. It's a zillion-billion times more powerful than the darkness. And when I follow You, Your Light shines *on* me and *inside* me too.

There are *crooked and mean people all around.* That means I have many chances to *shine like a star in this dark world.* Before I can shine, though, I need to spend time with You, soaking up Your Light. Please *change me to be more like You,* Jesus. I make a lot of mistakes, but I want more than anything to live in a way that *shows Your Light and Glory.* Please help me do that.

In Your wonderful Name, Jesus, *Amen*

READ ON YOUR OWN

JOHN 1:5; PSALM 62:8; PHILIPPIANS 2:14–15; 2 CORINTHIANS 3:18

LITTLE BY LITTLE

"I told you these things so that you can have peace in me."
—John 16:33

Dear Jesus,

Help me learn to be joyful—even when troubles are pulling me down. To do that, I'm going to need to spend plenty of time with You. Because even though it seems like trouble and worry are everywhere in this world, You are *the One who has defeated and overcome the world.* Only Your Light and Love can give me the power to face all those problems with *good cheer*, with joy, and maybe even with a smile.

When I sit with You, resting in Your Presence, You shine peace into my heart and mind. Little by little, the worries and troubles slip out of my thoughts and You slip in.

Soon, I begin to see my troubles the way *You* see them. I realize that some things aren't important, and I can just let them go. And for the things that *are* important, I know I can trust You to help me with them. Resting here in prayer with You blesses me with *a joy that no one will take away* from me.

In Your Joy-filled Name, Jesus, *Amen*

READ ON YOUR OWN

JOHN 16:33 NKJV; PSALM 42:5; JOHN 16:22

TASTE AND SEE

Taste and see that the LORD is good.
Oh, the joys of those who take refuge in him!
—Psalm 34:8 NLT

Dear Jesus,

Your Word invites me to *taste and see that You are good*. When I follow You, life is sweeter and better. It's not problem-free, but it is good.

I'm so thankful that *You are the God who sees me*. You're training me to look for You too. Help me remember that You are here with me and You're working in every moment of my life. As Your Love flows into me, I can share You with those around me, helping them see how close and caring You are.

Sometimes Your blessings come in mysterious ways. They might start out as a struggle, like changing schools. But then they bring me a blessing, like a new friend. I don't always understand what You're doing, but I'm learning to *trust* that You're busy doing something good. So I'm going to stick close to You!

Thank You for the gift of Your Peace. This was the first thing You gave Your followers after You died and were raised to life. They were upset and afraid, so You calmed their fears with Your Peace. You do the same for me when I'm upset and afraid. Please block out all the voices that tell me I should be worried—and help me listen only to You. I love to hear You saying, *"Peace be with you!"*

In Your peaceful Name, Jesus, *Amen*

READ ON YOUR OWN

PSALM 34:8 NLT; GENESIS 16:13–14; JOHN 20:19; COLOSSIANS 3:15

I BELIEVE!

*Your faith has a goal, to save your souls. And you
are receiving that goal—your salvation.*
—1 Peter 1:9

Dear Jesus,

I can't see You with my eyes, but *I believe in You.* You are more real than the things I can see! More real than the trees, my room, and this book—because You are endless and eternal. No matter what's going on in my life, You are the never-changing Rock that I can count on. *I can always run to You for safety.*

Believing in You comes with so many blessings! Of course, the biggest blessing is *the saving of my soul* from sin—forever. That's a priceless gift! Believing in You also makes my life so much better right now. I know who I am: Your child. And I know who I belong to: You! You help me find my way through this broken and sinful world. You pour the hope of heaven into my heart. You listen to my prayers, *and* You answer them.

Lord, You are making more and more room for joy in my heart. I want to make more and more room for *You* in my life. Spending time with You helps me get to know You better. And the better I know You, the more *You fill me with a joy so great that it cannot be explained*!

In Your Name that is greater than all other names, Jesus, *Amen*

READ ON YOUR OWN

1 PETER 1:8-9; PSALM 18:2; ROMANS 8:25

LEARNING TO TRUST

The person who trusts in the Lord will be blessed.
The Lord will show him that he can be trusted.
—Jeremiah 17:7

Dear Jesus,

The Bible tells me that *the person who trusts in You will be blessed.*
So please help me to trust You with everything in my life—the big stuff
and the little stuff. I know that there are no accidents in Your kingdom. *In*
everything that happens, *You are working for the good of those who love You.*

I waste a lot of time trying to figure things out so I can understand
them better. But what I really need to do is spend more time trusting
and thanking You. Nothing is wasted when I stay close to You. You even
recycle my mistakes and turn them into something good—like helping
me help others who've made the same mistake. That's what Your grace
does for *those who love You.* Grace takes my mess-ups and changes them
into good things.

Even before I began trusting You, You were already shining Your
Light into my life. And *You began lifting me out of the sticky mud* of my
mistakes. *You stood me on a rock and made my feet steady.* You helped me
know the right things to do.

Thank You for c*alling me out of the darkness* of this world so that I
can live *in Your wonderful Light.* I know I can trust You with every detail
of my life!

In Your amazing Name, Jesus, *Amen*

READ ON YOUR OWN

JEREMIAH 17:7; ROMANS 8:28; PSALM 40:2; 1 PETER 2:9

YOU ARE LORD

Give all your worries to him, because he cares for you.
—1 Peter 5:7

Dear Jesus,

When things in my life don't turn out like I want them to, help me accept them right away. Dreaming about how I wish things had happened is a waste of time. And I've seen that feeling sorry for myself can quickly turn into feeling angry. Anytime I start getting upset, help me remember that You are Lord over all the events of my life. I need to *humble myself under Your powerful hand* and *give all my worries to You*. Thank You for all the ways You're working to help me—even when I don't understand what You're doing.

Jesus, *You are the Way and the Truth and the Life*. You give me everything I need for this life—and for living forever with You. I don't want the things that are happening in this world to pull my attention away from You. My challenge is to keep *looking only to You* no matter what's going on around me.

Please keep teaching me the way *You want me to live*. When You're in the center of my thoughts, I begin to see things the way You see them. That helps me walk closer to You, and *being with You fills me with joy*.

In Your perfect Name, Jesus, *Amen*

READ ON YOUR OWN

1 PETER 5:6–7; JOHN 14:6; HEBREWS 12:2; PSALM 16:11

POWERFUL GOD!

Lord, I trust you.
I have said, "You are my God."
My life is in your hands.
—Psalm 31:14–15

Dear Jesus,

I *come to You* in prayer because *I'm feeling tired*—like *I'm carrying a heavy load*. I want to rest here in Your Presence. I need *You*, Jesus, and I need Your Peace.

When everything is going right in my life, I sometimes forget how much I need You. Then, as soon as things start to go wrong, I get worried and upset. But that reminds me that I need You, and I turn back to You—looking for Your Peace. I can't always receive Your Peace right away, though. First I have to calm down and stop being upset. It would be so much better if I just stayed close to You all the time!

Please help me remember that You, the *Prince of Peace*, are also *Powerful God*! *All power in heaven and on earth has been given to You*. There's never a time I can't come to You and tell You about my troubles. But I need to come to You humbly, remembering how great and wise You are. Instead of getting upset or demanding that You do things my way, I can pray like King David did: *Lord, I trust You. You are my God. My life is in Your hands*.

In Your mighty Name, Jesus, *Amen*

READ ON YOUR OWN

MATTHEW 11:28; ISAIAH 9:6; MATTHEW 28:18; PSALM 31:14–15

WAIT, TRUST, HOPE

Jesus said, "Don't let your hearts be troubled.
Trust in God. And trust in me."
—John 14:1

Dear Jesus,

As I read Your Word, I'm learning that waiting, trusting, and hoping are all connected. They're like three pieces of rope that are braided together to make a bigger, stronger rope. I think trusting must be the most important part because the Bible teaches about it over and over again. Waiting and hoping are braided with the trusting part. And together, the three pieces make a strong rope that connects me to You. Please help me hold on tight to this rope!

Being patient while I'm waiting for You to work shows that I really do trust You. Sometimes I've said, "I trust You," and then tried to force things to go my way. But that just showed that I *wasn't* trusting You. Help me to really, truly trust You!

Hoping is all about reminding myself that no matter how tough things get here on earth, I have Your promise of heaven to look forward to. I can trust You to keep that promise, and that makes me happy.

But waiting and hoping aren't only about "someday in heaven." Once I ask You into my heart, I belong to You. I can wait and hope as I'm trusting You to do what's best for me *today* too—knowing that You're taking good care of me.

In Your holy Name, Jesus, *Amen*

READ ON YOUR OWN

JOHN 14:1; PSALM 56:3–4; PSALM 27:14; 1 JOHN 3:3

A LOVE THAT LASTS FOREVER

Show your kindness to me, your servant.
Save me because of your love.
—Psalm 31:16

Dear Jesus,

If I score the winning run, You love me. If I flunk the big test, You love me. If I do something great, You love me. If I mess up and fall on my face, You still love me. You love me no matter what. Thank You!

Sometimes though, Lord, I still wonder: Am I doing enough good things for You to keep on loving me? Please help me remember that Your love doesn't depend on what I do. *You love me with a Love that will last forever.* I don't have to work for it or worry about losing it. *You have covered me with Your coat of goodness* for all eternity! That means nothing will ever change Your love for me!

You're also showing me that I'm not very good at judging myself. When I try to do something right and it doesn't turn out very well, I feel like I've completely messed up. But You're happy and pleased with me because I tried.

Instead of worrying about whether the things I'm doing are good enough, help me focus on *Your Love*. It never fails, and it lasts forever. That's something to be really excited about!

In Your precious Name, Jesus, *Amen*

READ ON YOUR OWN

JEREMIAH 31:3; ISAIAH 61:10; PSALM 31:16

BETTER THAN ANY DAYDREAM!

With God's power working in us, God can do much, much more than anything we can ask or think of.
—Ephesians 3:20

Dear Jesus,

You are teaching me that worry is like a flashing sign. It's telling me that I'm forgetting about You. So the best way to stay out of the Worry Zone is to talk to You. Talking to You in prayer reminds me that You're right here with me. I know I can *give all my worries to You because You care for me.*

When I pray, please help me remember not to do all the talking. I want my prayers to be a conversation with You. I talk while You listen, *and* I read the Bible and listen while You talk.

Thank You for showing me what I should do when worry tries to sneak in. First, I need to stop thinking about what might or might not happen in the future. That's when the weeds of worry really grow! Second, it's important for me to remember that You've promised to be with me all the time. So whenever I'm making plans, I need to include You. You are here with me now, and You'll be with me in the future too.

It's easy to daydream about what *I* want to happen, but I know that *Your* plans are perfect. I'm learning to trust that what You want to happen is much, much better than any daydream could ever be!

In Your beautiful Name, Jesus, *Amen*

READ ON YOUR OWN

LUKE 12:22–25; 1 PETER 5:7; EPHESIANS 3:20–21

CAPTURE EVERY THOUGHT

We capture every thought and make it give up and obey Christ.
—2 Corinthians 10:5

Dear Jesus,

When You made me, You gave me the wonderful ability to *choose* what I think about. That's a sign that I am *created in Your image.* So please help me choose to think about You.

There are times when my thoughts get stuck on worries and fears. Those thoughts can grow bigger and bigger until they're even bigger than my thoughts about You! But You're teaching me to push those worries right out of my mind by saying, "I trust You, Jesus!" Then You remind me that You've got this under control and You're taking care of me.

Lord, You know everything about me. You know every thought I think! I can hide my thoughts from other people—but not from You. So please help me guard my thoughts, only letting in the ones that honor You. Teach me to *capture every thought* as it zips through my mind and then bring it to You. If any thought doesn't please You, help me toss it out of my mind.

As I sit with You, the Light of Your Presence chases away the dark, worried thoughts. And You keep Your promise to *give perfect peace to everyone who trusts in You.*

In Your comforting Name, Jesus, *Amen*

READ ON YOUR OWN

GENESIS 1:27; 2 CORINTHIANS 10:5; PSALM 112:7; ISAIAH 26:3 NLT

NOTHING TO FEAR

God makes people right with himself
through their faith in Jesus Christ.
—Romans 3:22

Dear Jesus,

I love that You know me completely! *You have examined my heart and know everything about me. You know when I sit down or stand up. And You know all my thoughts.* You see everything I do and think. Even my most secret thoughts and feelings are easy for You to see. If *everyone* could see my secret thoughts, it would be scary! But I trust You with them because I am Your beloved child. When *I believe in You*, I have nothing to fear because You cover me with Your own goodness and righteousness. You make me a member of Your royal family forever and ever!

Anytime I'm feeling alone or afraid, please remind me to talk to You. Your Presence with me is what chases away my loneliness and fear. I know You always listen to my prayers, even the ones I only think in my heart. But sometimes it helps me to say them out loud. I never have to explain to You what's happening because You already understand me and the things I'm going through. So I can just dive right in and ask You to help me. Once I've talked to You, I like to spend time resting with You—knowing that You're glad to be with me, just like I'm glad to be with You.

In Your royal Name, Jesus, *Amen*

READ ON YOUR OWN

PSALM 139:1–3 NLT; 1 CORINTHIANS 13:12 NLT; ROMANS 3:22; PSALM 21:6

YOU FIGHT FOR ME

Letting the Spirit control your mind leads to life and peace.
—Romans 8:6 NLT

Dear Jesus,

You will fight for me. That's what the Bible says. I just need to *be still* and calm, trusting You to take care of me.

I keep trying to do the right things and work out my problems for myself. But sometimes things seem to get worse no matter what I do! And some of my problems are just too big for me. All this struggle makes me very tired. *Tired* is not what You want for me, though. I'm learning that You want me to stop trying to fix everything myself. That's not easy for me. A lot of times, I just keep trying harder and harder. But that means I'm counting on myself instead of counting on You. I'm sorry, Lord! Help me *be still and know that You are God*—remembering that *You* have the real power to fix things.

Lord Jesus, You're the One who keeps me safe. I ask You to keep working in me and changing me. Please calm my spirit with the Peace of Your Holy Spirit. Help me *rest in the shadow of Your Almighty Presence* while You fight for me.

In Your powerful Name, Jesus, *Amen*

READ ON YOUR OWN

EXODUS 14:14 NIV; PSALM 46:10; ROMANS 8:6 NLT; PSALM 91:1 NLT

I WON'T GIVE UP!

Trust the Lord with all your heart.
Don't depend on your own understanding.
—Proverbs 3:5

Dear Jesus,

I'm coming to You today because I need rest. There's so much happening right now! Some things have been really good and some not-so-good. But now I'm tired and exhausted. I used to get mad at myself for feeling tired. You're teaching me, though, that being tired isn't always a bad thing. It can actually be a blessing when it reminds me to lean on You.

Please don't let me forget how You can *work everything into Your good plan for me*—even the things I wish hadn't happened. I've seen You do it over and over again! When I come to You, I know You'll guide me through this day, one step at a time and one minute at a time. My job is to keep looking to You, asking You to guide me through every choice I need to make.

I wish that was as easy as it sounds. The devil is always trying to trick me and pull my attention away from You. He likes to make bad things look good and good things look bad. And he would love for me to give up on You. But I won't give up! Instead, I'm going to *trust You with all my heart* and follow You even when I don't really understand what You're doing. And I'm going to *keep praising You* for all the ways You help me every day.

In Your awesome Name, Jesus, *Amen*

READ ON YOUR OWN

ROMANS 8:28; PROVERBS 3:5; PSALM 42:5

I CAN CHOOSE

The Lord is good to those who wait for Him,
to the person who seeks Him.
—Lamentations 3:25 HCSB

Dear Jesus,

Help me *be strong and brave* today. You've been showing me that I can *choose* to be strong and brave even when I'm feeling a little weak and scared. I can do that by choosing where I look. If I look at my problems and what *I* can do to fix them, I don't feel brave at all—my courage melts away. But if I look to *You* for answers, trusting You to guide me through the tough times, I feel strong!

I need to remember that *You will be with me everywhere I go*. Knowing that You're with me makes all the difference! It's so much easier to be brave when I remind myself that You are *beside* me and You're fighting for me.

Even when everything seems to be turning out wrong, I can still trust You. With Your never-ending supply of creativity and power, *all things are possible for You*! So I'm giving You my worries and fears. And while I wait for Your answers, I'm going to remember that Your loving Presence is right here with me. The Bible promises that *You are good to those who wait for You*. And I know that's true. Waiting for You is a wonderful way to live!

In Your amazing Name, Jesus, *Amen*

READ ON YOUR OWN

JOSHUA 1:9; MATTHEW 19:26; LAMENTATIONS 3:25–26 HCSB

THE BEST THING I CAN DO

You lead me and give me good advice,
and later you will lead me to glory.
—Psalm 73:24 ERV

Dear Jesus,

Help me to trust that *Your love will never disappear.* Because sometimes, Lord, it seems like there's a lot more bad than good in this world. It feels like things are out of control. But *You* aren't worried or afraid. You're not wondering what to do next. No! You're in complete control. And You are always pouring Your goodness into this world and working to make things right—even when I can't see it. I praise You for that, Jesus!

There is *no end to Your wisdom and knowledge. No one can explain Your decisions or understand Your ways.* Especially not me. The best thing I can do is *trust You all the time.* When I'm worried and afraid, when I don't understand, I will still trust You.

Please help me remember that *You are always with me. You hold my hand. You are leading me* so I can stay close to You. And because I believe in You, You will someday lead me all the way to heaven. I can't see it yet, but one day I will. Thank You for such amazing blessings—now and in the future!

In Your holy Name, Jesus, *Amen*

READ ON YOUR OWN

ISAIAH 54:10; ROMANS 11:33; PSALM 62:8; PSALM 73:23–24 ERV

SAFE AND SECURE

*We set our eyes not on what we see but on what we
cannot see. What we see will last only a short time.
But what we cannot see will last forever.*
—2 Corinthians 4:18

Dear Jesus,

I'm happy that You're with me every moment of every day! You are with me when I wake up in the morning and when I go to sleep at night. You are with me in my good times and in my troubles. You are with me when I'm cleaning my room or taking out the trash. Because You love me so much, every detail of my life matters to You. *You even know how many hairs are on my head!*

When I remember all that, I feel so safe and secure. But sometimes, Lord, I forget. I get busy, or I start thinking about a problem. My thoughts wander away from You. That's when worry sneaks in and my peace sneaks out.

Please teach me how to keep my spiritual eyes—the eyes of my heart—on You every moment, even while I'm busy doing other things. That's something that only You can help me do. This world changes all the time, but *You* never change. You're always with me. So I want to keep *my eyes set on what I cannot see*—You!

In Your never-changing Name, Jesus, *Amen*

READ ON YOUR OWN

MATTHEW 10:29–31; HEBREWS 11:27; 2 CORINTHIANS 4:18

THE RIGHT WAY

All of you holy brothers and sisters, who were called by God, think about Jesus, who was sent to us and is the high priest of our faith.
—Hebrews 3:1 NCV

Dear Jesus,

Help me to see my struggles and challenges as a chance to trust You more. I know You are right here beside me, Lord. And when I choose to follow You, Your Spirit comes to live inside me. So there's nothing that You and I can't handle together. But when my day is filled with struggles, I start thinking about how *I* will face them. And that leads me straight to worry and fear—and away from You. Help me not to forget that I *always* need You.

Thank You for teaching me the *right* way to face challenges: by holding on tight to Your hand and talking to You. I'm learning that my day goes so much better when I remember to stay by Your side—trusting and thanking You all day long.

Instead of trying to solve all my problems, I can choose to *think about You*. Your Word promises that *You give true Peace. You give peace to those who depend on You. You give peace to those who trust You.* So please help me to keep doing that—trusting You and depending on You.

In Your great Name, Jesus, *Amen*

READ ON YOUR OWN

JAMES 1:2; PHILIPPIANS 4:13; HEBREWS 3:1 NCV; ISAIAH 26:3

YOUR KIND OF JOY

Yes, I am sure that nothing can separate
us from the love God has for us.
—Romans 8:38

Dear Jesus,

I want to live as close to You as I can—every minute of the day. But I'm still figuring out how to do that. My thoughts get pulled away so easily. Sometimes it's by fun things. Other times it's by problems.

I used to think that a good day was when everything was going my way. So I would try to make sure things went how I wanted. When it worked, I was happy. When it didn't work, I would get sad or upset. Then I learned what Your Word says: it's possible to *be happy at any time*, no matter what happens!

Instead of trying so hard to control everything, help me focus on trusting You. I want my joy to come from You and Your precious promises in the Bible. Because that's the kind of joy that teaches me how to be happy even when things aren't going my way. Thank You, Lord, for speaking these promises to me through Your Word:

I am with you, and I will protect you everywhere you go.

I will use My wonderful riches to give you everything you need.

Nothing in the whole world will ever be able to separate you from My Love.

In Your wonderful Name, Jesus, *Amen*

READ ON YOUR OWN

PHILIPPIANS 4:12; GENESIS 28:15; PHILIPPIANS 4:19; ROMANS 8:38–39

BECOMING LIKE YOU

God decided to let his people know this rich and glorious secret which he has for all people. This secret is Christ himself, who is in you. He is our only hope for glory.

—Colossians 1:27 NCV

Dear Jesus,

I'm so glad I can come to You anytime and talk about whatever is on my mind. I can just sit and rest with You, soaking up Your Love—knowing that You always understand what I'm feeling.

The world isn't like that. People aren't always kind, and they don't always understand me. So sometimes I don't feel loved. But the Bible tells me that I *am* loved—at all times! Help me to see myself the way *You* see me: as someone You love so much that You were willing to die on the cross to save me. You created me, and You want me to be with You in heaven. Even now, *You are changing me to be like You—to show Your Glory.* Thank You, Jesus, for loving me so much!

As I sit quietly in Your Presence, I realize more and more that You really are here with me. And when I trust You as my Savior, Your Spirit actually comes to live inside me. I don't understand how that works, but I believe it and I'm thankful for it. Because then the Light of Your Presence doesn't just shine *on* me, it shines *in* me too! *You are in me*, and I am in You. This means that nothing in heaven or on earth can ever separate me from You!

In Your magnificent Name, Jesus, *Amen*

READ ON YOUR OWN

PSALM 34:5; 2 CORINTHIANS 5:21;
2 CORINTHIANS 3:18; COLOSSIANS 1:27 NCV

WHERE JOY COMES FROM

We all show the Lord's glory, and we are
being changed to be like him.
—2 Corinthians 3:18

Dear Jesus,

It would be great if following You erased all my troubles so I could have a problem-free life. But I know that won't happen because Your Word tells me that *in this world I will have trouble*. So if joy can't come from having a problem-free life, then joy must come from belonging to You—and from knowing that one day I will be with You in heaven. Instead of trying to make the world around me perfect, I need to focus on seeking *You*, Jesus, because only You are perfect.

I'm learning all these things from You. You're also teaching me that it's possible to praise You even in the middle of my troubles. Your Spirit helps me trust You in these tough times. When I trust You, especially in my darkest times, Your Light shines through me. I really want to shine brightly for You, Jesus!

Please keep working on me, making me more and more the person You created me to be. Help me to get rid of things like selfishness and anger and pride. I'm sorry that I sometimes try to hurry You up or slow You down. I know Your timing is perfect! I'm so grateful that *You are always with me, holding my hand and guiding me*.

In Your mighty Name, Jesus, *Amen*

READ ON YOUR OWN

JOHN 16:33; 2 CORINTHIANS 3:18; PSALM 73:23–24

PUTTING DOWN THE PEBBLE-PROBLEMS

The Lord's love fills the earth.
—Psalm 33:5

Dear Jesus,

Help me to stop thinking about myself so much—about what I want and the problems I'm facing. Help me to think more about You instead!

Sometimes I imagine I'm standing at the edge of the ocean. The beach is covered with pebbles. Each one is like one of my problems. I pick up a small pebble-problem and hold it close to my eyes, looking at all the tiny details. But when I hold it that close, the pebble blocks out my view of the great big, beautiful ocean! Usually, as soon as I put down one pebble-problem, I pick up another one and hold it close to my eyes—looking at all its details. Focusing on problems like this keeps me from seeing the beauty of Your Presence and the blessing of *Your Love that fills the earth.*

Lord, I want to put down all the pebble-problems so that I can see *You.* I can almost hear You whispering: "Choose Me, dear one. Choose to see Me instead of focusing on your problems."

Please teach me to choose You all through the day—every day! That's the way to stay close to You. And when I'm close to You, *You fill me with Your Joy.*

In Your beautiful Name, Jesus, *Amen*

READ ON YOUR OWN

HEBREWS 12:2; PSALM 33:5; HEBREWS 11:27; PSALM 16:11

MY STRENGTH AND SHIELD

The LORD is my strength and my shield;
my heart trusts in him, and I am helped.
—Psalm 28:7 NIV

Dear Jesus,

You are *my Strength and my Shield*! Thank You for all the ways You protect me and make me stronger. I'm learning that the more I trust You, the happier I am—sometimes *my heart even leaps for joy*!

Help me to trust You with my whole heart. You're in control of the entire universe. You keep the sun and moon and stars shining in the sky. Because You can do all that—and so much more—I know You're able to take care of me! When my life gets crazy and everything feels like it's spinning out of control, remind me to reach out and grab on to Your hand. Because You know what You are doing. You hold everything in Your hands, and You are always good. I can't expect to understand all the things You're doing, Lord. *Your ways are higher than my ways, just as the heavens are higher than the earth.*

When trouble comes, I want to remember to thank You because I know that You can bring something good out of my situation. Thanking You during tough times gives You glory and gives me strength. So *I will give thanks to You in song*!

In Your joyful Name, Jesus, *Amen*

READ ON YOUR OWN

PSALM 28:7 NIV; PSALM 18:1–2; ISAIAH 55:9; ROMANS 8:28

MAY

"Come to me, all of you who are tired and have heavy loads. I will give you rest."

—Matthew 11:28

WORTH MORE THAN GOLD

Troubles come to prove that your faith is pure. This
purity of faith is worth more than gold.
—1 Peter 1:7

Dear Jesus,

Help me to find joy everywhere I go, especially in the places where I don't think I'll find it. I know I'm going to have to do my part—I'll need to search for the good and the wonderful. Please open my eyes to see it. Teach me to look past what is right in front of my face to find Your hidden treasures, like a tiny flower poking up through a crack in a sidewalk or a bird making its nest in a tree outside my window.

This world is so broken and full of sin that sometimes it's hard work to find joy. It's even harder when I'm having troubles of my own. But the Bible tells me to *look at troubles as an opportunity to find great joy.* It's like a challenge or a test! Searching for joy and finding it makes my faith in You even stronger. And a strong *faith is worth more than a mountain of gold.*

Jesus, You chose to *suffer death on the cross for the Joy put before You.* Your Joy was knowing that You were making a way *to bring many children into Glory*—children like me! Thank You for choosing to save me so I can live with You forever in heaven!

In Your bold and brave Name, Jesus, *Amen*

READ ON YOUR OWN

JAMES 1:2–3 NLT; 1 PETER 1:6–7; HEBREWS 12:2; HEBREWS 2:10 NLT

YOU DELIGHT IN ME!

He will take delight in you with gladness.
With his love, he will calm all your fears.
He will rejoice over you with joyful songs.
—Zephaniah 3:17 NLT

Dear Jesus,

Sometimes I hear You whispering in my heart, "*I delight in you.*" That makes me smile. Your delight doesn't depend on me doing everything right, either. No! You delight in me because You love me with a never-ending Love. Please help me learn to relax while *You calm all my fears with Your Love.*

This world is not an easy place to live. There's so much sadness and badness and sin all around me. And honestly, Lord, it's inside me too. You chose to die on the cross so that You could wash away my sins. Please wash me clean and help me to spend more time thinking about *You*—instead of focusing on all the things that are wrong.

Thank You for adopting me into Your own royal family. *I am saved by Your grace because I believe.* I don't ever have to work for Your Love. It's a wonderful gift that I'll have forever! Your gift of Love makes me want to stay close to You, ready to follow You wherever You lead.

In Your wonderful Name, Jesus, *Amen*

READ ON YOUR OWN

ZEPHANIAH 3:17 NLT; PSALM 27:8; NUMBERS 6:25–26; EPHESIANS 2:8

BECAUSE YOU LOVE ME

About three o'clock Jesus cried out in a loud voice,
"Eli, Eli, lama sabachthani?" This means, "My God,
my God, why have you left me alone?"
—Matthew 27:46

Dear Jesus,

Your Word tells me that *You have made a wide path for my feet to keep them from slipping.* You don't want me to fall into wrong ways of thinking or living, so You walk ahead of me—protecting me from things that might confuse me or hurt me. You make the path of my life easier to follow.

Sometimes You let me see the troubles that You've saved me from. Other times, You hide them from me so that I won't worry or be afraid. You do all these things because You love me!

Even though You clear away so many of my troubles, You still leave some of them on my path. I don't really understand why. But then I remember that You had lots and lots of troubles during Your life in this world. People said terrible things about You. They laughed at You. You were arrested and beaten, and You were hung on a cross to die. While You were on the cross, there was even a time when Your Father-God turned away from You. You were all alone and hurting, Jesus. You suffered through all those things so that I would never have to be alone when I'm hurting. *You are with me always*, and I'm so thankful that You are!

In Your marvelous Name, Jesus, *Amen*

READ ON YOUR OWN

PSALM 18:36 NLT; PSALM 121:3; MATTHEW 27:46; MATTHEW 28:20

OUT ON A LIMB

*"Anyone who wants to serve me must follow me,
because my servants must be where I am."*
—John 12:26 NLT

Dear Jesus,

There are days when I feel like You're asking me to go "out on a limb"—putting myself in a scary situation as if I'd climbed up a tree and gone out onto a shaky branch. You might be asking me to forgive that kid who said ugly things behind my back or to reach out to the new kid in my class. Or You might be asking me to trust You and do what You say is right, even when I'm afraid. Climbing out on a limb can be scary. But I also know that You'll be out there on that limb with me. And that makes it the safest place for me to be.

You've been teaching me that I shouldn't try to just "play it safe" all the time—never taking any risks. *That's* not the way You want me to live. You want me to step out and do things that challenge me. Because it's doing those hard things that helps me learn to be more like You. You never ask me to do it alone, though. You are always there, holding my hand and guiding me.

Life with You is an adventure, Jesus. And You promised that I can count on You *to be with me and protect me wherever I go.* Please help me to trust You and not be afraid.

In Your ever-watchful Name, Jesus, *Amen*

READ ON YOUR OWN

PSALM 23:4; JOHN 12:26 NLT; PSALM 9:10; GENESIS 28:15 NLT

141

NEW THINGS

"The things I said would happen have happened.
And now I tell you about new things."
—Isaiah 42:9

Dear Jesus,

Help me to live in the present—not in the past or the future. I want to *give all my attention to what You are doing right now.* I don't want to be wondering *about what may or may not happen tomorrow.* But I'll be honest: it's not easy for me to live this way. Instead of trusting You to take care of my tomorrows, I like to have an idea of what's going to happen. I often try hard to control things and make them go *my* way.

I admit that I waste a lot of time focusing on the future. Mostly, I worry that there will be a problem I don't know how to handle. But Your Word promises that *You will help me deal with whatever hard things come up—when the time comes.*

Sometimes, the more I try *not* to think about the future, the more I end up thinking about it! It's like hearing someone say, "Don't touch your nose." Then all I can think about is touching my nose! But You're teaching me that the way to stop worrying about the future is to look for what *You* are doing in my life right now. And You are always doing *new things* for me!

In Your perfect Name, Jesus, *Amen*

READ ON YOUR OWN

MATTHEW 6:34 THE MESSAGE; HEBREWS 12:2; ISAIAH 42:9

THE INVITATION

"Come to Me."
—Matthew 11:28 NASB

Dear Jesus,

You are always inviting me closer to You. I can almost hear You whispering, *"Come to Me*, dear child. *I love you with a Love that will last forever. I became your Friend because of My Love and My kindness."*

Jesus, I like to say yes to Your invitation by being still in Your Presence—relaxing and *thinking about You*. One of my favorite things to think about is the wonderful truth that *You are always with me*. It's one of my favorites because this world is changing all the time. My friends change, my teams change, my schools change—even *I'm* changing as I learn and grow up and get bigger. But *You* never change. I can count on You to be the same loving, wise, and ready-to-help Lord that You have always been.

That's what I need to remember, to help me stay alert to the truth that You are with me every second of every single day. When I forget, please remind me that Your loving Presence is here with me right now.

I'm learning that the closer to You I live, the happier I am. You bless me with Your Joy and help me bring joy to others.

In Your blessed Name, Jesus, *Amen*

READ ON YOUR OWN

MATTHEW 11:28 NASB; JEREMIAH 31:3; HEBREWS 3:1; PSALM 73:23

THE GOD WHO HELPS PEOPLE

From long ago no one has ever heard of a God like you.
No one has ever seen a God besides you,
who helps the people who trust you.
—Isaiah 64:4 NCV

Dear Jesus,

I'm learning to do more and more things on my own. Sometimes I like to think I can do *everything* on my own. But that's not really true. Actually, it's good that I can't do everything because it reminds me how much I need You.

I need You to help me forgive when I don't want to, be kind and helpful when I'd rather not, and trust You when I'm feeling worried. Jesus, I mess up so many times! All my mistakes and messes show me that I need Your help. But most of all, I need *You*—the Savior who is strong and perfect. Help me trust You to *give me everything I need.*

I know I can ask You for anything. You don't always show me Your answers right away, but I'm learning to wait for You, believing that You *will* answer at just the right time and in the perfect way. Your Word promises that *You help the people who trust You.* You take care of the things I can't do. And *You give me the strength* to do what I can. Thank You for always being ready to listen and help.

In Your saving Name, Jesus, *Amen*

READ ON YOUR OWN

PHILIPPIANS 4:19; ISAIAH 64:4 NCV; 1 PETER 4:11; 2 CORINTHIANS 12:9

I CAN LEAN ON YOU

Even children become tired and need to rest,
and young people trip and fall.
But the people who trust the Lord will become strong again.
—Isaiah 40:30–31 NCV

Dear Jesus,

You give strength to those who are tired. And *You give more power to those who are weak.* So please help me not to give up when I'm feeling tired and weak. Remind me to turn to You and ask for Your help instead.

Some days really wear me out, and there's just too much to do. Some days my body just doesn't feel strong enough. On other days I feel sad, worried, or scared. But I'm learning that when I feel any of those things—or all of those things—I can lean on You. You promise that if I lean on You and *trust in You, I'll become strong again.*

This isn't something I should do just when I feel weak or tired, though. I should lean on You all the time! You want me to live every day looking for You—because *You are the Living One who sees me.*

The more time I spend thinking about who You are and all that You've done for me, the more I trust You. And the more I trust You, the more time I *want* to spend with You. As I relax with You, *Your unfailing Love surrounds me*—wrapping me in comfort and increasing my strength.

In Your loving Name, Jesus, *Amen*

READ ON YOUR OWN

ISAIAH 40:29; ISAIAH 40:30–31 NCV;
GENESIS 16:14 NLT; PSALM 33:20–22 NLT

CREATED TO PRAISE

Through Jesus let us always offer to God our sacrifice
of praise, coming from lips that speak his name.
—Hebrews 13:15 NCV

Dear Jesus,

I want to live every moment in Your Presence, enjoying Your Peace. Your Presence and Your Peace are amazing gifts, and they're for everyone who believes in You. Ever since You rose up from the grave, You have comforted Your followers with these wonderful messages: *"Peace be with you"* and *"I will be with you always."*

Each day You offer me the gifts of Your Peace and Your Presence. Help me to accept these precious gifts with a happy heart. I'm learning that the best way to accept them is to thank You for them.

Lord, You created me to praise You. That means I can never spend too much time praising You. The more I sing and thank You in this way, the more You fill me with Your Joy! How wonderful is that?

One of the best things about praising You is that it helps me remember who You are—the Lord of everything. It also helps me remember who *I* am—the child You will love forever. That gives me even more reasons for praise! This is a gift that You never stop giving. Thank You, Jesus!

In Your amazing Name, Jesus, *Amen*

READ ON YOUR OWN

MATTHEW 28:20; LUKE 24:36; HEBREWS 13:15 NCV; 2 CORINTHIANS 9:15

A FAITH TEST

These [troubles] are testing your faith.
And this will give you patience.
—James 1:3

Dear Jesus,

Help me learn to praise You and rest in Your Presence even when everything around me is going wrong. Times like this are like a test of my faith. To pass the test, I need to believe in You and trust You to take care of me.

But that's tough sometimes, Lord. It's almost like I'm living in two different worlds—the natural world that I can see, and the spiritual world that I can't see. In the natural world, troubles pop up around me like popcorn—I see them everywhere. But when I come to You and spend time in Your Presence, I'm focusing on the spiritual world. My troubles don't seem so big anymore because I'm paying attention to *You*. I remember that You are in control and You're so much greater than all my problems—and all the troubles in the world! Each time I choose to trust You instead of worrying, I'm "exercising" my faith. And every time I see You keep Your promises, my spiritual muscles get stronger.

I can also exercise my trust-muscles by studying Your Word. I need to keep *searching for You* in the Bible. You promise to *give me the strength I need to do all the things You want me to do.* And I know You always keep Your promises!

In Your faithful Name, Jesus, *Amen*

READ ON YOUR OWN

JAMES 1:2–3; PSALM 105:4 NLT; PHILIPPIANS 4:13

I WON'T BE AFRAID

He won't be afraid of bad news.
He is safe because he trusts the Lord.
—Psalm 112:7

Dear Jesus,

In this world, it seems like there's some sort of bad news all the time. But I don't want to *be afraid of bad news* or to worry about what's happening. Help me remember that *I am safe because I trust You.* You will take care of me.

When I think about how You were willing to die on the cross for me, I'm so thankful. And when I remember how You rose up from the grave, I'm amazed at how strong and powerful You are. Jesus, You're my living Savior, and You are Almighty God! You're bigger and stronger than any bad news could ever be. You hold the whole world in Your hands!

When everything around me feels like it's spinning out of control, I can come to You and *tell You all my problems.* Instead of worrying or being afraid, I can put that energy into talking to You. As I spend time with You, please comfort me and show me the right way to go. I want to stay close to You, Jesus.

Because I belong to You, I don't have to worry about bad news or let it scare me. I can stay calm by trusting in You—no matter what happens.

In Your comforting Name, Jesus, *Amen*

READ ON YOUR OWN

PSALM 112:7; ISAIAH 9:6; ISAIAH 40:10 NCV; PSALM 62:8

ONE CHOICE THAT'S ALWAYS RIGHT

Yes, God's riches are very great! God's wisdom and knowledge have no end!
—Romans 11:33

Dear Jesus,

Whenever I start to feel sorry for myself, please remind me that I need to trust You more. And when I wish I could just run away and hide, help me remember that You are with me.

It's hard to think clearly and make good choices when I'm in the middle of a big problem. Sometimes it seems like *way* too many choices are swirling around me—so many that I get a little dizzy. That makes it even tougher to know what to do. But I know there's one choice that's always right: choosing to *trust You with all my heart*.

When I start slipping into worry, or when I feel like giving up, I can stop all that by saying, "I trust You, Jesus!" I can shout it, say it, or just whisper it. Then I can think about all the reasons I have for trusting in You: You always keep Your promises, You're always with me, and You never stop loving me. Thank You for letting me soak in Your *Love that lasts forever.*

Anytime I feel like hiding under the covers, remind me to talk to You instead. You know everything about me, *and* You know about all the things happening in my life. You understand me perfectly!

In Your encouraging Name, Jesus, *Amen*

READ ON YOUR OWN

PROVERBS 3:5; PSALM 52:8; ROMANS 11:33

TEACH ME TO SEEK YOU

"You will search for me. And when you search for
me with all your heart, you will find me!"
—Jeremiah 29:13

Dear Jesus,

Thank You, Lord, for changing me and helping me find *a new way of thinking*. Because when I just let my thoughts go wherever they want, they usually go toward problems. Before I know it, my mind is stuck on one pesky problem. Then it will spin round and round in my head as I try to figure it out. But I can't, and that makes me feel even worse. It also makes me tired. I end up feeling drained, and I don't have enough energy left to do the things I need to do. Worst of all, I forget about *You*!

Even though I sometimes forget You, Lord, You never forget me! Please keep reminding me that You are near, ready to help. Teach me to seek You—to *go to You for help*—in every situation, including my problems. And thank You for blessing me with little reminders of Your loving Presence, like the smile of a friend, sunlight shining through the clouds, and a bird's pretty song.

I love being able to sit quietly and find that You are right here with me. But I'm learning that the most important place to search for You is in the Bible. The more *I search for You*, the more *I find You*—and the more You change me to become like You.

In Your magnificent Name, Jesus, *Amen*

READ ON YOUR OWN

ROMANS 12:2; HEBREWS 3:1; PSALM 105:4; JEREMIAH 29:13

TRUST AND THANKS

I trust in your love.
My heart is happy because you saved me.
—Psalm 13:5

Dear Jesus,

There are days when it feels like *everything* is going wrong. I wake up late, spill my milk, and stub my toe before I've even stepped outside the door! And then things get even worse. When I'm having one of those days, my life feels like it's being turned upside down. That's when I need to remember to thank You and tell You that I trust You. It sounds kind of crazy. But I'm learning that when I trust *and* thank You in the middle of these rough days, I start to feel better. And my problems seem a little smaller.

If I choose to whine and complain about everything that's going wrong, I get grumpy. *That* makes me want to grumble even more. Then I end up feeling grumpier than before! It's like being on a slippery downhill slide that keeps getting steeper and steeper—the more I complain, the faster I slide. The only way to stop sliding down is to tell You "I trust You" and to *thank You for everything.* This can be really hard for me to do, but it works!

Please help me remember to turn back to You whenever I start whining and complaining. If I stop whining, and I trust You and thank You instead, You bless me with *a peace that is so great I cannot understand it.* And that *peace keeps my heart and mind safely in You*, Jesus.

In Your all-powerful Name, Jesus, *Amen*

READ ON YOUR OWN

PSALM 13:5; EPHESIANS 5:20; PHILIPPIANS 4:6–7

MORE ROOM FOR YOU

Let your unfailing love surround us, LORD,
for our hope is in you alone.
—Psalm 33:22 NLT

Dear Jesus,

Sometimes my plans and problems take up too much room in my mind. That's when I need to turn to You and whisper Your Name: "Jesus." Just saying Your Name brings me into Your Presence, where I can rest with You and enjoy *Your unfailing Love.*

Thank You for watching over me all the time and for loving me—now and forever. I love You, Lord, and I trust You to shine Your Light into each day. You show me what I need to do today *and* what I don't need to do. Help me not to worry about problems that *might* come up either.

The more I pay attention to You, the better I can see things the way You see them. A wonderful way to keep my attention on You is to fill my mind and heart with Your Word. Reading, studying, and memorizing verses brings me closer to You. It's just like the Bible says: *Your Word is like a lamp for my feet and a light for my path.*

The more I think about and study the Bible, the less I think about my own plans and problems. That leaves room in my mind for more of You. As I spend time with You, Lord, please *fill me with the joy of Your Presence!*

In Your delightful Name, Jesus, *Amen*

READ ON YOUR OWN

PSALM 33:22 NLT; 1 PETER 5:7; PSALM 119:105 NCV; ACTS 2:28 NLT

THIS WAY

If you go the wrong way—to the right or to the left—
you will hear a voice behind you. It will say, "This
is the right way. You should go this way."
—Isaiah 30:21

Dear Jesus,

Your Word promises that if I belong to You, then *I am not judged guilty for my sins*. Because You died on the cross, I am set free. I am *free from the law that brings sin and death*. Your sacrifice not only frees me from guilt and punishment for my sins, but it also helps me live free from worry and fear. All of that happens when I choose to trust in You.

If I want to live in Your freedom, I have to keep You in the center of my thoughts. In this world, there are plenty of voices trying to tell me what to do and which way to go. Some of them are good, like my parents' voices. But many others are not so good—and some are really bad. I can easily get confused by the voices that are trying to lead me away from You!

Jesus, You are the Good Shepherd—You are *my* Shepherd. Help me to be content and happy to be one of Your sheep. I want to listen for Your voice and follow You, because only *You* lead me perfectly. *You give me rest in green pastures. You lead me to calm waters. You give me new strength. For the good of Your Name, You lead me on paths that are right.*

In Your lovely Name, Jesus, *Amen*

READ ON YOUR OWN

ROMANS 8:1–2; ISAIAH 30:21; JOHN 10:27; PSALM 23:1–3

IN GOOD TIMES AND TOUGH TIMES

God is the one who saves me;
I will trust him and not be afraid.
—Isaiah 12:2 NCV

Dear Jesus,

I love to hear You whisper in my heart: *"Don't worry, because I am with you. Don't be afraid, because I am your God."* These loving words feel like a soft, warm blanket wrapped around me—protecting me from the cold of fear and worry.

On those days when troubles seem to follow me wherever I go, remind me to hold tight to Your hand and keep talking to You. Help me to *trust You and not be afraid because You give me strength and make me sing.* You are powerful, and You are always with me. I don't have to face anything alone. Not ever! Thank You for promising *to make me strong and help me.*

Sometimes, when everything is good and happy in my life, I forget how much I need You. But when *I'm walking through the darkest valley,* I really see how weak I am without You. I need to keep holding on to Your hand so I'll be able to take the next step—and the next one after that. Help me learn to trust You in the good times *and* the tough times. Please bless me with peace and joy in Your Presence, Lord.

In Your strong Name, Jesus, *Amen*

READ ON YOUR OWN

ISAIAH 41:10; ISAIAH 12:2 NCV; PSALM 23:4 NLT

LIVE IN TODAY

Jesus, our high priest, is able to understand our weaknesses.
When Jesus lived on earth, he was tempted in every way. He was
tempted in the same ways we are tempted, but he never sinned.

—Hebrews 4:15 ERV

Dear Jesus,

This is the day that You have made! Help me to *rejoice and be glad in it.*

Lord, I come to You this morning with my hands lifted up and empty. I'm ready to receive everything You want to pour into me today. You are writing the story of my life, so I don't want to complain about any of it. Not the weather, not my homework, not brothers or sisters—not one single thing.

I'm learning that the best way to handle troubles is to start by thanking You for them. This helps me not to grumble. And it reminds me to look for the blessings hidden in my problems. Sometimes You show me those blessings right away—like quickly making a friend on my new team. Other times, I have to wait to find Your blessings. At *all* times, You give me the wonderful gift of Your Presence with me!

You know that I can't handle the trouble of more than one day at a time. That's why You're teaching me to live in *this* day—not yesterday or next week. I don't want to *worry about tomorrow* or get stuck thinking about the past. Instead, I want to focus on *today*, the day that You have made, enjoying Your Presence!

In Your joyful Name, Jesus, *Amen*

READ ON YOUR OWN

PSALM 118:24 NLT; HEBREWS 3:13; HEBREWS 4:15 ERV; MATTHEW 6:34

NOTHING IS AS GOOD AS KNOWING YOU!

*People might make many plans, but what
the Lord says is what will happen.*
—Proverbs 19:21 ERV

Dear Jesus,

Every time something messes up my plans or what I want, I have a choice to make. I can choose to be upset, or I can choose to talk with You.

When I choose to talk with You, I'm blessed in so many ways. Just telling You about what's bothering me helps me feel better and brings me closer to You. Also, You're able to take my disappointments and change them into something good. This makes it possible for me to be joyful even when things don't go the way I wanted.

Please help me to keep telling You about all the little disappointments that happen in my day—from the yucky lunch to the rained-out game. And teach me to look for the good that You bring out of them. Thinking like this helps me feel better and remember that I am blessed. Someday I hope I can feel this way about my big disappointments and losses. But for now, I'm practicing on the smaller things. I want to become more like the apostle Paul. He wrote that he believed everything he had lost was like *worthless trash compared to the greatness of knowing You*!

In Your marvelous Name, Jesus, *Amen*

READ ON YOUR OWN

PROVERBS 19:21 ERV; COLOSSIANS 4:2; PHILIPPIANS 3:7–8

MY SAFETY NET

"Be sure of this: I am with you always, even to the end of the age."
—Matthew 28:20 NLT

Dear Jesus,

I love hearing You whisper to my heart, *"I am with you. I am with you. I am with you."* These words give me so much comfort. When I feel like giving up, or like I'm falling into a deep pit of sadness, Your encouraging words catch me like a safety net.

Even though I'm young, there are already plenty of ups and downs in my life. But Your promise that You are with me keeps me from falling too far down. Please open my eyes to see all the ways You're helping me— and catching me when I fall.

Sometimes I count on other people and they let me down. That hurts, but then I remember that You *never* let me down. So instead of crying or complaining, I can turn to You and tell You everything. This totally changes my attitude! You help me see that there are still so many things to be thankful for. You remind me that *You are with me and You are holding my hand. You are guiding me* and, one day, You will lead me all the way home to heaven. This is just what I need: Your loving Presence with me now and the promise that I can live with You forever in heaven!

In Your glorious Name, Jesus, *Amen*

READ ON YOUR OWN

MATTHEW 28:20 NLT; ZEPHANIAH 3:17; PSALM 73:23–24

WHAT OTHER PEOPLE THINK

Being afraid of people can get you into trouble.
But if you trust the Lord, you will be safe.
—Proverbs 29:25

Dear Jesus,

It's easy to see myself the way I *think* others see me. But that's a dangerous trap that can really hurt me. Lord, help me not to fall into that trap.

The truth is, there's no way to know what other people are actually thinking. I can't read their minds. Plus, people change their minds all the time! Friends might be grouchy with me because they're having a bad day, not because they don't like me. But the biggest problem with worrying about what others think is that I try too hard to please them. I might even start to care more about pleasing *them* than about pleasing *You*. This can lead to all kinds of problems—like saying something mean about someone or making up a lie, just to try to fit in. Please forgive me when I do these things. Jesus, I want You to be the most important Person in my life!

You're showing me that the only way to see myself as I really am is to look through *Your* eyes. I am Your wonderfully made creation. You love me perfectly and endlessly. And You never change Your mind about that. Help me to see myself and others the way You do, Lord. As I focus on You and Your amazing Love, I want to *worship You in spirit and truth*.

In Your great Name, Jesus, *Amen*

READ ON YOUR OWN

PROVERBS 29:25; HEBREWS 11:6; ROMANS 5:5; JOHN 4:23–24

I'M BUILDING ON SOLID ROCK

"Everyone who hears these things I say and obeys them is like a wise man. The wise man built his house on rock."
—Matthew 7:24

Dear Jesus,

With each new day I'm seeing more and more how wonderful it is to depend on You! I feel safe and secure because I know You won't let me down. It's like I'm *building a house on solid rock*, and that house is my life. When winds and storms come my way, I can keep standing because I've built my life on You.

I'm also learning that depending on myself—or other people or things—isn't a good plan. It's like *building a house on sand*. Sometimes the storms and troubles of life are just too big, and people don't always keep their promises. The winds and storms come, and the house built on sand falls with a *splat!*

Lord, help me depend on You in the storms and also on sunny days when my life is peaceful. I need to practice relying on You every day, so I can be ready for whatever happens. It's not just about getting ready for stormy days, though. Depending on You gives me so much joy! Because relying on You means staying close to You. You encourage me, guide me, and make me strong. As I *live in the Light of Your Presence, I rejoice in You*, Lord. Building my life on You is the best way to live!

In Your joyous Name, Jesus, *Amen*

READ ON YOUR OWN

MATTHEW 7:24–27; PSALM 89:15–16; 1 THESSALONIANS 5:16

MY SHEPHERD

God can do anything!
—Luke 1:37 NCV

Dear Jesus,

You are my Shepherd, the One who watches over me. So I know I can come to You with all my problems and struggles—the struggles in my spirit, in my feelings, and in my life. As I rest with You, You comfort me with Your Presence. I remember that *You can do anything*, and that *fills me with joy*.

Help me to stop thinking so hard about my problems and to spend more time thinking about You, Lord. You're the One who is able to *do much, much more than anything I can ask or imagine*. Instead of telling You what I think You should do, I need to look for what You are *already* doing. Because I know that what You're doing and planning is so much better than anything I could plan!

If worry tries to sneak into my thoughts, remind me that You are my Shepherd. Since You are taking care of me, I don't have to be afraid of anything! Instead of trying to fix everything myself, I want to let You take more and more control of my life. Honestly, trusting You like that can be a little scary! But I'm learning that the safest place to be is right beside You.

In Your comforting Name, Jesus, *Amen*

READ ON YOUR OWN

LUKE 1:37 NCV; PHILIPPIANS 4:4; EPHESIANS 3:20–21 NCV; PSALM 23:1

GENTLE AND KIND

Whoever is wise will remember these things.
He will think about the love of the Lord.
—Psalm 107:43

Dear Jesus,

Help me be *full of Your Joy always*. I want to be *gentle and kind* to everyone, so that they'll know that *You* are gentle and kind.

My problem is, I can get grouchy when things don't go my way. Sometimes I complain. And my bad attitude spills out and all over others. That's not how You want me to be. You want me being gentle with others, not grouchy. And now I'm starting to see that praising You is the best way to stop the grouchiness and complaining. I can do that because You give me so many things to be thankful for!

I can rejoice because You never change. *You're the same yesterday, today, and forever.* And I can be joyful because You are near. You love me and comfort me and bless me with reasons to be happy—more reasons than I can count!

Please help me remember to thank You and praise You all the time. I don't want to just thank You at bedtime or praise You at church. I want to thank and praise You all through the day, every day. And that's easy to do when *I think about how much You love me!*

In Your wonderful Name, Jesus, *Amen*

READ ON YOUR OWN

PHILIPPIANS 4:4–5; GALATIANS 5:22–23; HEBREWS 13:8; PSALM 107:43

REASONS TO BE GLAD

Thank the Lord because he is good.
His love continues forever.
—Psalm 118:1

Dear Jesus,

This is the day that You have made! That's all the reason I need to *rejoice and be glad.* But You don't stop there! You fill my day with blessings and with so many chances to grow closer to You. I want to walk through this whole day with You—searching for all the delights and treasures You've prepared for me. And I want to thank You for every single one I find! Every day, I can *thank You because You are good and Your Love continues forever.*

Yes, this world is full of troubles and sadness—that's what sin does. But I'm figuring out that whenever I spend too much time thinking about the problems and sadness, I miss all the reasons You give me to be glad today. I miss the bright and beautiful treasures You've poured into this day.

Lord, please help me to focus on You and Your blessings, not on the troubles around me. When I'm thankful, I can walk through the darkest day with joy in my heart. That's because I know that *the Light of Your Presence* is still shining on me. I'm so grateful for You, Jesus, the Friend who is always by my side.

In Your bright and beautiful Name, Jesus, *Amen*

READ ON YOUR OWN

PSALM 118:24; COLOSSIANS 4:2; PSALM 118:1; PSALM 89:15–16

THE LIGHT OF YOUR GOOD NEWS

God once said, "Let the light shine out of the darkness!" And this is the same God who made his light shine in our hearts.
—2 Corinthians 4:6

Dear Jesus,

The Light of the Good News about Your Glory is a priceless treasure! This amazing news tells me about who You are and how You save people who believe in You. The thing that makes the Good News so wonderful is that it gives me a way to know *You*, my perfect Savior.

When I decide to trust You as my Savior, You put me on a path that leads to heaven. You forgive my sins, and You make a home for me in heaven, where I can live with You forever. Those are such amazing gifts. But You give me even more! *You shine Your Light into my heart.* That Light *shows me that the Glory of God is in Your Face,* Jesus. Help me *come to You* and give You my whole heart. I want to know You better!

I learn more and more about You as I read Your Word. I learn that You are always with me and always working in my life, and so many other wonderful truths! *The devil has blinded the minds of those who do not believe.* But I believe in You, Jesus, and the Bible shows me clearly who You are. Help me live close to You, enjoying the Light of Your glorious Presence.

In Your wonderful Name, Jesus, *Amen*

READ ON YOUR OWN

2 CORINTHIANS 4:4; 2 CORINTHIANS 4:6; PSALM 27:8 ERV

TASTE AND SEE

The Lord is close to everyone who prays to him,
to all who truly pray to him.
—Psalm 145:18

Dear Jesus,

I know You are always with me, but sometimes I can't feel Your Presence. Sometimes it seems like You're very far away. But even then, I can call out to You and know that You have never left my side. The Bible promises that *You are close to everyone who prays to You.* All I have to do is whisper Your Name and You'll help me let go of my doubts and questions. As I whisper "Jesus," I know You are here!

I like to spend time telling You about all that is happening in my day. Please show me what You want me to do about my problems. While I wait for You to guide me, I will praise You, Lord. You are so great and majestic, so powerful and glorious! I enjoy thinking about You—about how amazing You are! Thank You for all the good things You're doing in my life.

The Bible tells me to *taste and see that You are good.* The more I focus on You and your blessings, the more I can taste Your goodness. Your *unfailing Love* is sweeter than honey or candy. Your strength encourages me and reminds me of good food that make me strong. When my heart is hungry, You fill it with the joy and peace of Your Presence. And You promise, *"I am with you, and I will protect you everywhere you go."*

In Your sweet Name, Jesus, *Amen*

READ ON YOUR OWN

PSALM 145:18; PSALM 34:8 NLT; ISAIAH 54:10 NIV; GENESIS 28:15

YOU ARE WRITING MY STORY

I pray that the God who gives hope will fill you with much joy and peace while you trust in him. Then your hope will overflow by the power of the Holy Spirit.

—Romans 15:13

Dear Jesus,

Help me remember that challenges and troubles come and go. But *You are always with me.*

I'm so grateful that You are writing the story of my life! You can see the whole story all at once. So You know everything that has happened and everything that will happen—from the moment I was born until I meet You in heaven. You know exactly what I'll be like when I'm living in heaven with You. Meanwhile, You never stop working on changing me. You're always helping me become the person You created me to be. Your Word comforts me and tells me that I'm already a member of Your royal family.

One of my favorite ways to be close to You is to say Your Name. "Jesus" is the simplest prayer—just one word. But it tells You that I trust You, I believe You are here with me, and I know You're taking care of me. You are *the God who gives hope. You fill me with much joy and peace while I trust in You.* When I sit quietly with You, I can almost hear You whisper: *"Come to Me, all of you who are tired and have heavy loads. I will give you rest."* Your loving Presence is my greatest treasure!

In Your comforting Name, Jesus, *Amen*

READ ON YOUR OWN

PSALM 73:23; 1 PETER 2:9; ROMANS 15:13; MATTHEW 11:28

IN THE MORNING

Tell me in the morning about your love.
I trust you.
—Psalm 143:8

Dear Jesus,

Tell me about Your Love in the morning, every morning. Even when my life isn't easy, help me to *trust You* and enjoy the Love You shine down on me. And whenever I feel like giving up, help me choose to trust You instead. Remind me of who You are: the Creator of the whole universe, the One who keeps the earth spinning and the sun shining, my Savior, my Lord, and my Friend.

I know I can count on You, Jesus, because Your Love never changes and never ends. It never runs out and never stops shining into my life. Best of all, Your Love is always mine to enjoy—whether I mess up or whether I do great. Your perfect Love never changes because *You are the same yesterday, today, and forever.*

I'm blessed when I take time to *lift my prayers up to You*. I'm learning to wait in Your Presence—praising You and enjoying You. You use this waiting time to work in my heart and help me get ready for the day. Then You show me *what I should do* and *You guide me* step by step. I'm so thankful that *You are my God forever and ever!*

In Your guiding Name, Jesus, *Amen*

READ ON YOUR OWN

PSALM 143:8; HEBREWS 1:2–3; HEBREWS 13:8; PSALM 48:14

NOTHING BETTER

Let everything that breathes praise the Lord.
Praise the Lord!
—Psalm 150:6

Dear Jesus,

I praise You because Your Love is better than anything—even better than life! There's no limit to it either. That makes me so happy! Your Love is greater than anyone else's love. There's always more of it than I can ever dream of. And it never ends. Your Love is better than anything this world has to offer. It's the greatest treasure in the universe!

Your precious Love makes my life so much better—in so many ways. It gives me a rock-solid foundation to stand on. That means that no matter what else happens in my life, I can count on You because You Love me perfectly. Knowing that You love me like this helps me to love others more. And it helps me grow into the person You created me to be.

When I think about *how wide and how long and how high and how deep Your Love is,* I just have to stop and worship You. My praises bring me closer to You, where I can celebrate and enjoy Your wonderful Presence.

The psalm says, *Let everything that breathes praise You, Lord.* And that's what I say too!

In Your loving Name, Jesus, *Amen*

READ ON YOUR OWN

PSALM 63:3; PSALM 36:7; EPHESIANS 3:16–18; PSALM 150:6

THINK ABOUT GOOD THINGS

Think about the things that are good and worthy of praise. Think about the things that are true and honorable and right and pure and beautiful and respected.
—Philippians 4:8

Dear Jesus,

Your Word tells me I should *think about the things that are good and worthy of praise.* That sounds pretty easy, but it's really hard for me to keep my mind on good things.

People like to complain in this world. And it's the bad news that seems to get all the attention online and on TV. Sometimes it's a struggle to find good news. Especially good news about what You and Your people are doing.

If I'm honest with You, Lord, I have to admit that I complain a lot too. When Adam and Eve ate that forbidden fruit, and sin came into the world, it messed up *everything*, even people's minds. This changed the way everyone thinks—the way *I* think. It's easier for me to think about the bad things than the good things. I have to work hard to keep my attention on all the good that is around me—and there is a lot! Please help me choose to look for good things every hour of every day, and to be full of joy.

I know it's true that this world has lots of problems, but there are so many *more* things that I can praise You for. One of the best things is the promise that *You are always with me*—even closer than my thoughts!

In Your excellent Name, Jesus, *Amen*

READ ON YOUR OWN

PHILIPPIANS 4:8; GENESIS 3:6; PHILIPPIANS 4:4; PSALM 73:23

JUNE

This God is our God forever and ever.
He will guide us from now on.

—Psalm 48:14

THINKING ABOUT YOU

God, we come into your Temple.
There we think about your love.
—Psalm 48:9

Dear Jesus,

I love spending time with You and *thinking about Your Love* for me. *You are my God forever and ever.* Please turn my thoughts back to You anytime my mind wanders away.

Long ago, Jacob from the Bible said, *"Surely the Lord is in this place."* I know that's still true today, and thinking about that encourages me a lot. No matter where I am, You are with me. I'm so grateful that You are my God—today, tomorrow, and forever!

You are also *my Guide.* I can easily get a little spooked when I start thinking about the future. I forget that You lead me through every step of this day and all my tomorrows. You've been guiding me step by step ever since I trusted You as my Savior. Help me remember that You are with me every moment—when I wake up in the morning, during my classes, at my music lessons or games, when I'm playing with my friends, when I'm eating dinner with my family, and when I lie down to sleep at night.

One way I'm learning to get closer to You, Jesus, is by whispering Your Name. This reminds me that You are here beside me. Instead of *worrying about anything*, I can *pray and ask You for everything I need.* I know You are already working on the answers!

In Your blessed Name, Jesus, *Amen*

READ ON YOUR OWN

PSALM 48:9–10, 14; GENESIS 28:16; PHILIPPIANS 4:6

YOUR HELP

*God wanted them to look for him and perhaps search all
around for him and find him. But he is not far from any of us.*
—Acts 17:27

Dear Jesus,

Sometimes I need You to help me ask You for help—because I don't always remember to do that. I run as fast as I can from one thing to the next, from practice to chores to homework, trying to get everything done. Except that I don't really finish any of it, and I don't do anything well. Clothes are just stuffed in the drawers, my homework is sloppy, and I don't stop to read my Bible. When I race through my day, I get worried and stressed. Anytime that happens, please remind me to *stop*, take a deep breath, and whisper Your name. Talking to You calms me down. *Then* I remember: *You lead me on the paths that are right.*

I usually think to ask You for help when I'm about to do something difficult. But if it's just regular, everyday stuff, I often tell myself, "Oh, it's nothing big. I'll just handle it." The truth is, I need You for *all* of it—the big stuff *and* the little stuff.

Teach me to be humble and admit that I need You in everything I do. As I wait here now in Your loving Presence, I love to hear You whispering this promise: *"I will guide you along the best pathway for your life."*

In Your comforting Name, Jesus, *Amen*

READ ON YOUR OWN

PSALM 23:3; ACTS 17:27; PSALM 32:8 NLT

YOU UNDERSTAND ME COMPLETELY

Lord, you have examined me.
You know all about me.
—Psalm 139:1

Dear Jesus,

You know me better than anyone else—even better than I know myself! You understand everything I'm thinking and feeling. There's no detail that You don't know. You've counted every hair on my head and You can hear every beat of my heart. You also know all the not-so-great stuff that I try to hide. But I don't have to be worried or scared about that. You love me because I'm Your child, not because of what I do or don't do.

Please shine the Light of Your Presence into my heart. Wash away all the hateful and hurtful things I've done and said. Heal the sadness, the fear, and the worry that I feel inside. And please give me Your Strength, Joy, and Peace.

Help me trust You enough to accept Your wonderful offer to forgive every one of my sins. To receive this amazing gift, which You paid for on the cross, I just need to believe in You and ask You to be my Savior. Thank You for dying for my sins and for comforting me with this promise: *"I will not leave you or forget you."*

When I'm thinking that no one could ever understand me, *You* do, Jesus. I can come to You anytime and be filled all the way up with Your Love. That's what I want—to be so full of Your Love that it spills out onto everyone I meet.

In Your loving Name, Jesus, *Amen*

READ ON YOUR OWN

PSALM 139:1–4; JOHN 1:16–17; JOSHUA 1:5 NCV

IT'S OKAY TO REST

By the seventh day God finished the work he had been doing.
So on the seventh day he rested from all his work.
—Genesis 2:2

Dear Jesus,

Thank You that I can *come to You* whenever *I'm tired* or I feel like I'm carrying *a heavy load*, and *You will give me rest.* This is something I'm learning from You—that there's a time to keep going and a time to just stop and relax. Even You took time to rest! On the seventh day, after You had created everything in the world, *You rested from Your work.*

Please teach me to make room in my life for You-and-me time, where I can just sit and enjoy Your loving Presence. When I'm with You, the Light of Your Face *smiles on me* and I feel Your kindness all around me. Lord, You know everything I'm feeling. I can't hide anything from You—and I don't want to! As we spend time together, Jesus, You help me remember some of my favorite Bible verses. Your Love soaks deep down inside me, and I get to tell You how much I love You—using whispers and praises and songs.

Help me really and truly believe that I don't have to work to earn Your Love. And help me believe that it's okay to rest. Because every time I rest in Your Presence, You bless me with Your Joy and You give me the strength I need.

In Your joyful Name, Jesus, *Amen*

READ ON YOUR OWN

MATTHEW 11:28; GENESIS 2:2; NUMBERS 6:25–26 NLT

CHANGING ME

We know that in everything God works for
the good of those who love him.
—Romans 8:28

Dear Jesus,

Sometimes I can feel the Light of *Your Glory* shining on me. It's warm like the sun and makes me smile. These moments—when I'm praising You and You're pouring Your Love into me—are like treasures glowing brightly in my heart!

I'm learning that when *I look to You* through prayer and worship, I'm able to take in the Light of Your Glory and then let it shine out into the world around me. But there are days when I'm so busy with friends or sports or my schoolwork that I forget You're right beside me, just like a best friend is. Thankfully, You've created me with the ability to think about more than one thing at a time. Help me to make sure that one of the things I'm thinking about is *You*!

Thinking about You helps me in many ways. When I remember that You're with me, I try harder not to do or say things that would make You unhappy. Also, when I'm struggling with a problem, thinking about You comforts me and cheers me up.

Thank You for using our time together to *change me to be more like You*, Jesus. I know that You can use *everything* in my life *for good*!

In Your wonderful Name, Jesus, *Amen*

READ ON YOUR OWN

HEBREWS 12:2; 2 CORINTHIANS 3:18; ROMANS 8:28

I BELONG TO YOU!

Don't you realize that your body is the temple of the Holy Spirit, who lives in you and was given to you by God? You do not belong to yourself.
—1 Corinthians 6:19 NLT

Dear Jesus,

On those days when I'm only thinking about making myself happy, I usually end up feeling upset and disappointed. No matter how hard I try, I can't make things go my way. But pretty soon You show me the problem: I'm acting like I'm the center of my world. The truth is, *You* are really the center of everything! You're the One who is in control! So it's okay for me to make plans, but please remind me to *go to You* and talk to You about them. I need to be ready to change my plans if You have a different idea.

This is actually a great way to live. If things go how I've planned, I can thank You and be happy. But if Your plan is different, I know it's the *perfect way*, because that's what the Bible says. So I can trust You and follow Your plan instead of mine.

Help me remember that *I don't really belong to myself.* Because You paid for my sins when You died on the cross, I belong to You. What a relief! I can stop thinking so much about what *I* want. I can quit trying to force things to fit my plans—and think about how to please *You*. That sounds like it might be hard work, but *the work You ask me to do is easy. And the load You give me to carry is not heavy.* Best of all, knowing that I belong to You gives me *rest for my soul.*

In Your restful Name, Jesus, *Amen*

READ ON YOUR OWN

PSALM 105:4; PSALM 18:30 NLT;
1 CORINTHIANS 6:19 NLT; MATTHEW 11:29–30

A TASTE OF JOY

Then I will know everything completely, just
as God now knows me completely.
—1 Corinthians 13:12 NLT

Dear Jesus,

Help me trust You with my whole heart and to follow wherever You lead. As we walk along together, I know there will be plenty of problems and challenges. In fact, the Bible is teaching me that *each day has its own troubles*. So I should expect to have some troubles every day, and some of those struggles may be really hard to get through.

Help me not to let the daily troubles keep me from enjoying Your Presence. My life with You is an adventure, and every adventure includes some dangers. There are rivers that have to be crossed and mountains that must be climbed. But with You by my side, I can bravely face whatever challenges are on my path—and never stop trusting You.

Following You makes me happy. It fills me with *a joy that is too big to be explained*. I can't find this kind of joy anywhere else—only with You! And even though this joy is wonderful, it's only a taste of the happiness that I'll have in heaven. Because that's where I'll see You face to Face, and I will *know You completely*. I can't even imagine how huge and awesome that joy will be!

In Your powerful Name, Jesus, *Amen*

READ ON YOUR OWN

MATTHEW 6:34; 1 PETER 1:8; 1 CORINTHIANS 13:12 NLT

YOU ARE EVERYTHING!

*Jesus has the power of God. His power has given us
everything we need to live and to serve God.*
—2 Peter 1:3

Dear Jesus,

You are everything I could ever need in a Savior. And when I choose to believe in You, *You come to live in me*, filling me with bright, shining life and love! I want Your Life and Love to grow so huge inside of me that they spill over and "splash" onto everyone around me.

Please live through me and love through me as I talk and work and play with others. Let my words show Your Love—not just to my friends and family but to my neighbors too. Help me be polite to my teachers and coaches, and also to the people who work in stores or bring the mail or drive the trash truck. And let my actions be like a light that shows others who You are.

I admit that sometimes the world gets me down, and then I feel like I'm not good enough. But with You *I have a full and true life. You give me everything I need to live and serve You.* It's Your power that will get me through this day, through my whole life, and all the way to heaven.

You've said that You want me *to know You* and be close to You. Thank You for inviting me to share my happiest moments with You—and my biggest struggles too. And best of all, because You were willing to die on the cross, all my sins can be forgiven. You are my Savior and my forever Friend. I love You, Lord!

In Your amazing Name, Jesus, *Amen*

READ ON YOUR OWN

GALATIANS 2:20; COLOSSIANS 2:9–10; 2 PETER 1:3

MY SHIELD OF FAITH

*Use the shield of faith. With that you can stop
all the burning arrows of the Evil One.*
—Ephesians 6:16

Dear Jesus,

I'm bringing You *all* my feelings today. Even the ones I wish I didn't have—like my fears and worries. Sometimes those feelings just won't go away. Mostly that's because I'm thinking of everything I'm worried about instead of trusting You.

Fear and worry are like arrows that the devil has set on fire. And he keeps shooting them right at me! He wants me to be so busy with the arrows that I don't look to You for help. Teach me to use my *shield of faith*—my trust in You. That's the only thing that will *stop all those burning arrows*.

I'm tired of hiding my fears and worries, Jesus. Stuffing them down inside my heart only makes them grow bigger. Instead, I need to bring them out into the Light of Your loving Presence and let You show me what to do with them.

I'll say it right now: "I trust You, Lord." Please help me to keep saying that short prayer, no matter how I feel. Because when I tell You that I trust You, that's how I raise up my Shield. And when I remember how near You are, those flaming arrows don't stand a chance!

In Your mighty Name, Jesus, *Amen*

READ ON YOUR OWN

EPHESIANS 6:16; 1 JOHN 1:5–7; ISAIAH 12:2

PLAYING CATCH

The LORD himself watches over you!
The LORD stands beside you.
—Psalm 121:5 NLT

Dear Jesus,

The Bible tells me to *cast all my cares on You because You care for me.* "Cast" means toss or throw, like a baseball. So You want me to just throw my cares to You. And since You're such a great Catcher, that's exactly what I'm going to do. I'm going to toss You every single one of my cares—my worries and fears. You might end up with a bucket full of them, but I know You're okay with that.

Letting go of all those things feels so good! I can breathe a sigh of relief and relax in Your Presence. Remind me to do this whenever a fear or worry sneaks into my thoughts. It doesn't matter if it's day or night. You are always awake—ready to catch my cares and help me feel better.

Your power is gigantic, Lord. It's so huge that there's no end to it! So helping me is easy for You, even if my troubles are really big. I've found that "playing catch" with You gives me joy and peace in my heart. No matter how much I throw at You, You never drop the ball or miss a catch!

Anytime I realize I'm wrestling with a problem, I can stop and just toss it to You. I can even smile a little when I throw it. Thank You, Jesus, for always *watching over me* and catching all my cares!

In Your perfect Name, Jesus, *Amen*

READ ON YOUR OWN

1 PETER 5:7 NKJV; PSALM 139:23; PSALM 68:19; PSALM 121:5–6 NLT

HEADED THE RIGHT WAY

The Lord will always lead you.
He will satisfy your needs in dry lands.
He will give strength to your bones.
You will be like a garden that has much water.
You will be like a spring that never runs dry.
—Isaiah 58:11

Dear Jesus,

I want to walk through this day with joy. I can do that when I walk with *You*, holding Your hand and trusting You to take care of me. You are the perfect Guide! With You by my side, I can laugh and be happy and enjoy the good things that happen. If something not-so-great happens, or even something bad, I can trust You to help me get through it. You fill each day with many wonderful gifts: a colorful sky, new adventures, people who love me, and a safe place to rest with You when I'm tired. I'm so thankful for how You guide me through each day, from morning to night.

Because *You are the Way*, I know I'll be headed the right way as long as I stay close to You. Help me to keep *thinking about You* and talking to You. Teach me not to worry about what might happen later today or even tomorrow or next week. And whenever I feel alone, please remind me that You are always right by my side. Then I can just focus on enjoying Your Presence and staying close to You as we walk through this day together.

In Your joyful Name, Jesus, *Amen*

READ ON YOUR OWN

PHILIPPIANS 4:13; ISAIAH 58:11; JOHN 14:6; HEBREWS 3:1

A REASON TO BE THANKFUL

Give thanks whatever happens. That is what
God wants for you in Christ Jesus.
—1 Thessalonians 5:18

Dear Jesus,

I'm going to stop everything and sit quietly with You for a few minutes. This way I can just enjoy being in Your Presence in *this* present moment. If my thoughts get stuck on something I did in the past, I start to feel farther away from You. The same thing happens if I worry about the future. I can only live in this moment right now. And this is where You come to meet me.

Jesus, You're teaching me to keep talking to You all the time. Even short, little prayers keep me close to You—like "I trust You, Jesus" and *"I love You, Lord"* and "Help me, Jesus." These prayers also remind me that You're always watching over me with love in Your heart. You never sleep, and You never go on vacation or even take a day off. Thank You for that, Lord.

I'm learning that having a thankful heart helps me stay close to You. When I forget to thank You, my friendship with You gets weaker. Please help me remember that You're making a home for me in heaven—in Your *kingdom that cannot be shaken.* So no matter what happens, I always have a great reason to *be thankful!*

In Your precious Name, Jesus, *Amen*

READ ON YOUR OWN

PSALM 18:1; HEBREWS 12:28–29 NIV; 1 THESSALONIANS 5:18

THE SECRET TO BEING HAPPY

It is good to praise the Lord,
to sing praises to God Most High.
—Psalm 92:1

Dear Jesus,

The apostle Paul figured out *the secret to being happy*—to being content—*at any time and in everything that happens.* I want to learn that same secret. I know it's something You'll have to train me to do.

Some days it's easy to be content, like when everything is going my way. The sun is shining, I get a good grade on my test, and I score a goal for my team. But on other days, when it's pouring rain and I wake up late and miss the bus, it's hard for me to be happy.

One thing that really helps me is to *tell You all about my problems.* I don't have to hide my feelings from You, not even when I'm grumpy and upset. Telling You actually helps me feel so much better! That's because You understand all my feelings and everything that's going on in my life.

Lord, please keep showing me that You are right here with me. Don't let me forget to talk to You and read the Bible—even memorizing some verses that speak to my heart. And remind me to keep singing too, because *it's good to sing praises to You. It's good to tell of Your Love in the morning and Your loyalty at night.* Thank You for being so faithful—sticking with me always, no matter what! *You* are the secret to being happy and content.

In Your loving Name, Jesus, *Amen*

READ ON YOUR OWN

PHILIPPIANS 4:12; PSALM 62:8; PSALM 92:1–2

MORE STRENGTH AND GLORY

I have seen your strength and glory.

—Psalm 63:2

Dear Jesus,

Your Word reminds me that You can do so *much, much more than anything I can ask or even imagine.* So when I come to You, I need to be ready for big and wonderful things to happen. There is no limit to what You can do. You can do everything!

But I have to tell You, Lord, that sometimes I do get discouraged. I pray for things—for someone who's sick to feel better, or for other kids to quit teasing me—and then I wait and wait for Your answer. That's hard for me. I want to keep trusting You, even when I'm not sure what Your answer will be. You promise that *those who trust in You will find new strength.* And I definitely need new strength to keep waiting! Please help me learn to wait patiently.

Instead of letting my problems worry me, I'm going to look at them in a different way. I'm going to look at my troubles as a chance to see You do something amazing. You're teaching me that the bigger my problem is, the more of Your *Strength and Glory* I'll be able to see. Please open my eyes to see everything that You are doing in my life!

In Your holy Name, Jesus, *Amen*

READ ON YOUR OWN

EPHESIANS 3:20–21; ISAIAH 40:30–31 NLT; PSALM 63:2

YOU WILL HELP ME

God, my strength, I will sing praises to you.
God, my protection, you are the God who loves me.
—Psalm 59:17

Dear Jesus,

You are *my Strength*! I'm feeling tired and worn-out this morning, but that's okay. It reminds me that I need *You*. You are always with me, and *You will help me* as I go through my day. Whether I'm at home or at school, riding the bus, or on the playground, I'm going to hold tight to Your hand and trust You to take care of me. Please *give me strength* and guide me.

Whenever I'm feeling like I'm too weak to handle a tough problem, that's a great time to stop and think about You. Because You make me strong. And You never run out of anything!

When You and I work together, there's no limit to what can happen—anything is possible. I may be having trouble making friends; I may need to study harder so I can pass all my tests, or I might need to tell someone about the bully in my class. No matter how tough the problem is, I'm going to count on You to give me everything I need. You might help me solve my problem quickly, or it could take a long time. But I know You'll get me through it at the perfect time.

Help me to keep moving forward—step by step—holding on to Your hand. No matter what happens, I trust that You know exactly what You're doing!

In Your strong Name, Jesus, *Amen*

READ ON YOUR OWN

PSALM 59:16–17; ISAIAH 41:13; PHILIPPIANS 4:13; ISAIAH 40:28–29

IN FULL CONTROL

Trust the Lord always.
Trust the Lord because he is our Rock forever.
—Isaiah 26:4

Dear Jesus,

Teach me to trust You—to *really* trust You—with all my heart! If I can learn this lesson, nothing will be able to take Your Peace away from me.

The devil likes to toss problems into my day, hoping I'll turn my back on You. But You are the Lord, and You can use those troubles to grow my faith and help me trust You more. The bigger my faith gets, the less I worry about my problems. The devil really hates that!

It's like the story of Joseph in the Bible. His brothers sold him as a slave, and he was taken away to Egypt, where he suffered for many years. But You used that terrible thing to make Joseph a powerful leader. Then Joseph saved his family and many other people from starving. Joseph told his brothers, *"You meant to hurt me. But God turned your evil into good."*

You are Lord over every single detail of my life and every hour of my day. You know exactly what's going to happen, and You are in full control. Nothing can happen to me unless You let it. You're always standing guard, ready to take care of me.

When I remember that these things are true, I can relax in Your Presence. *I will not be afraid because You are with me.*

In Your trustworthy Name, Jesus, *Amen*

READ ON YOUR OWN

ISAIAH 26:4; GENESIS 50:20; 2 CORINTHIANS 4:17; PSALM 23:4

A PATH OF PEACE

The Lord is my shepherd.
I have everything I need.
—Psalm 23:1

Dear Jesus,

I want to *rest in green pastures* of peace with You, *my Shepherd.* There's so much noise in this world. Phones are beeping and buzzing and ringing. Televisions and computers talk at us. Even the refrigerator makes sounds now! It's getting harder and harder to relax. But You created me to need rest.

Sometimes I even feel guilty for wanting to rest awhile. So instead of slowing down for a little quiet time, I go faster! But that's not what You want for me. You want me to come to You so that You can give me Your strength. Right now, nothing sounds better than having a few minutes to just relax and spend some peaceful time with You.

Jesus, I ask You to *guide me into Your path of peace.* As I walk with You, it'll be like we're making a trail that others can follow too. But it won't be my strength that gets us through this adventure. You've been showing me how weak I really am. And that shows me how much I need You! With each new day, I'm learning that the more I depend on You, the more peace I have—and the more ready I am for our next adventure.

In Your peaceful Name, Jesus, *Amen*

READ ON YOUR OWN

PSALM 23:1–3; GENESIS 2:2–3; LUKE 1:79 NCV

YOU FORGIVE ME

[God] will make us clean from all the wrongs we have done.
—1 John 1:9

Dear Jesus,

I'm so happy that *You cover me with the clothes of salvation. You give me a coat of goodness*—and it's mine to keep forever. Thank You, Jesus! You are the perfect Savior. That means I don't have to be afraid of facing my sins and mistakes. I just need to confess them to You, agreeing with You that they're wrong and telling You I'm sorry. Then *You will forgive me and make me clean from all the wrong things I've done.*

Please help me also to forgive myself. You don't want me to keep feeling bad about sins that You've already forgiven. That's one of the devil's traps to keep me away from You. Remind me to look at *You*, not at those sins in my past.

I love the way You keep telling me that I'm precious in Your sight. I'm so thankful I don't have to work to earn Your Love. You *already* love me, and You'll never stop!

Before I was even born, You knew I would make lots of mistakes. That's why You came and lived a perfect life on earth—so that You could give me Your perfect "report card" and take away all my sins. The Bible says that *those who belong to You are not judged guilty.* Thank You for inviting me to belong to You!

In Your forgiving Name, Jesus, *Amen*

READ ON YOUR OWN

ISAIAH 61:10; MATTHEW 1:21; 1 JOHN 1:9; ROMANS 8:1

SURROUNDED BY LOVE

The Lord's love surrounds those who trust him.
—Psalm 32:10

Dear Jesus,

You are *the One who makes my faith perfect*. And You've been teaching me that when a problem comes into my life, I need to *look to You* for the answers. The bigger the problem, the more I need to keep my eyes on You.

If I look at a problem for too long, I'll probably get discouraged. When that happens, please remind me to turn to You. I don't want to let my thoughts just wander wherever they want to—like ants going in lots of different directions. I want to keep turning my thoughts toward You. You're always by my side, listening to my prayers and speaking to me through Your words in the Bible.

Please help me learn to rest in Your Presence. I like to imagine curling up in Your lap as You wrap Your arms around me. You promise that *nothing in the whole world will ever be able to separate me from Your Love*. No matter how bad or sad things might look, I know that You're in control and You're taking care of me. You fight for me and *You laugh at* anyone who thinks they can beat You.

Lord, I praise You for Your Love that never fails and never ends. The Bible tells me that *Your Love surrounds those who trust You*. I trust You, Jesus!

In Your powerful Name, Jesus, *Amen*

READ ON YOUR OWN

HEBREWS 12:1–2; ROMANS 8:38–39; PSALM 2:4; PSALM 32:10

A NEW HABIT

The Lord is like a strong tower.
Those who do what is right can run to him for safety.
—Proverbs 18:10

Dear Jesus,

Help me live close to You—talking to You, reading Your Word, and just taking time to rest with You. I think of You as my quiet place, Jesus. Since You're the *Prince of Peace*, I can always find peace in You.

I want to learn to stay calm during days that are crazy and full of problems. Turning to You really helps me deal with my problems. That way, I don't have to worry when things seem to be getting out of control. But I admit, Lord, that the bigger the trouble, the harder it is for me *not* to worry. Sometimes I even forget that You're with me and *You give me strength*.

As soon as I start to wander away from You, please remind me to come running back! Just whispering Your Name calms me down. Then I suddenly remember: You haven't gone anywhere—You're right next to me, Jesus!

I do get frustrated with myself because my thoughts wander away from You so many times. But remembering to keep thinking about You is a new habit that I'm learning. I'll need to practice it over and over again. I don't mind, though. Because the more I *come to You*—my quiet place—the more peace and joy I have. Thank You for patiently teaching me!

In Your wonderful Name, Jesus, *Amen*

READ ON YOUR OWN

ISAIAH 9:6; PHILIPPIANS 4:13; PROVERBS 18:10; MATTHEW 11:28

SMALL TROUBLES

We have small troubles for a while now, but they are helping us gain an eternal glory. That glory is much greater than the troubles.
—2 Corinthians 4:17

Dear Jesus,

You are making me more and more like You as I'm being changed into Your glorious image. Thank You for working to change me—through Your Spirit who lives in me. Help me say yes to everything the Spirit is doing in me.

I'm so thankful that You don't give up on me when I mess up. In fact, You're able to use my troubles and mistakes to change me in lots of ways. One way You're working on me is to make me kinder and more patient. You're also teaching me to look to You for answers. I know this won't be easy, so please help me trust that Your wisdom, Your ways, and Your plans for me are perfect. *I need to be ready to suffer* through some hard times—like You did—s*o that I can also share in Your Glory.*

Some troubles seem so big that it feels like they'll never end. But all my problems are really *small troubles* compared to how much You suffered for me. And my troubles last only *a little while*, but I'll get to live *forever* in heaven with You.

The truth is, I still don't like having problems, but I'm learning to thank You for them. They remind me that You are God and You're always taking care of me. *Thanking You for everything*—the good things and the not-so-good things—helps me become more like You.

In Your beautiful Name, Jesus, *Amen*

READ ON YOUR OWN

2 CORINTHIANS 3:18 NLT; ROMANS 8:17; 2 CORINTHIANS 4:17; EPHESIANS 5:19–20

YOU ANSWER MY PRAYERS

Because of his glory and excellence, he has
given us great and precious promises.
—2 Peter 1:4 NLT

Dear Jesus,

Help me trust You to take control of my day. I want to let go and stop trying to handle everything myself. *You are God.* This is Your world. You made it, and You're in charge of everything. My job is to follow You. I can do that without being afraid because I know You love me so much. You've created my heart to *trust You all the time.*

Thank You for inviting me to talk to You and *tell You all my problems.* I like to tell You everything I'm thinking and feeling. I can ask You for anything and You always listen. I know that You start answering as soon as I pray—even if I don't see Your answers yet.

Help me not to worry about when You're going to answer my prayers, no matter how long I have to wait. And remind me that I don't need to keep telling You my problems—over and over and over. Instead, I want to trust that You *will* answer and that You will do the very best thing for me. So I thank You for the answers that are already on the way. Thanking You gives me peace and calms my worries. When I'm feeling peaceful, I can focus on You and all the ways You keep *Your great and precious promises* to me.

In Your amazing Name, Jesus, *Amen*

READ ON YOUR OWN

PSALM 46:10; PSALM 62:8; COLOSSIANS 4:2; 2 PETER 1:4 NLT

YOU SHOW ME THE WAY

When I am afraid,
you, Lord, know the way out.
—Psalm 142:3

Dear Jesus,

There are times when I have no idea how to find my way through a problem. But You always *know the way out* of my troubles. So, whenever I'm feeling tired or confused or scared, I can choose to look away from those feelings and turn to You—trusting You to lead me.

It's such a relief to be able to tell You everything I'm wondering or worried about! Because You listen to me and guide me, I don't have to be led by my feelings or fears. You comfort me and help me rest in Your Presence.

Even when I think I know the right thing to do, I need to talk to You about my plans. Your plan is perfect. You know which way is best. So please keep leading me step by step—today and tomorrow and all the way to heaven.

I need to remember that *Your ways are higher than my ways, just like the heavens are higher than the earth.* Remembering this great truth helps me want to worship You, Lord. *You are holy and You live forever.* And even though *You live in the high and holy place* of heaven, You still reach down and show me the way I should go. Thank You, Lord!

In Your holy Name, Jesus, *Amen*

READ ON YOUR OWN

PSALM 142:3; ISAIAH 55:9; ISAIAH 57:15

FOLLOW AND SING

"You follow me!"
—John 21:22

Dear Jesus,

The Bible tells me to *sing to You because You take care of me*. There are days when I love to do that. Sometimes I even wake up with a song in my heart! But I admit, Lord, that there are other days when I don't want to sing at all. I'd rather grumble and complain. Like those days when I forget my homework, trip on the playground, or have a fight with my friend. But I know *that's* when I need to sing the most! Help me remember that You're always taking care of me whether it feels that way or not. Singing to You on the tough days is something I can do that will bring me closer to You. Because praising You reminds me how awesome You are!

Sometimes I look at the kids around me and wonder, *Why are their lives so much easier than mine?* But really, I don't know all the things they're facing. I don't see all their troubles. Maybe they feel lonely because they don't know You, Jesus. Or maybe they're so sad about something that they cry in their beds at night. Instead of comparing my life to theirs, I need to turn to You and listen to what You tell me. You say in Your Word, *"Follow Me!"* Help me do that, Lord—and to sing praises to You while I do!

In Your loving Name, Jesus, *Amen*

READ ON YOUR OWN

PSALM 13:6; 2 SAMUEL 22:33–34; JOHN 21:22

LIKE THE PIECES OF A PUZZLE

The Lord your God will go with you. He will not leave you or forget you.
—Deuteronomy 31:6

Dear Jesus,

Only You know how weak I really am. Only You know about all the times I'm not sure what to do. But I'm learning that those are the times You give me even more of Your strength. And I'm seeing how well my weakness and Your strength fit together—like the pieces of a puzzle! They make the most beautiful picture. It's a picture that You designed before I was even born.

Your Word tells me that *Your power is greatest when I am weak.* Being able to lean on You when I'm feeling weak or overwhelmed is like having my mom's or dad's arm around me in a big crowd. When I trust You to *give me strength,* I can do whatever I need to do and go wherever I need to go. I find so much joy in Your promise to stay close beside me and *hold my hand.* And I love hearing You say, *"Don't be afraid. I will help you."*

Remind me to lean on You always, even when I feel like I can handle things by myself. You are so much wiser than I could ever be! Your wisdom is awesome and endless! And our friendship grows stronger each time I trust You to help me. Thank You, Lord, for promising that *You will never leave me or forget me.*

In Your wise and comforting Name, Jesus, *Amen*

READ ON YOUR OWN

2 CORINTHIANS 12:9 GNT; PHILIPPIANS 4:13;
ISAIAH 41:13; DEUTERONOMY 31:6

LEARNING TO BE JOYFUL ALWAYS

"The mountains may disappear, and the hills may become dust,
but my faithful love will never leave you."
—Isaiah 54:10 ERV

Dear Jesus,

You're teaching me to *always be joyful.* That's possible because my greatest joy comes from *You*—and You are always with me. All I have to do is remember that You love me all the time and in every situation. Then suddenly my heart feels lighter! The Bible tells me that no matter what happens—even if *the mountains disappear*—Your faithful *Love will never leave me.*

Anytime I fail, or when things don't go the way I want them to, it would be easy for me to start wondering if You still love me. Please help me not to do that, Lord. Your Love is more sure and steady than anything in this whole world. I'm so glad that You're *the Lord who loves me!* Thank You, Jesus!

I'm learning that when I praise You, my joy gets bigger and bigger. It doesn't matter what's happening! Even during the toughest times, You scatter blessings into my day. To help me be more thankful, I need to *think about the things that are good and worthy of praise.* I need to *think about the things that are true and right and pure and beautiful and respected.* Teach me to look for all Your blessings and to praise You for each one that I find.

In Your amazing Name, Jesus, *Amen*

READ ON YOUR OWN

1 THESSALONIANS 5:16–18 NCV; ISAIAH 54:10 ERV; PHILIPPIANS 4:8

WAITING FOR YOUR ANSWER

Lord, every morning you hear my voice.
Every morning, I tell you what I need.
And I wait for your answer.
—Psalm 5:3

Dear Jesus,

I'm learning that troubles and challenges are not just things I have to get through. They give me a chance to be on Your team, working together with You.

Some problems are so big and tough that they feel like a huge rock—a boulder—sitting on my chest. So I start trying everything I can think of to push it off. But what I really need to do is *go to You for help.* Your Word says that I should *tell You what I need and wait for Your answer.* Please remind me, though, that it may take some time for You to answer. It could be a day, a month, or even longer. But I know that You are working and doing important things in my life, even if I don't see them right now.

You've been showing me that my troubles are part of a bigger battle that You're fighting. My job is to trust You to take care of me and to *ask You for everything I need—always remembering to thank You.* When I keep praying to You and trusting You, Your Spirit works to *change me and make me more like You.* And as people see how great and powerful You are, You receive more and more glory!

In Your wonderful Name, Jesus, *Amen*

READ ON YOUR OWN

PSALM 105:4; PSALM 5:3; PHILIPPIANS 4:6; 2 CORINTHIANS 3:18

ALL FOR YOU!

Whatever you do, do it all for the glory of God.
—1 Corinthians 10:31 NLT

Dear Jesus,

You came and died on the cross to save me from my sins, but You didn't stay in that grave. You rose to life again! You are *my living God*— more alive and full of energy than I could ever imagine!

Please help me to walk boldly through this day with You, trusting You no matter what happens. Thank You for promising that You'll never let go of my hand. I might not be able to feel Your hand with my fingers, but I can feel it in my heart and know that You are with me.

I love thinking about all the blessings You give me: Your Love, Your Presence, forgiveness of all my sins, and a home in heaven with You one day. I don't even fully understand just how amazing these gifts are, but they make me want to worship You. And they keep me walking with You, with a hopeful heart, when hard things happen.

I can worship You in so many different ways: singing songs of praise, studying and memorizing Your Word, praying by myself or with others—or simply being amazed by the wonders You've created. I can also worship You by serving and loving other people. *Whatever I do*, Lord, help me to *do it all for Your Glory*! I want others to know You and to praise You too!

In Your glorious Name, Jesus, *Amen*

READ ON YOUR OWN

MATTHEW 28:5–6; PSALM 42:2;
COLOSSIANS 2:3; 1 CORINTHIANS 10:31 NLT

THE GREATEST VICTORY

My heart has heard you say, "Come and talk with me."
And my heart responds, "Lord, I am coming."
—Psalm 27:8 NLT

Dear Jesus,

Your Word says, *"If God is for us, then no one can defeat us."* When I decide to trust You as my Savior, then You *are* for me. Of course, I know You're not saying that I'll never have another problem, or that the devil will stop trying to trick me and trap me. But You're telling me that You are on my side and nothing can ever defeat You.

When You died on the cross and were raised to life again, You won the greatest victory of all time! By choosing to follow You, I get to share in Your victory and celebrate with You. My future home in heaven is ready and waiting for me because of the amazing victory You won! This means I don't have to be afraid of what problems might pop up—I can bravely and boldly follow You.

You're teaching me to *talk with You* about everything and to go wherever You lead. The more I trust You, the easier it is to let go of worry and fear and just enjoy the adventure of living my life with You. I rejoice because You are always beside me and *You're always ready to help me*. No matter what happens today, I'm on the winning side—*Your* side!

In Your great Name, Jesus, *Amen*

READ ON YOUR OWN

ROMANS 8:31; PSALM 27:8 NLT; PSALM 46:1 NLT

THIRSTY FOR YOU

A deer thirsts for a stream of water.
In the same way, I thirst for you, God.
—Psalm 42:1

Dear Jesus,

I thirst for You, just like I thirst for a drink of cold water on a hot day. I'm so thirsty for You, Jesus, because I really want to know You better. I want to be close to You.

When You created me, You put this deep "want" in my heart. You made me so that when I *seek You*—and find You—I feel full of joy! Sometimes, though, it still seems strange to spend time just sitting in Your Presence. I feel like I should be busy doing something. Help me to see that being still with You is one of the best things I could ever do.

You made me in Your image, and heaven is my true home—my forever home with You. So this wanting to be close to You is like being homesick. It's kind of how I feel when I spend the night with a friend. It's fun being with my friend, but I also miss my family.

There are lots of things I enjoy here on earth, but I sometimes get homesick for heaven too. Please help me stay close to You every day. Because I'm starting to see that the closer I am to You, the more *Your Glory* can shine through me and into the world.

In Your bright and shining Name, Jesus, *Amen*

READ ON YOUR OWN

PSALM 42:1–2; 1 CHRONICLES 16:11 NLT;
PSALM 34:5; 2 CORINTHIANS 3:18

JULY

Those who are in Christ Jesus
are not judged guilty.

—Romans 8:1

YOU ARE GOOD

I tell you, "Don't be afraid.
I will help you."
—Isaiah 41:13

Dear Jesus,

You are good—all the time and in every way. But I don't always see Your goodness right away. I see a lot of sadness in this world, Jesus. And sometimes I hear stories about how mean and evil people are being. All of that can make me feel a little worried and scared. I start to wonder where You are and why You're not doing something to help.

Then I remember that You are always good. You're working in this world and in my life all the time. Getting worried or scared is a sign that I need to start talking to You and then keep on talking to You. I can pray silently in my heart, or I can pray out loud. Either way, Lord, help me learn to *trust You with all my heart*. Instead of *depending on my own understanding*—trying to figure things out by myself—I need to come to You when I'm confused.

I don't want to be a pushy person who demands that You explain why things happen the way they do. But I'm learning that I can always ask, "How do You want me to see this situation?" and "What do You want me to do right now?"

Please teach me to trust You one day at a time and not worry about what might happen tomorrow, next week, or next month. I love to hear You whispering this precious promise to me: *"Don't be afraid. I will help you."*

In Your trustworthy Name, Jesus, *Amen*

READ ON YOUR OWN

PSALM 37:12–13; PROVERBS 3:5; ISAIAH 41:13

MIGHTY TO SAVE

It is Christ who lives in me. I still live in my body, but I live by faith in the Son of God who loved me and gave himself to save me.
—Galatians 2:20 NCV

Dear Jesus,

I'm so grateful that *You are with me* and You are mighty. Just like the sun is the center of our solar system, You are the center of my life—and everything about me. The planets never forget to go around the sun, and I don't want to forget to think about You, Jesus. You are the *Mighty One* who created the whole universe.

When I trust You as my Savior, You come to *live inside me*! I need to take some time and really think about how amazing that is! I want that truth to soak deep down into my heart. It means I don't need to worry about whether or not I have enough strength or courage to do the things You want me doing. I have Your power to help me—and that will always be enough!

I like knowing that *Your power can work through me*. You even say that *Your power works best in my weakness*. When I think about all these things, I stop worrying—and I feel peaceful.

Jesus, please keep reminding me that You live in me *and* You are mighty! Being sure of those wonderful facts chases away my worries and fills me with joy. Thank You for using Your mighty power to strengthen me and help me.

In Your mighty Name, Jesus, *Amen*

READ ON YOUR OWN

ZEPHANIAH 3:17; GALATIANS 2:20 NCV;
EPHESIANS 3:20; 2 CORINTHIANS 12:9 NLT

IN ALL TIMES

Even the darkness is not dark to you.
The night is as light as the day.
—Psalm 139:12

Dear Jesus,

Help me to look for You—and find You—in the tough times of my life. It's easy for me to find You when everything is good and happy. I see You in answered prayers, in the beauty of nature, and when I'm laughing and having fun with people I love. But I know that You are with me in all my hard times too. That's where I need to search for You the most, and where I really need to find You.

So, when I start to think about sad things that happened in the past, please show me how You helped me get through them. Help me to see You right where You *actually* were: close by my side. And show me how You've used the hard times to grow my faith and love for You. Then, when troubles come into my life again, please remind me to keep holding tight to Your hand.

The Light of Your Presence shines on even my darkest days, blessing me and lighting up my way like sunshine pushing through the clouds. You comfort me, guide me, and show me which path to take, step after step after step. Thank You for always leading me closer and closer to You.

In Your comforting Name, Jesus, *Amen*

READ ON YOUR OWN

PSALM 73:23–24; JOHN 1:5; PSALM 139:11–12

CAPTURED BY YOU

The Holy Spirit is in you. You have received the Holy Spirit from God.
You do not own yourselves.

—1 Corinthians 6:19

Dear Jesus,

Your Love has both captured my heart and *set me free*! For a long time I was *a slave to sin—sin controlled me*. Selfishness controlled me. I was always thinking about what *I* wanted. And because what I wanted wasn't always good for me, I was often unhappy. But as soon as I prayed, "Please save me from my sins, Jesus," You set me free. Now I'm *like a slave to You and Your goodness. I don't own myself. You bought me* by dying on the cross for my sins. I'll never be able to pay You back for this, but I can give You my heart. And when I do, You fill me up with joy.

Because You are perfect and good in everything You do, I don't have to be afraid of being a slave to You. *I was bought by You*, so I belong to You. But I know You would never be mean to me. Instead, You protect me and watch over me. You're working to make me free from sin and selfishness and worry and fear—they can't rule over me anymore.

As I learn to follow You more closely, Your Spirit takes over more and more of my heart. It's just like Your Word says: *Where the Spirit of the Lord is, there is freedom.* Thank You, Lord, for making me free to love and be loved by You. Help me to love You with all my heart!

In Your powerful, loving Name, Jesus, *Amen*

READ ON YOUR OWN

ROMANS 6:17–18; 1 CORINTHIANS 6:19–20; 2 CORINTHIANS 3:17

I'LL SING PRAISES TO YOU

Praise the Lord!
My whole being, praise the Lord.
I will praise the Lord all my life.
—Psalm 146:1–2

Dear Jesus,

You are so great, so glorious, and so understanding that I could never praise or thank You too much! You are worthy of all my praises—and so much more! *The praises of Your people are Your throne.* So, when I worship You, I get to come really close to You! Sometimes my praises burst out big and loud, like when You surprise me with a special blessing or when You paint a colorful rainbow or sunset across the sky. Other times, especially on tough days, I need to remind myself of all the reasons I have to be thankful. Then I can quietly praise You for those things.

Being thankful is a wonderful way to enjoy spending time in Your Presence. A grateful heart has plenty of room for You. When I thank You for the good gifts You pour into my life, I remember that every blessing comes from You. Help me to thank You in the tough times too—trusting in Your goodness at *all* times! It comforts me to know that You are always in control, no matter what is happening.

Please teach me to fill my days with praises to You—for the big things *and* the little things. Joyful praise like this helps me live closer to You, Lord.

In Your great Name, Jesus, *Amen*

READ ON YOUR OWN

PSALM 22:3; PSALM 146:1–2; 1 THESSALONIANS 5:18; PSALM 100:4

MY PRINCE OF PEACE

Jesus came and stood among them. He said, "Peace be with you!"
—John 20:19

Dear Jesus,

Spending time with You is one of my favorite things! You are my *Prince of Peace*. I love hearing You whisper the same words that You spoke to Your disciples when they were afraid: *"Peace be with you!"*

I'm able to have Your Peace—anytime and all the time—because You are always with me. You're my constant Companion and my forever-Friend. When I keep You in my thoughts, I can feel Your Peace and Your Presence in my heart. You are the King of all kings, the Lord of all lords, and the Prince of Peace. Jesus, You are worthy of all my worship and praise!

I need Your Peace all day long. It helps me do the things You want me to do—like stay calm when others are getting upset, or sit with the new kid at lunch even though I'm a little shy too. Sometimes, though, I like to take shortcuts. Taking a shortcut to get to class faster is fine, but taking a shortcut in my faith is *not* fine. Rushing through my prayers or Bible reading doesn't do me any good. If I want to be closer to You, I need to take my time.

Please keep *showing me how to live* and *guiding me to the path of peace*. Help me enjoy every moment of walking along my path with You.

In Your worthy Name, Jesus, *Amen*

READ ON YOUR OWN

ISAIAH 9:6; JOHN 20:19; PSALM 25:4; LUKE 1:79 NLT

MY GOD AND MY SAVIOR

I will look to the Lord for help.
—Micah 7:7

Dear Jesus,

You are the Creator of the universe. I'm so happy that You are *with me* and *for me*. You are everything I need! If I feel like something is missing in our friendship, it's because I need to reach out to You more often. My life is overflowing like a fountain with Your blessings. Help me to see all the good things You pour into each day and to thank You for each one. Because I trust You, I don't have to worry about anything. I can bring my problems and prayers to You, Jesus, knowing that You'll take care of them.

One of the things I'm learning about myself is that it's not the hard times in my life that upset me the most. It's the way I think about them that makes things worse. I start trying to figure out how to fix my problems or make them go away—I act like it's all up to me. And what keeps going through my mind is, "I need to fix this!" These thoughts run around in my head like a pack of hungry wolves that eat up all my peace! I forget that *You* are in charge. Whenever I forget, please help me to stop thinking about the problems and think about Your Presence instead. Teach me to *look to You for help* and to *wait for You to save me*. I know that *You will hear me* and answer my prayers because You are God—my Savior!

In Your saving Name, Jesus, *Amen*

READ ON YOUR OWN

ISAIAH 41:10; ROMANS 8:31–32; JOHN 10:10; MICAH 7:7

ON AND ON FOREVER!

Give thanks to the Lord because he is good.
His love continues forever.
—Psalm 136:1

Dear Jesus,

You are good, and Your Love continues forever. That's a beautiful promise from You to me. The best way to say how I feel is to *give thanks to You* and *sing songs of praise—praising Your name.* Please help me do this more and more each day.

I'm so grateful for Your goodness, Lord. There isn't one single speck of badness in You. You're never mean or cruel. Even when things are looking bad in this world, I can know that You're doing something good. You're actually working to do what's best for me and for *all* Your people. Help me to *live by what I believe*—that You are good—*not by what I see* happening in the world around me.

Giving thanks to You and praising Your Name give me strength to keep going day after day. Thanksgiving and praise take my eyes off my worries and put them on the treasure that I have in You. Being thankful also reminds me that You are my Creator and my Savior. The more I praise You, the closer we grow. And the closer we grow, the happier I am that Your Love for me goes on and on forever!

In Your loving Name, Jesus, *Amen*

READ ON YOUR OWN

PSALM 100:4–5; 2 CORINTHIANS 5:7; PSALM 136:1

THE BEST FRIEND!

You hide them with you, where they are safe.
—Psalm 31:20 NET

Dear Jesus,

I can come to You when everything is wonderful, and I can *come to You when I'm tired and carrying a heavy load* of trouble. I find rest and new strength in the peace of Your Presence. I'm thankful for *Your Peace. It's bigger and greater than I could ever understand.* And it's waiting for me anytime I need it. All I have to do is come to You and ask.

Teach me to *hide with You, where I am safe.* Even as I do all the everyday things of life—like hanging out with friends, finishing my chores, and memorizing multiplication tables—I can be in the safe place of Your Presence and protection. You aren't limited by time and space the way I am. That means You can be by my side right now *and* You can be in the future at the same time, clearing a path for me to follow. You are the best Friend I could ever have!

Remind me to bring my troubles to You and let You carry them for me. Your Word tells me that *in this world I will have troubles.* But I don't have to let that scare me. *You have already defeated the world. I can have peace* because You are with me and Your power protects me.

In Your powerful Name, Jesus, *Amen*

READ ON YOUR OWN

MATTHEW 11:28; PHILIPPIANS 4:7; PSALM 31:20 NET; JOHN 16:33

IF THE WORLD WAS PERFECT

I was very worried.
But you comforted me and made me happy.
—Psalm 94:19

Dear Jesus,

You *comfort me when I'm worried. And that makes me happy*! This world gives me lots of reasons to be worried. There are so many that I can't even count them all. Everywhere I look, I can see trouble and problems. Please help me to stop spending so much time looking at those problems, and teach me to look at *You* more and more. If I just whisper Your Name, Jesus, I remember that You're with me—and that You're bigger and stronger than any trouble could ever be. This helps me feel better right away. My heart feels lighter and my day looks brighter.

Sometimes I start to imagine how great it would be if I didn't have any troubles or problems. But then I realize that if the world was perfect, I wouldn't ever know what Your comfort feels like. Instead of letting troubles scare me, I can choose to see them as reminders to look for Your Presence, Your Peace, and Your Love. You're always ready to give me these precious, invisible gifts when I come to You. And You fill me up with *a joy that no one can take away from me.*

I'm cheered up and blessed by Your comforting invitation: *"Come to Me, all of you who are tired and have heavy loads. I will give you rest."* Jesus, I come to You!

In Your wonderful Name, Jesus, *Amen*

READ ON YOUR OWN

PSALM 94:19; JOHN 16:21–22; MATTHEW 11:28

211

FIRST THING

All the days planned for me
were written in your book
before I was one day old.
—Psalm 139:16

Dear Jesus,

I'm thankful that *You can do so much more than anything I could ask or imagine*. I like to pray for big and wonderful things, but I know You're able to do *much* bigger and more wonderful things! You're always working in my life, even when I can't see what You're doing.

Sometimes, when I can't see the good things You're doing right now, I start to feel stuck. And I just wish that my situation could change. But because You are God, You're able to look at the big picture—the past, the present, and the future—all at the same time. And You're working in ways I can't even begin to understand.

Please help me learn to keep thinking about You all day long. I really want to remember to start my day by talking to You. The longer I wait, the harder it seems to get. But when I pray to You first thing in the morning, it's easier to keep talking to You all through the day. I'm happy that I can bring You both my prayer requests and my praises.

Sometimes I think I'm too busy to pray. Then I remember that I'm not alone when I'm doing my tasks. You are working right here with me in my chores and homework and practices. And *Your power is working in me*. I feel strong when I think about how You can do much, much more than anything I can ask or imagine!

In Your mighty Name, Jesus, *Amen*

READ ON YOUR OWN
EPHESIANS 3:20 NCV; MATTHEW 19:26; PSALM 139:16; PSALM 5:3

THREE WORDS

He has showered his kindness on us, along
with all wisdom and understanding.
—Ephesians 1:8 NLT

Dear Jesus,

Help me to *be joyful always* and to *never stop praying*. I'm learning that being "joyful always" isn't the easiest thing to do. But it *is* possible to always find something to be joyful about—when I think about You. You pour so much comfort and encouragement into my days. This makes it possible for me to *be joyful* and to *have hope* even when I'm struggling with the biggest problems.

The Bible tells me to *be thankful in all circumstances,* no matter what is happening. When I'm having trouble being thankful, it helps me to pray, "Thank You, Jesus." This prayer is only three words long, but it's always the perfect thing to say to You. Just saying those words helps me look around and see how much I have to be thankful for. And the greatest thing is that You were willing to suffer and die on the cross so that You could be my Savior.

Even when I'm feeling sad or discouraged, it's still a good time to thank You. Please teach me to praise You for every good thing as soon as I see it. These praises add sparkle to my blessings and joy to my heart. Thank You, Jesus!

In Your joyful Name, Jesus, *Amen*

READ ON YOUR OWN

1 THESSALONIANS 5:16–18 NLT; ROMANS 12:12;
EPHESIANS 1:7–8 NLT; PSALM 95:2

MY GUIDE FOREVER

This God is our God for ever and ever; he
will be our guide even to the end.
—Psalm 48:14 NIV

Dear Jesus,

You are my Shepherd. You guide me and shield me. You're the perfect Shepherd and You are taking wonderful care of me! You love me with an *unfailing Love* that never ends. You know *everything* about me—the things I'm great at and the things I'm not so good at. You know my strengths and my weaknesses, my struggles and my sins. You know all my secrets—even the ones that no one else knows about. Because You know all these things, You are able to guide me perfectly.

Help me to walk through this world trusting and depending on You, Jesus. I'm learning that even while You are here with me in the present, You are also in the future. And You are carefully preparing the path I will follow. You move many dangers and problems out of my way. And You give me everything I need to get through the challenges and troubles that are still there.

Even if I walk through the darkest valley, I will not be afraid because You are close beside me. Your closeness gives me comfort and joy. As I talk with You, I'll trust You to guide me carefully through this day—and every day of my life. You are *my God and my Guide for ever and ever.*

In Your comforting Name, Jesus, *Amen*

READ ON YOUR OWN

PSALM 23:1 AMPC; EXODUS 15:13 NLT; PSALM 23:4 NLT; PSALM 48:14 NIV

POWER AND JOY

The Lord has glory and majesty.
He has power and joy in his Temple.
—1 Chronicles 16:27

Dear Jesus,

Please fill every moment with Your Presence so that I can see things the way You see them. When I'm around someone who gets on my nerves, I usually focus on everything I think is wrong with that person. But instead of that negative focus, I need to look at *You* through the eyes of my heart. When I'm looking at You, I can just let those things that are bothering me wash over me. The Bible teaches me that *judging other people* is a dangerous trap—and I've seen how it pulls me away from You. I want to stay close to You, so please help me to focus on You and *be joyful because You are my Savior.*

There is so much *power and joy in You*, Jesus! The more *I keep my eyes on You*, the more strength and joy You give me. Please teach me to stay aware of You even while I'm busy with other things. I can do that because You created me with this amazing brain that's able to think about several different things all at the same time. Thank You for that! I want to learn to keep looking to You, Lord, enjoying Your Presence every minute of the day.

In Your strong Name, Jesus, *Amen*

READ ON YOUR OWN

MATTHEW 7:1; HABAKKUK 3:18 NIV;
1 CHRONICLES 16:27; HEBREWS 12:2 NLT

YOU ARE HOLY

Praise the Lord for the glory of his name.
Worship the Lord because he is holy.
—Psalm 29:2

Dear Jesus,

Help me to *praise You and worship You because You are holy*. Lord, I'm grateful for all that You give me, but I don't want Your gifts to be the only reason I praise You. You are God! And I know that You are perfectly and completely holy. I don't understand that very well yet, but one day *I will know fully* just how perfectly holy You are.

Even now, thinking about how perfect You are makes me want to worship You. There isn't a single speck of sin in You. Your pure goodness delights me and amazes me. I can't wait to sing with the angels one day, *"Holy, holy, holy is the Lord Almighty. The whole earth is full of Your Glory"*!

I'm discovering that when I praise You, I begin to change. I become more and more like the person You created me to be. I can't understand You perfectly or completely, but I *can* learn more about You from the Bible. Please use Your Word to teach me who You really are and how You want me to live. Then I can praise You even better!

In Your amazing Name, Jesus, *Amen*

READ ON YOUR OWN

PSALM 29:2; 1 CORINTHIANS 13:12; ISAIAH 6:3 NIV

NOTHING IN THE WHOLE WORLD

"I came to give life—life in all its fullness."
—John 10:10

Dear Jesus,

Help me to stop and just rest in Your Presence. And please remind me that *nothing in the whole world will ever be able to separate me from Your Love.* Because when it's been a really rough day—when I've messed up and it seems like I'm doing everything wrong—it's hard to remember that You love me. Sometimes little doubts sneak into my thoughts, and I wonder if I've messed up too many times. When I'm feeling *really* bad about myself, I even wonder if You might stop loving me. But Your Word promises me that's impossible! Your Love doesn't depend on me doing everything right. It's a gift from You to me, and it's mine forever.

If I remember that I won't ever lose Your Love, I can relax and live my *life in all its fullness.* When things are going well, I want to enjoy those good times without worrying that some problem might be waiting for me on the path up ahead. And when I *am* dealing with a problem, I can count on You and Your Love to make me strong. I know there are always going to be some troubles. That's just the way this world is. But I'm learning that I can still *have peace* because I have *You.* I can smile and *be brave* in tough times because You give me this wonderful promise: *"I have defeated the world!"*

In Your all-powerful Name, Jesus, *Amen*

READ ON YOUR OWN

ROMANS 8:38–39; JOHN 10:10; JOHN 16:33

YOU GIVE AND GIVE AND GIVE

Some people did accept him. They believed in him. To them he gave the right to become children of God.
—John 1:12

Dear Jesus,

You never run out of joy, and You're always willing to share it with me. But sometimes I forget to ask for it—and sometimes I'm too busy being upset or worried or feeling sorry for myself. When that happens, please remind me that You are right here with me, just waiting to bless me with Your Joy. Help me to open up my arms all the way and accept Your Joy—just like getting a big hug.

As soon as I turn to You and spend some time in Your Presence, the blessings begin. I feel the Light of Your Love shining on me as *You change me to be more like You*—one little bit at a time. The more moments we spend together, the more I begin to *understand how wide and how long and how high and how deep Your Love is*.

You pour Your Life and Your Love into me, and all I have to do is *receive* these amazing gifts. That almost seems too good to be true. So many people are only interested in what they can take for themselves, but You give and give and give. The more I believe and trust You, the more I can receive the blessings You give me. Help me, Lord, to *be still* in Your Presence and to *know that You are God*—the One who helps me and loves me forever!

In Your blessed Name, Jesus, *Amen*

READ ON YOUR OWN

2 CORINTHIANS 3:18; EPHESIANS 3:16–18; JOHN 1:12; PSALM 46:10

RESTING IN YOU

He gives me new strength.
For the good of his name,
he leads me on paths that are right.
—Psalm 23:3

Dear Jesus,

Please help me relax and enjoy this day. Sometimes I rush through the day thinking about all I need to do. I take care of school stuff and pets and chores. I go to practice, eat, and hang out with friends. But I get so busy hurrying from one thing to the next that I sometimes miss the blessings You sprinkle into my day. Like the fluffy, white clouds in the sky, the golden sunshine, or that new friend I just ran right by.

Remind me that You love me just as much when I'm relaxing as when I'm working hard to get everything done. I'm not saved because of what I do. *I'm saved by grace because I believe in You*, Jesus. What an amazing *gift from You*! When I believe in You, I become Your child—a part of Your family forever!

Help me to *rest in You*, even on my busiest days. Resting in You helps me think more clearly. You teach me about what's important and what doesn't really matter. *You give me new strength,* and *You lead me on paths that are right*. Resting with You is like lying down *in a green pasture, next to calm waters*—enjoying Your Peace.

In Your peaceful Name, Jesus, *Amen*

READ ON YOUR OWN

EPHESIANS 2:8–9; PSALM 62:5 NCV; PSALM 23:3; PSALM 23:2

LEARNING TO LET GO

Happy are the people who know how to praise you.
Lord, let them live in the light of your presence.
—Psalm 89:15

Dear Jesus,

You're teaching me that I need to learn to let go. I don't want to hold on so tightly to money or toys or other stuff that I'm not willing to share with others. I also need to learn how to let go of trying to be in charge of everyone and everything. But I can only let go with Your help. That starts when I take time to rest in Your Presence. As I sit with You in the Light of Your Love, You help me see what matters the most: loving You and loving others. I don't have to be afraid of sharing what I have because I can trust You to give me everything I need.

I'm so happy that You are always with me *and* You never change. *You are the same yesterday, today, and forever!* As I learn to trust You to take care of every situation I face, I remember Your promise to never let go of my hand. I love hearing You whisper to me through Your Word, *"I am the Lord your God, and I am holding your right hand. Don't be afraid. I will help you."*

Thank You that I can *live in the Light of Your Presence.* That's a blessing no one can ever take away from me.

In Your loving Name, Jesus, *Amen*

READ ON YOUR OWN

PSALM 89:15; HEBREWS 13:8; ISAIAH 41:13

YOUR JOY AND PEACE

All of God lives fully in Christ (even when Christ was on earth). And in him you have a full and true life. He is ruler over all rulers and powers.
—Colossians 2:9–10

Dear Jesus,

Thank You for all the ways You make me complete, putting the pieces of my life together. You are my faithful Friend when I'm feeling alone. You give me hope and courage when I feel like giving up. And You are the Light that keeps shining through every moment of my life. I don't like feeling alone, or hopeless, or afraid, Jesus. But You use those feelings to remind me to turn to You. And turning to You is *always* a good choice. Anytime I'm feeling sad or lonely or afraid, help me remember that You're right here with me.

I'm learning that the best thing I can do to start my day is say, "I trust You, Jesus." Then I need to keep saying and doing that all day long. If I depend on You like that, I discover something wonderful when bedtime comes around. I realize that You have sent Your Joy and Peace to be my companions through the day. I don't remember exactly when it happened, but it did! Those two friends were with me every step of the way.

Thank You, Lord, for Your Joy and Peace—and for all the blessings You give me! The perfect way to end my day is to think about these blessings and praise You. *Let everything that breathes praise You.* Especially me!

In Your holy Name, Jesus, *Amen*

READ ON YOUR OWN

2 CORINTHIANS 4:6; COLOSSIANS 2:9–10; JAMES 1:4; PSALM 150:6

MY MESS OF MISTAKES

It is wise to be humble.

—Proverbs 11:2 NCV

Dear Jesus,

When I mess up, it's hard not to keep thinking about my mistake. Then I end up feeling awful. Help me not to be so hard on myself. I know that You can bring something good out of everything—even my mistakes. I can't go back and change what I've already done, so it's just a waste of time to keep thinking about it. Instead, help me to bring that mistake to You. Because You are amazingly creative, You can find a way to weave my good choices *and* my bad choices into a beautiful work of art.

The thing is, I'm going to keep on making mistakes. I don't want to, Jesus, and I'll try not to. But You and I both know I'm going to mess up sometimes—because I'm only human. Thinking that I can or should be perfect is a kind of pride. Help me to *be humble* and admit my mistakes. After all, it's those mistakes that remind me how much I need You. And it's those mistakes that help me be more kind and understanding when the people around me mess up too.

I'm so grateful that You know how to make something beautiful out of the messes I make. My job is to trust You and watch to see what You will do in my life.

In Your marvelous Name, Jesus, *Amen*

READ ON YOUR OWN

ROMANS 8:28; PROVERBS 11:2 NCV; PROVERBS 3:5; MICAH 7:7

THE CLIMB

Our homeland is in heaven, and we are waiting for our
Savior, the Lord Jesus Christ, to come from heaven.
—Philippians 3:20

Dear Jesus,

Sometimes my life feels like I'm climbing a huge mountain. Help me to keep climbing it with You instead of trying to do it alone.

There are days when the trail is so flat that it's easy to keep going. I'm learning that You provide those restful days to give me a break from climbing *and* to prepare me for tougher days ahead. Today is one of those tough days. This mountain we're climbing is so tall that I can't even see the top—it's hidden in the clouds. I can't tell how far we've come, and I can't tell how far there is left to climb. But the higher up the mountain You take me, the better I can see the beautiful scenery all around.

Every day has a challenge, another trail to hike. Some are short and easy to get through quickly. Others are really long and tough to climb. But whether the trail is short and easy or long and hard, it's an amazing adventure because I'm traveling it with You, Lord.

The higher up this mountain we go, the steeper the trail becomes. But my adventure becomes greater too! Please keep reminding me that the higher I climb with You, the closer I get to my greatest goal—living forever in heaven with You!

In Your breathtaking Name, Jesus, *Amen*

READ ON YOUR OWN

MATTHEW 17:1–2; HABAKKUK 3:19; PHILIPPIANS 3:20–21

LEARNING TO THINK MORE LIKE YOU

"The Helper will teach you everything. He will cause you to remember all the things I told you. This Helper is the Holy Spirit whom the Father will send in my name."
—John 14:26

Dear Jesus,

When I think about how great You are, I want to celebrate. *Your thoughts are not like my thoughts. Your ways are not like my ways. Just as the heavens are higher than the earth, so are Your ways higher than my ways. And Your thoughts are higher than my thoughts.* You are the King of the universe, but I can still talk to You anytime! My mind can't understand why You would do this—why You would stoop down and pay attention to me—but thank You, Jesus. Thank You for loving me that much!

Even though You are so much greater and higher than I am, You're teaching me to think like You—with love and kindness and wisdom. As I spend time with You, reading Your Word and praying, my thoughts are slowly becoming more like Yours. When I trust You as my Savior, Your Spirit comes to live inside me. And He always keeps working on changing me! He guides my thoughts and even reminds me of Bible verses I need to remember, right when I need them.

Talking to You and learning from You makes my faith stronger, helping me be ready for any troubles or challenges that are coming. Lord, spending time with You blesses me more than I could ever ask or imagine!

In Your majestic Name, Jesus, *Amen*

READ ON YOUR OWN

ISAIAH 55:8-9; COLOSSIANS 4:2; JOHN 14:26

NEVER BORING

I will trust you.
—Psalm 56:3

Dear Jesus,

Thank You for this day of life, Lord. It's a precious, one-of-a-kind gift. And I trust that You will be with me each moment of this day. Even if I can't feel Your Presence all the time, I know that You are always here.

When I thank You and trust You, it's easier for me to see things the way You see them. I learn to see others as people who You love—and see troubles as a chance to learn more about You. That makes my faith grow stronger. So please teach me to thank You and trust You more and more.

Help me to look at this day as an adventure that You've carefully planned out for me. You are my Guide, and You know every detail of my life. So instead of looking for the easiest way to get through this day, I'll try to follow You—wherever You lead me. I'm excited to see everything You have planned for me.

Living close to You is never dull or boring. I'm learning to look for surprises every day. Please help me to find each and every one. Some days, our adventures together are fun and easy. Other days, they are challenging and hard. But I won't be afraid. Because I know that You are always near!

In Your protecting Name, Jesus, *Amen*

READ ON YOUR OWN

PSALM 118:24; ISAIAH 41:10; PSALM 56:3; PSALM 145:18

LIVING CLOSE TO YOU

I will see the goodness of the Lord in the land of the living.
—Psalm 27:13 NIV

Dear Jesus,

I come to You, wanting to rest in *the safe place of Your arms*. There are times when doing the right thing is easy—I barely have to think about it. Other times it's so much harder, and I get tired. I'm trying to see those times as chances to practice living close to You, but I need Your help to do that.

When I'm worn-out, I sometimes start to feel sorry for myself. But what I really should do is thank You because You're always here to give me everything I need. You have a never-ending supply of energy, strength, wisdom, and love—and You're willing to share it all with me!

Help me to lean on You all through this day and to enjoy being so close to You. I'm learning to be thankful that I need You like I do. Because the more I lean on You, the more I see how much I can trust You, Jesus. You never let me down! When I think about the tough days I've had in the past, I end up thinking about You and how You've always been right there with me—helping me every step of the way. Having You by my side makes everything better!

In Your guiding Name, Jesus, *Amen*

READ ON YOUR OWN

DEUTERONOMY 33:27; ROMANS 8:26;
PHILIPPIANS 4:19; PSALM 27:13–14 NIV

BRIGHTER AND BRIGHTER

*I keep running hard toward the finish line to get
the way that is mine because God has called me
through Christ Jesus to life up there in heaven.*
—Philippians 3:14 ERV

Dear Jesus,

The Bible tells me that *the way of the good person is like the light of dawn. It grows brighter and brighter until it is full daylight.* This wonderful verse is for me! I can shine brightly because You have covered me in Your perfect goodness—Your righteousness. These *clothes of salvation* that You have given me can't be lost or stolen, and they won't ever turn into rags. They won't get holes in them or go out of style. This *coat of goodness* from You is *mine* forever, just like I am *Yours* forever!

As I go through this day, help me stay aware of You. Thank You that Your loving Presence is always with me. In any problems I face, remind me to look to You. Help me to walk close to You and keep my eyes on the goal: my home in heaven with You. Right now, my picture of heaven is kind of fuzzy and blurry. It's like when the sun begins to rise in the morning, and all I can see are those first few rays of light. But one day I will see all the glory of heaven. And it will be so much brighter than the sun shining in the middle of a clear summer day. Heaven will be brighter and more beautiful than anything I can imagine!

In Your bright, shining Name, Jesus, *Amen*

READ ON YOUR OWN

PROVERBS 4:18; ISAIAH 61:10 NCV; PSALM 23:3; PHILIPPIANS 3:14 ERV

I'M IN TRAINING

You were taught to be made new in your hearts. You were taught to become a new person. That new person is made to be like God—made to be truly good and holy.
—Ephesians 4:23–24

Dear Jesus,

I'm so thankful to be *a child of God*! Someday, when we're face to Face in heaven, *I will see You as You really are*! But for now, I'm in training. You're teaching me to *become a new person and to be made new in my heart.* That doesn't mean I'm not myself anymore. I still have my own personality. But You're helping me to be more loving and kind and wise—to be more like *You.* The amazing thing is that the more I become like You, the more I grow into the unique, one-of-a-kind person You created me to be!

The moment I ask You to save me from all my sins, I am adopted into Your royal family. I become *an heir of God* our Father, just like You are. That means I get to share in all the wonderful blessings that He has for You as His Son. But that also means I will *share in Your suffering.* That's why I still have hard times and troubles. When they come along, help me remember to turn to You. No matter how tough things get, help me to act like a child of God—a member of Your royal family. Please remind me that those tough times can make me more like You, Jesus. Plus, I have an awesome goal: to one day *see Your Face* in heaven. When I see You there—face to Face—*I will be satisfied*!

In Your royal Name, Jesus, *Amen*

READ ON YOUR OWN

1 JOHN 3:2; EPHESIANS 4:22–24; ROMANS 8:17 NLT; PSALM 17:15

I RAISE MY HANDS

Raise your hands in the Temple
and praise the Lord.
—Psalm 134:2

Dear Jesus,

Whenever I'm feeling weak and tired, I love to hear You say, *"Come to Me."* With You, Jesus, I find a safe place to rest, where I can become stronger.

I know that You're always right by my side, but sometimes I forget, letting others steal my attention away from You. Sometimes it's because I get busy doing things like practice and homework and chores. Other times it's because my friends aren't being all that nice to me. Before I know it, I start to feel like I'm carrying a *heavy load.* Then it gets harder and harder for me to keep going.

When that happens, please remind me to come to You for help. You promise to take my load and carry it for me. As I talk with You about my problems, Your Light shines on each one and shows me the way to go. That same Light soaks into my heart, comforting me and giving me the strength to keep going.

Lord, I open my heart to Your loving Presence. And *I raise up my hands in joyful praise* to You. I love spending time with You because *I find rest in You*—I can relax and be myself with You. I'm so grateful that *You give strength to Your people and You bless Your people with peace.*

In Your peaceful Name, Jesus, *Amen*

READ ON YOUR OWN

MATTHEW 11:28; PSALM 134:2; PSALM 62:1 NCV; PSALM 29:11

MY GUARD AND GUIDE

*"I give my sheep eternal life. . . . No one
can take them out of my hand."*
—John 10:28 ERV

Dear Jesus,

Your Word promises that no matter what happens, I don't need to *be
afraid because You are close beside me—guarding and guiding me all the
way*. Even though You never leave me, I have to admit that a lot of the time
I forget that You're with me.

Whenever I start to feel afraid, help me to use that fear like an alarm
clock that wakes me up and reminds me to come to You. Instead of letting
my fear get bigger and bigger, I can turn to You and let the Light of Your
Presence shine on me. As I relax in the warmth of Your Love and Light,
my fears melt away like ice cubes in the sun on a summer day. Your
wonderful Love makes me feel so much better! I want to love *You* more,
Jesus—and trust You more too.

I'm grateful that You keep guarding and guiding me everywhere I go.
You protect me from so many problems and dangers—things that I never
even know about. And because I belong to You, my soul is safe forever.
No one can take me out of Your hand! You will stay with me and *guide me*
all the way to heaven.

In Your guarding and guiding Name, Jesus, *Amen*

READ ON YOUR OWN

PSALM 23:4 TLB; JOHN 10:28 ERV; PSALM 48:14

YOU ARE MY ROCK

The Lord is my rock, my protection, my Savior.
My God is my rock.
I can run to him for safety.
—Psalm 18:2

Dear Jesus,

You're like a *towering rock of safety.* You are *my* Rock—*I can run to You and be safe,* anytime and anywhere. No matter what is going on around me, I can rest in the peaceful place of Your Presence, taking a break from trying to figure out the answers to my troubles.

There are so many things I don't understand. And so many things I can't control. But this shouldn't surprise me. The Bible tells me that *Your ways are higher than my ways. And Your thoughts are higher than my thoughts—like the heavens are higher than the earth.*

When the world around me is confusing, and it seems like the bad guys are winning, help me to think about You instead of worrying about all those troubles. You're the Light that keeps on shining no matter what's happening. And when I choose to trust You, Your Light can shine through me into this troubled world. I can tell others *the good news that brings joy to all people*: that *You are Christ,* our Lord and Savior.

I like to come close to You by whispering Your Name and by singing songs of praise. As I keep looking to You, Your Light brightens up my day.

In Your shining Name, Jesus, *Amen*

READ ON YOUR OWN

PSALM 61:2 NLT; PSALM 18:2; ISAIAH 55:9; LUKE 2:10–11

YOU KEEP ME SAFE

As I lie in bed, I remember you.
—Psalm 63:6 GNT

Dear Jesus,

Help me remember to *cling to You*, staying as close to You as I can. I know that You hold on to me, and *Your hand keeps me safe*. Thank You for using the tough times in my life to make my faith stronger and more more pure. A strong, *pure faith is worth more than gold. Gold can be destroyed*, but real faith can never be ruined or lost.

As I hold tight to You, my faith grows, and I find comfort in You. When I count on You in hard times and see how You take care of me, I learn that I can trust You with my troubles in the future too. You've been showing me that I can always trust You to help me when I need You.

Lord, sometimes *I think about You while I'm lying in bed*. In the middle of the night or in the middle of a tough time, Your hand is holding me and keeping me safe. Your hand is super-strong! It's strong enough to handle all the troubles in the whole world! So anytime I feel like giving up, I'll choose to look up at You instead. The Bible tells me to always *look to You and Your strength*.

I love the promise that You give me in Your Word: *"Don't worry, because I am with you. Don't be afraid, because I am Your God. I will make you strong and will help you. I will support you with My right hand."*

In Your powerful Name, Jesus, *Amen*

READ ON YOUR OWN

PSALM 63:6, 8 GNT; 1 PETER 1:7; PSALM 105:4 NIV; ISAIAH 41:10

AUGUST

"You will search for me. And when you search for me with all your heart, you will find me!"

—Jeremiah 29:13

I CAN WALK IN YOUR LIGHT

[Jesus] said, "I am the light of the world."
—John 8:12

Dear Jesus,

Teach me to *live in the Light of Your Presence, rejoicing in You and prais-ing Your goodness.* There's a lot of darkness in this world. So many sad and bad things happen. But Your Light shines much, much brighter than all that—brighter than the sun ever could—and it never stops shining!

When Your goodness meets the evil of this world, it creates a way for You to show just how powerful You really are. So I'm going to be on the lookout for Your miracles, Lord. I can't wait to see all the awesome things You will do!

Whenever I'm struggling with my troubles, it's important for me to keep praising You and rejoicing in You. One of my favorite ways to do that is to whisper Your Name. *Jesus.* This one-word prayer praises You and it also protects me. Your mighty Name never loses its power to help me!

I can praise You for Your goodness even on my darkest days. When I believe in You, Jesus, You weave the Light of Your Glory into *clothes of salvation.* And You give them to me to wear forever! I can walk joyfully through this day because I'm walking in Your Light with Your *coat of good-ness* wrapped around me.

In Your powerful Name, Jesus, *Amen*

READ ON YOUR OWN

JOHN 8:12; PSALM 89:15–16; ACTS 4:12; ISAIAH 61:10

THE GREATEST GIFT

Let's come to him with thanksgiving.
Let's sing songs to him.
—Psalm 95:2

Dear Jesus,

Thank You for the gift of this brand-new day! I want to be thankful for every moment. That's the way to find joy in my day. In fact, I'm discovering that good things become even better when I remember to thank You for them. And since every blessing in my life really comes from You, I need to be thanking You all through my day. Praising and thanking You brings me closer to You—which is exactly where I want to be!

I trust You as my Savior, and You have blessed me with Your grace. Grace is the amazing gift of Your forgiveness. I didn't earn it, and I don't deserve it. But You forgive all my sins anyway. No one can ever take this gift away from me. I belong to You forever, Jesus! *Nothing in the whole world will ever be able to separate me from Your Love.*

Please keep reminding me that You're always with me—through every step of my day. Help me find all the blessings and happy moments You sprinkle all around me. I don't want to miss even one! I know, though, that even with all the good things You send my way, my greatest treasure is *You*, Jesus. You are the *Gift that is too wonderful to explain*!

In Your treasured Name, Jesus, *Amen*

READ ON YOUR OWN

PSALM 95:2; EPHESIANS 2:8–9; ROMANS 8:38–39; 2 CORINTHIANS 9:15

SPARKLES OF JOY

Let them give thanks to the Lord for his love.
—Psalm 107:8

Dear Jesus,

You are teaching me that joy is something I can choose. I can't control what happens in my day, but I *can* choose to be joyful instead of grumpy. I can do that because *You made me a little lower than the angels*. You gave me this amazing brain that lets me think through things and make decisions.

You've been showing me that my thoughts really matter—because those thoughts turn into feelings and actions. That's why choosing to think good thoughts is extra-important. If I spend time thinking about all the things I don't like, I start to feel sad and discouraged.

Whenever I'm feeling unhappy, I need to stop and remember the things that are *always* a reason for joy. Like knowing that *You are always with me*, always *watching over me*, and that You love me with *a Love that never fails*.

Thank You for giving me Your Spirit to remind me of all these wonderful truths from the Bible. Anytime I'm stuck in the middle of a problem, that problem is all I can see at first. But if I remember to search for *You*, soon I can see the Light of Your Presence shining through my problem. I see sparkles of Your Joy shining back at me—*filling me with joy*!

In Your joyful Name, Jesus, *Amen*

READ ON YOUR OWN

PSALM 8:5; GENESIS 28:15 NIV; PSALM 107:8 NIV; ROMANS 15:13

EVERY SECOND

*"I am the good shepherd. The good shepherd
gives his life for the sheep."*
—John 10:11

Dear Jesus,

You are my *good Shepherd*. I really want to keep my focus on You so that You're in the center of my thoughts.

I can't even count how many things I think about during my day. Family and friends, my animals, sports, homework, and classes—there are so many things on my mind! Help me not to let any of those things crowd You out. Because the more I think about You, the more You're able to do in me and through me. Thinking about You makes me happy because I love You, Jesus.

Help me remember that You are with me every minute of every day, watching over me and loving me perfectly. You're *always* thinking about me! And the Bible tells me that *Your unfailing Love surrounds those who trust You.* Please help me trust You more, Lord.

You care about every thought and feeling I have, and everything I say or do. You're teaching me to be aware of Your Love and Your Presence even when I'm busy with other things.

This world is changing fast, but You stay *the same yesterday, today, and forever.* So I can always count on You to help me. As I keep You in my thoughts, please show me the way You want me to go—and *give me Your Peace.*

In Your always-loving Name, Jesus, *Amen*

READ ON YOUR OWN

JOHN 10:11; PSALM 32:10 NLT; HEBREWS 13:8; JOHN 14:27

THE GOD WHO SAVES ME

The Lord lives!
May my Rock be praised.
Praise the God who saves me!
—Psalm 18:46

Dear Jesus,

Thank You for being my *living Lord, my Rock, and the God who saves me!* Help me spend time with You every day, thinking about Your greatness and how good You are to me. I don't know many people in this world who like to make promises. And even when they do, they don't always keep them. But *You* keep every promise You ever make.

Instead of thinking about the things that are going wrong in my day and in the world, I want to spend more time thinking about You. Starting today—starting right this minute. Not only are You my living Lord and my strong Rock, but You are also *the God who saves me.* I trust You as my Savior, Jesus. Your death on the cross pays for my sins and *saves me completely.* You're able to do this because You are *the everlasting God*—the God who lives forever and rules heaven and earth.

I don't have to worry that You'll stop loving me if I'm not good enough. It's *Your* goodness that keeps me safe and secure in Your Love! You will never leave me or give up on me. That promise gives me strength and comforts me as I walk through this world with all its troubles. One day, I will live with You forever, and I'll never have another worry, problem, or trouble!

In Your awesome Name, Jesus, *Amen*

READ ON YOUR OWN

PSALM 18:46; HEBREWS 7:25 NIV;
DEUTERONOMY 33:27; 2 CORINTHIANS 5:21

SAFE AND SECURE

*"In this world you will have trouble. But be
brave! I have defeated the world!"*
—John 16:33

Dear Jesus,

Please help me to stop trying to make everything perfect—and also to stop worrying because things aren't perfect. Instead of worrying and getting upset, I want to come talk to You. I know I can tell you anything and everything. I can *give all my worries to You, because You care for me* and You are taking care of me. I'm *safe in the shelter of Your Presence.*

There are times that I get busy with my thoughts and other things, and before long, I start to wander away from You. When that happens, I don't feel safe and secure anymore; I feel scared and worried. But those feelings are actually a gift from You. They remind me to turn back to You and to *the love I had for You in the beginning.* Jesus, I want to keep You in the center of my thoughts and feelings, my plans and actions—where You belong. When You are the Center of my life, everything works better. Help me live this way every day!

You have set my feet on the path that leads to heaven, and You are walking right beside me every step of the way. Whenever I run into trouble in this world, You whisper this promise from the Bible: *"Be brave! I have defeated the world!"* Thank You, Jesus, for always helping me. In Your Presence, I am wonderfully safe and secure!

In Your comforting Name, Jesus, *Amen*

READ ON YOUR OWN

1 PETER 5:7; PSALM 31:20; REVELATION 2:4; JOHN 16:33

WAITING PATIENTLY

The Lord is a faithful God.
Blessed are those who wait for his help.
—Isaiah 30:18 NLT

Dear Jesus,

The Bible says that *those who wait for Your help are blessed.* Lord, You know I'm not very good at waiting. But You're teaching me that it's all worth it. I like to make plans, make decisions, and make things happen. And You've been showing me that there's a time to do all those things, but there is also a time to wait. A time to sit and talk to You and read Your Word and trust Your plans for me.

As hard as this can be for me, it really makes me feel better. I've seen how many wonderful blessings You give me through our time together. Many of the good things You've promised are in the future. While I'm resting in Your Presence, You're preparing me for those future blessings. I can't see them clearly yet, but I'm trusting that they are there.

Other blessings are for right now. I've discovered that one of those right-now blessings is actually the waiting, because I get to wait *with You.* As I do, I remember that You are good and You're in control. When I'm struggling to wait patiently—wondering why I have to wait so long— remind me to *trust You with all my heart and not depend on my own understanding.*

In Your hope-filled Name, Jesus, *Amen*

READ ON YOUR OWN

ISAIAH 30:18 NLT; PSALM 40:1; PSALM 143:8; PROVERBS 3:5

MY HELP AND MY SHIELD

Our hope is in the Lord.
He is our help, our shield to protect us.
—Psalm 33:20

Dear Jesus,

You are my Help and my Shield. I love that I get to use the word "my." You are not just *a* help or *a* shield. You are *mine*—now and forever! This forever-promise makes me strong and encourages me as I walk with You through each day. You have said *You will never leave me or forget me.* I can always count on You!

Because You are *my Help*, I don't have to be afraid I can't do something I need to do. Anytime the task I'm facing seems too hard—like forgiving someone who has hurt me a lot or inviting a new friend to church—I can turn to You and say, "I can't do this on my own." Then suddenly I find it easier to trust You. I'm learning that *I can do all things through You,* Jesus. You're the One *who gives me strength.*

I really need You to be *my Shield* too. Thank You for protecting me from so many dangers—not just dangers to my body but also to my thoughts and feelings. Sometimes I see the way You protect me. Other times You sweep away the trouble before I even know it's there. It's comforting to know that Your powerful Presence is always watching over me. *I will not be afraid because You are with me.*

In Your shielding Name, Jesus, *Amen*

READ ON YOUR OWN

PSALM 33:20; DEUTERONOMY 31:8; PHILIPPIANS 4:13; PSALM 23:4

PERFECTLY LOVED

Thank the Lord because he is good.
His love continues forever.
—Psalm 107:1

Dear Jesus,

I'm so thankful that You understand me completely. I rejoice because You love me with a perfect Love that never ends. Sometimes I worry, though, that if other people really knew me, they wouldn't like me. That can make it hard to make friends. Some days I do get a little lonely. But my heart smiles as soon as I remember that You know absolutely everything about me—and You still love me!

I don't have to pretend with You, Jesus. Not ever! You know the real me. I can't hide anything from You. And I don't want to. Help me rest in this wonderful truth: *You know me completely*, yet You delight in me!

Instead of working to earn Your Love, I can relax in Your Love. There's nothing that could ever stop You from loving me. I am Yours, Jesus. I was bought with Your precious blood on the cross, so I belong to You forever. You call me Your friend, *and* You are my Brother. I'm a member of Your royal family! I need to keep telling myself this truth over and over again, so that I never forget it. Your Love changes me and helps me see myself the way You do—as someone who is perfectly loved!

In Your joyful Name, Jesus, *Amen*

READ ON YOUR OWN

PSALM 107:1, 43; 1 CORINTHIANS 13:12 NLT;
PSALM 149:4–5; EPHESIANS 1:5–6

WHAT I THINK ABOUT

Look at Jesus' example so that you will not get tired and stop trying.
—Hebrews 12:3

Dear Jesus,

Sometimes I feel like the problems of this world—mine and other people's—are shouting for my attention. These troubles can start to take up so much room in my thoughts that *I get tired and I want to stop trying.* When this happens, please remind me that I can choose what I think about. Instead of letting ugliness fill up my mind, I can decide that I'm going to think about *You.* Then Your Light will shine into every corner of my mind, chasing those dark thoughts away.

Please help me not to get stuck on remembering the mistakes I've made in the past either. Those kinds of repeating thoughts just make me feel terrible. Remind me that today is a new day, and You are helping me to become a new, better person. Every moment is another chance for me to be with You and get closer to You—enjoying Your Presence. Even on my worst days, I can choose to search for *You* in the middle of my problems instead of just thinking about the things that are going wrong.

Jesus, You cheer me up and cheer me on with Your strong words: *"You can have peace in Me. In this world You will have trouble. But be brave! I have defeated the world!"*

In Your powerful Name, Jesus, *Amen*

READ ON YOUR OWN

HEBREWS 12:3; PSALM 34:6–7; JOHN 16:33

YOU KNOW THE WAY

"Remember that I commanded you to be strong and brave. So don't be afraid. The Lord your God will be with you everywhere you go."
—Joshua 1:9

Dear Jesus,

Thank You for Your comforting words, straight from Your heart: *"I am with you, and I will protect you everywhere you go."* I love that, Lord! This life is a real adventure, and it's just waiting for me to dive in. As excited as I am, it also makes me a little nervous. I'm eager to discover all the joys and wonders and blessings along the way. But I know there will be challenges and troubles too.

Whenever fearful thoughts creep in, please remind me that You'll be watching over me and protecting me—no matter where I am. If I'm in another country, You're there. If I'm at someone else's house, You're right beside me. If I'm at school or at the park, You are with me. Thank You that the comfort of Your Presence is mine forever!

I'm learning that the most important part of this adventure is Your promise that You're on the journey with me. Your Presence goes with me every step—sort of like my shadow on a sunny day. No matter how many steps I take, You're still right there by my side. As we walk along together, I like to remember that You're holding on to my hand. You are my faithful Guide. Help me trust You to show me which path to take. You know the way perfectly, so I don't have to worry about getting lost. I can relax in Your Presence and just enjoy the wonder of sharing my whole life with You!

In Your comforting Name, Jesus, *Amen*

READ ON YOUR OWN

GENESIS 28:15; JOSHUA 1:9; PSALM 32:8; PSALM 48:14

MY WHOLE LIFE IS YOURS

Since God has shown us great mercy, I beg you to offer your lives as a living sacrifice to him.
—Romans 12:1

Dear Jesus,

When I start the day feeling like I can't get through it, I need to stop and hear You say, *"My grace is enough for you. When you are weak, then My power is made perfect in you."* I'm so glad that this promise uses the word "is." Not *was* or *will be* or *might be*. You say *is*, and that means Your grace is always there for me. So, I don't have to worry about feeling weak. Instead, I can be happy because my weakness reminds me that I need *You*. And when I come to You feeling weak, You give me all the strength and help I need.

Whenever I go through my day depending on You, I get so much more done. I'm blessed and amazed that I get to live and work with You every moment of every day. You are the *King of kings and Lord of lords*, and You want to be with me and help me! That seems almost too good to be true, but it *is* true. Thank You, Jesus!

Thinking about these wonderful blessings makes me want to give my whole life to You—like *a living sacrifice*. The Bible says that giving myself to You is a way of worshiping You. I know that the joy You give me now is only a tiny taste of the feast of joy waiting for me in heaven. *That joy is full of Your Glory*!

In Your joyful Name, Jesus, *Amen*

READ ON YOUR OWN

2 CORINTHIANS 12:9; REVELATION 19:16; ROMANS 12:1; 1 PETER 1:8

LIFE WITH YOU

It is through him that we are able to live, to do what we do, and to be who we are.
—Acts 17:28 ERV

Dear Jesus,

Living my life with You is the most amazing adventure! I see so many people just rushing through their days. They go from one thing to the next as if they can't stop—and they're trying to do things without Your help. Sometimes that seems to work for them, and sometimes it doesn't. But I know that they're really missing out. Because living and working with You is the best!

When I depend on You, Lord, the way I see myself and this world changes completely. I start to notice all the wonderful ways You are working. I wake up in the morning happy and excited to see what You're going to do.

I know I need You and Your help. Some days I forget how much I need You, but I always know it deep down in my heart. You're showing me that being weak is really a gift from You because *Your power works best in my weakness*. I've seen it with my own eyes! That's why I try to stay ready to change my plans if You ask me to—trusting that Your plans are much, much better than mine. When I *believe in You*, I'm *able to live, to do what I need to do, and to be who I am through You*. I'm grateful that You live inside me, Jesus.

It's amazing to know that *I am in You and You are in me*! Thank You for this awesome adventure of sharing my life with You!

In Your beautiful Name, Jesus, *Amen*

READ ON YOUR OWN

2 CORINTHIANS 12:9 NLT; JOHN 3:16; ACTS 17:28 ERV; JOHN 14:20

IN THE NIGHT

On his robe and on his leg was written this name:
"KING OF KINGS AND LORD OF LORDS."
—Revelation 19:16

Dear Jesus,

Help me to *remember You when I'm lying in bed*, ready to sleep. And if I wake up during the night, please help me *think about You* then too. In those times when I can't sleep, all kinds of thoughts start flying around in my brain—like moths flying around a light. If I don't take control of those thoughts and turn them toward You, I start to worry and feel anxious.

I'm learning that the best way to stop worrying is to think about *You* and tell You everything that's cluttering up my mind. The Bible teaches me to *give all my worries to You because You care for me*. When I remember that You are taking care of me, then I can relax and rest in Your Presence.

As I think about You during the night, please remind me of who You really are. I like to think about all the ways You are perfect—in Your wonderful Love, Joy, and Peace. I feel comforted and safe when I think about Your names: Shepherd, Savior, Prince of Peace. I rejoice in Your majesty, wisdom, mercy, and grace. I delight in Your Power and Glory— You are the *King of kings and Lord of lords*! I worship You, Lord, and I enjoy this time of being with You. These thoughts clear my mind and help me rest peacefully.

In Your peaceful Name, Jesus, *Amen*

READ ON YOUR OWN

PSALM 63:6; 1 PETER 5:7; REVELATION 19:16

THIS PLACE AND TIME

Each one should continue to live the way God has given
him to live—the way he was when God called him.
—1 Corinthians 7:17

Dear Jesus,

Help me to *live the life You have given me to live*—and to learn to be happy and satisfied. I need to be careful not to compare my life with anyone else's. Also, I shouldn't be comparing the way things are *today* with the way they used to be in the past. You're teaching me to stop all that comparing by remembering that You've *called me* to live in this place and time for a reason. Then even my tough times start to feel better. I know You'll help me shine no matter where I am, no matter what's going on. If I'm in a tough situation, I can trust You to give me everything I need to get through it. You'll even help me find some reasons to be thankful and joyful.

Because You are so amazingly and endlessly wise, I don't have to wonder if Your way is the best. When I don't understand what You're doing, help me to trust You anyway. Open my eyes to see all the ways You're working in every moment of my day. Please remind me to search for the good that You're bringing out of my troubles—*and* to expect to find it!

Day by day, I'm learning to accept the way things are, even while I'm hoping that You will make things better. I can be joyful now because I know that someday I'll have perfect, never-ending joy with You in heaven!

In Your wise Name, Jesus, *Amen*

READ ON YOUR OWN

1 CORINTHIANS 7:17; ROMANS 11:33–34; PHILIPPIANS 4:12

I NEED TO PRAISE YOU

Shout joyful praises to God, all the earth!
Sing about the glory of his name!
Tell the world how glorious he is.

—Psalm 66:1–2 NLT

Dear Jesus,

Help me find my joy in You because You love me and You are *my Strength*. I'm seeing that it's really important to keep joy in my life—especially in the middle of tough times. Whenever I'm struggling with a problem, I need to be extra-careful with my words and thoughts. If I think too much about all the things that are going wrong, I get more and more discouraged. Those kinds of thoughts steal my strength. As soon as I realize this is happening, I need to stop those thoughts right away, turn to You as quickly as I can, and ask You to *show me what I should do*.

When I'm struggling, that's a good time to spend time praising You. Because praising You brings me closer to You. I can worship You with my own words and with songs of praise. Also, I can read promises and pray praises from Your Word: *"God, my Strength, I will sing praises to You. I will sing about the glory of Your Name!"*

It's important for me to remember that my problems come and go, but *You* never go away. You stay right here with me. I can count on You, Jesus! You are forever—and so is my relationship with You. Just being in Your Presence gives me joy. As I delight in Your Love that never fails, You make me strong.

In Your glorious Name, Jesus, *Amen*

READ ON YOUR OWN

PSALM 59:17; JAMES 1:2; PSALM 143:8; PSALM 66:1–2 NLT

YOUR GENTLE WHISPER

Jesus quickly spoke to them. He said, "Have
courage! It is I! Don't be afraid."
—Matthew 14:27

Dear Jesus,

Whenever my day seems like it's just too much to handle, please remind me to turn to You. As I spend time with You, I love to hear You saying, *"Have courage! It is I! Don't be afraid."* Those words make me feel brave, Jesus. Help me remember to listen to You every day.

When I'm upset or worried about something, listening to You isn't always easy for me to do. My thoughts get so loud that they zoom through my mind like a race car—and I have trouble hearing Your *gentle whisper*. But when I ask You to help me, You calm my thoughts and I can hear better. Thank You, Lord!

I'm happy that You are the *Prince of Peace*, and You are with me all the time. You never stop helping me, and there's never a day when You're not in control. *Nothing* happens to me that You don't already know about! That doesn't mean I'll never be sad or hurt or upset. But it does mean that You're able to take even my hard times and use them for good. So, whenever I feel like I'm in a thunderstorm of troubles, I'll listen for Your voice saying, "Have courage! It is I!" Then I'll start searching for signs that You are with me in the storm. The Bible promises that if I *search for You with all my heart, I will find You.*

In Your calming Name, Jesus, *Amen*

READ ON YOUR OWN

MATTHEW 14:27; 1 KINGS 19:12 NIV; ISAIAH 9:6; JEREMIAH 29:13

THE *WHOLE* STORY

David found strength in the Lord his God.
—1 Samuel 30:6

Dear Jesus,

Help me to *trust in You and not be afraid*. Sometimes this world is a scary place. Things are happening all over that I just don't understand, and I start to feel afraid. But I'm learning that those scary stories don't tell the *whole* story. They leave out the most important part—they leave out *You*! They don't talk about who You are, and they don't say anything about the amazing things You are doing on this planet.

Whenever my world is feeling like a scary place, I need to turn to You. You are always there to comfort me and encourage me. I like to think about David in the Bible. Even when men were threatening to attack and stone him, *he found strength in You, Lord*. I can do what David did. I can come to You in prayer and remember how awesome You are! I feel safe when I think about Your Power and Glory and *Your unfailing Love*. I'm on an exciting journey with You, Jesus, and our path will take me all the way to heaven!

As I keep thinking about You, my fear slips away. *I will trust in You and not be afraid. You are my Strength and my Song.*

In Your strong Name, Jesus, *Amen*

READ ON YOUR OWN

ISAIAH 12:2 NLT; 1 SAMUEL 30:6; PSALM 33:5 NLT

THE ADVENTURE OF LIVING WITH YOU

Praise be to the God and Father of our Lord Jesus Christ. God has great mercy, and because of his mercy he gave us a new life.
—1 Peter 1:3

Dear Jesus,

You speak to me through the Bible, and I love to hear You saying these words: *"I give you eternal life, and you will never die. And no person can steal you out of My hand."* This is the best news! You have promised me great *blessings, kept for me in heaven. They cannot be destroyed or be spoiled or lose their beauty.*

When I trust You as my Savior, You give me the gift of life that lasts forever. That wonderful gift is like a light that never stops shining—not even on my darkest, toughest days. Its brightness encourages me to keep trying to do what is good and right, and to keep following You. Then the wickedness of this world can't drag me down.

I know there will be troubles to face. Some days I'll feel like I'm swimming through dark, cold waters. But You promise: *"When you go through deep waters, I will be with you. When you go through rivers of difficulty, you will not drown."* Help me to keep holding tight to Your hand—trusting that *nothing in the whole world will ever be able to separate me from Your Love.* Instead of worrying or being afraid, I want to enjoy the adventure of living with You!

In Your strong, dependable Name, Jesus, *Amen*

READ ON YOUR OWN

JOHN 10:27–28; 1 PETER 1:3–4; ISAIAH 43:2 NLT; ROMANS 8:39

A NEW WAY OF THINKING

The word of God is alive and powerful.

—Hebrews 4:12 NLT

Dear Jesus,

Help me to think more and more like You. When I'm worried, that's when I need to stop and take time to think things out with You. As I relax in Your Presence, *Your arms* wrap around me in a strong, comforting hug— filling me with Your Peace. It feels wonderful to take a break from thinking so much about all my problems and just enjoy this time of *looking to You.*

Sometimes I like to sit quietly with You, resting in Your Presence. Other times I like to read my Bible, say words of praise to You, or sing to You. I'm learning that I can use Bible verses in my prayers and praises. When my prayers are filled with Your own Word, I feel more confident that I'm praying the way You want me to.

Lord, there is so much noise in this world. All the phones, computers, tablets, and other screens are tugging at me, trying to make me think the world's way—not *Your* way. But I'm asking You to *change me and give me a new way of thinking.* I want to think more like You, Jesus. As You change my way of thinking, please help my thoughts and attitudes show more and more of Your Love.

In Your powerful Name, Jesus, *Amen*

READ ON YOUR OWN

DEUTERONOMY 33:27; PSALM 34:5 NLT; HEBREWS 4:12 NLT; ROMANS 12:2

IT'S A BATTLE

God says, "Be still and know that I am God."
—Psalm 46:10

Dear Jesus,

Sometimes it's hard for me to sit quietly in Your Presence, especially when it seems like everything and everyone else is on the move. I can always think of something else I could or should be doing: Like my chores. Or my homework. Or practicing my music lessons. But taking time to talk with You brings me closer to You, and that's a blessing worth fighting for. So I won't give up!

Please help me win this battle to spend quiet time with You, Jesus. I want to focus on You and Your Word. I'm so grateful that You are *Immanuel— God with us.* As I relax in Your Presence, my worries and fears start to slip away. I can hear You whispering, *"Be still and know that I am God."*

The longer I focus on You, the more I can rejoice in how great You are—and trust that You're in control of everything. *You are my Protection and Strength. I will not be afraid,* even *if the earth shakes or if the mountains fall into the sea.* You are the unshakable Rock I can always count on to be there for me!

As I think about how huge Your Power and Glory are, my troubles seem so small. I know *I will have trouble in this world.* But I can *be brave* when I remember that *You have already defeated the world!*

In Your unbeatable Name, Jesus, *Amen*

READ ON YOUR OWN

MATTHEW 1:23; PSALM 46:10; PSALM 46:1–2; JOHN 16:33

EVEN ON MESSY DAYS

*"I give you peace in a different way than the world
does. So don't be troubled. Don't be afraid."*
—John 14:27 ERV

Dear Jesus,

Help me trust You every day, but especially on the messy days, when nothing seems to be going right. You give me so much peace when I'm in Your Presence—I don't want that peace to be shaken by what's going on around me. Even though I live in this world right now, my soul belongs with You in eternity. So when I start to feel stressed-out, I need to step away from the world and step into Your Presence—like I'm coming to see my very best Friend. As I stop trying to be in control of everything in my life, You help me relax. Then You fill me up with *a peace that is so great I cannot understand it.*

The Bible tells me to *depend on You and Your strength, always going to You for help.* Don't let me forget to do that. Please teach me to see my life, my troubles, and this world the way You see them. Jesus, I love to hear You saying these comforting words: *"Don't be troubled. Don't be afraid. Be brave! I have defeated the world!"* I can rejoice even on tough days because You give me *Your Peace,* and that is great enough to help me face *anything* in this world!

In Your all-powerful Name, Jesus, *Amen*

READ ON YOUR OWN

PHILIPPIANS 4:6–7; PSALM 105:4; JOHN 14:27 ERV; JOHN 16:33

UNTANGLING THE KNOTS

I say to myself, "The Lᴏʀᴅ is mine,
so I hope in him."
—Lamentations 3:24 ɴᴄᴠ

Dear Jesus,

Please smooth out the tangled-up places in my life. Sometimes my thoughts and feelings get twisted up like a knot, and I have no idea what to think or do, or even how to pray. So I come to You just as I am—with my knots of problems and mixed-up feelings—and I ask You to straighten them all out.

Some of my troubles are a mixture of my own problems and a problem that belongs to someone else: a friend or someone in my family. Sometimes they're not my troubles at all—they're someone else's problem, but I'm getting dragged into the mess. I need to figure out what *is* my problem and what *isn't*. I want to take responsibility for my mistakes, but not for anyone else's. Please help me untangle all these troubles, Lord.

I'm realizing that becoming a better Christian is something I'll be learning more and more about for my whole life. Instead of trying to untangle all my knots myself, I need to keep *going to You for help*. I can trust You to smooth out the tangled-up places in Your timing. Please show me how to keep You in the center of my thoughts—even when I'm having troubles. I'm so grateful that You are always with me and that *I can say to myself, "The Lord is mine." I can depend on You and Your strength.*

In Your amazing Name, Jesus, *Amen*

READ ON YOUR OWN

2 CORINTHIANS 3:18; 1 CHRONICLES 16:11; LAMENTATIONS 3:24 ɴᴄᴠ

YOU ARE *FOR* ME

May the Lord watch over you
and give you peace.
—Numbers 6:26

Dear Jesus,

If You are for me, who can ever be against me? Please help me understand and believe this powerful truth that You really are *for* me. You really are on my team and by my side—helping me, guiding me, and fighting for me.

When things don't go my way, or when a friend turns against me, it's easy to feel like I'm all alone. That's when it's so important to remember that You're with me and You are for me—all the time. It's true on the days when I'm getting good grades and able to smile at everyone, *and* on the days when I'm grumpy or feel like I'm messing everything up.

I can face troubles calmly and bravely when I'm trusting that You're with me in those tough times, cheering me on. You're so faithful and loyal that I know You'll never betray me or turn against me. That gives me the confidence and courage to keep going when things get tough. Because You're my Savior and I belong to You forever, I'm always in Your loving Presence.

It's *Your* opinion of me that matters, Lord, and You say that You love me. In fact, You promise that *nothing in the whole world will ever be able to separate me from Your Love*!

In Your loving Name, Jesus, *Amen*

READ ON YOUR OWN

ROMANS 8:31 NLT; MATTHEW 28:20; NUMBERS 6:26; ROMANS 8:39

MY FOREVER HOME

In Christ all of us will be made alive again.
—1 Corinthians 15:22

Dear Jesus,

You're teaching me that heaven is both now and in the future. It's *now* because You are with me every moment. So, as I walk through life holding Your hand, it's like I'm already touching a little bit of heaven— just by being close to You. You also sprinkle bits of heaven all through my day: Like the shining light of the sun, which helps me remember *Your* Light that shines so much brighter! And like the pretty flowers and birds and the blue skies and green trees that remind me to praise Your holy Name. Help me to see more and more of Your wonders as I walk in the Light of Your Love.

One day I will come to the end of my journey through this world, and I'll find a door to heaven. Only *You* know when I'll come to that door. Until then, You are preparing me every day, with each step we take together. You're teaching me to think and see more like You. I know I'll face troubles and challenges, but You promise that I will someday see heaven—my forever home. Thinking about this wonderful truth *fills me with so much joy and peace*! While I'm walking with You down *the path of life*, the promise of heaven gives me strength and hope.

In Your heavenly Name, Jesus, *Amen*

READ ON YOUR OWN

1 CORINTHIANS 15:20–23; HEBREWS 6:19;
ROMANS 15:13; PSALM 16:11 NKJV

YOU GIVE ME SO MUCH

God gave his Son for us all. So with Jesus,
God will surely give us all things.
—Romans 8:32

Dear Jesus,

This is such a good and joyful time in my life! *My cup*—my life—
overflows with blessings. Sure, there have been times when I've felt like
I was climbing up a steep hill because I was having so many problems.
But now it feels like I'm skipping through a field of flowers soaked in sun-
shine. Help me enjoy this happy, easy time with my whole heart. Thank
You for giving it to me!

Sometimes I feel a little guilty about accepting Your good gifts. I think
about the ways I've messed up, and I know I don't deserve all the blessings You give me. But You've been teaching me that this kind of thinking
is wrong. The truth is, no one is good enough to *deserve* Your wonderful
gifts. But You give them anyway! I'm so thankful that Your kingdom is *not*
about earning and deserving. It's about believing and receiving.

Instead of worrying about receiving so many gifts from You, I want
to open up my hands and my heart to accept all Your blessings. Help me
be grateful for each and every one. Then Your Joy in giving and my joy in
receiving can join together to create an even greater joy!

In Your giving Name, Jesus, *Amen*

READ ON YOUR OWN

PSALM 23:5 NLT; JOHN 3:16; LUKE 11:9–10; ROMANS 8:32

COUNTING ON YOU

I love you, Lord. You are my strength.
—Psalm 18:1

Dear Jesus,

You've been showing me that the best way to live is to count on You to help me. I'm learning to be more thankful for tough times, because they aren't all bad—something good can come out of them. That's because they remind me that You are with me, ready to help. You're teaching me not to worry about difficult tasks that I have to do. I'm starting to see them as things You can use to bring me closer to You. I love remembering that You are *my Strength*. Especially when I'm feeling tired. The more I depend on You, the easier it gets and the happier I feel.

Please help me to keep You in the center of my thoughts. This is much easier to do when I'm by myself. I admit that when other people are around, I often forget that You are with me. I start worrying about pleasing others, and they become my focus. When this happens, please remind me to whisper Your Name: "Jesus." This one-word prayer shows that I trust You—and it puts You back in the center of my thoughts, where You belong.

Your nearness is such a wonderful blessing! Living close to You helps me feel fully alive. You came into this world to *give life—life in all its fullness*!

In Your blessed Name, Jesus, *Amen*

READ ON YOUR OWN

PSALM 18:1–2; PROVERBS 29:25; JOHN 10:10

IT'S ALL IN YOUR HANDS

My future is in your hands.

—Psalm 31:15 NLT

Dear Jesus,

My future is in Your hands—tomorrow, next week, next year. So the best thing I can do is *trust You* in every situation. You're teaching me to feel safe and secure even when everything around me is changing. It's actually a relief to know that *You* are the One in charge of my life, not me. It sets me free—free from worrying and wondering about what I should do.

That doesn't mean it's okay for me to sit around all day doing nothing, just wasting time. You've given me energy and abilities, and I know You want me to use them. But I need to talk with You *first* about what You want me to do. You're teaching me to pray about everything and to look for You in every moment. And I'm learning to look for You in the most unexpected places—because You are a God of surprises!

Help me to *rejoice and be glad in this day that You have made*. Please work out all the details just the way You want them, Lord. Since You're in charge of my future, I don't have to worry about making things happen faster. I've seen how hurry and worry go hand in hand. And You tell me *not to worry about anything*. So, while I wait with You, please bless me with *Your Peace—a peace so great that I cannot understand it.*

In Your faithful Name, Jesus, *Amen*

READ ON YOUR OWN

PSALM 31:14–15 NLT; PSALM 118:24; PHILIPPIANS 4:6–7

HAPPY RIGHT NOW

*Happy are the people whose God is the L*ORD*!*
—Psalm 144:15 NKJV

Dear Jesus,

Please help me not to be afraid of being happy. I know that might sound a little silly. But sometimes, when good things are happening, I start to worry about what could go wrong and mess it all up. I start thinking about ways to protect my happiness and not lose it—which worries me even more! Sometimes I feel like it isn't even safe to just relax and enjoy the good things that are happening. But this kind of thinking is all mixed up and wrong. Since I belong to You, there's always something I can be happy about.

The Bible teaches me to *stop striving*, to quit trying so hard. I can relax because I *know that You are God*. I used to think I needed to have everything figured out before I could take a break and just enjoy being in Your Presence. I'm learning that I'll never have everything figured out—not even most things. But You understand everything about everything, and You are in control! Thinking about that makes me feel safe, Jesus.

The Bible says You will protect me even *if the earth shakes, or if the mountains fall into the sea*. So I don't have to wait until all my problems are solved to be happy. This moment, right now, is the perfect time to be happy and *take delight in You*. And that's exactly what I'm going to do!

In Your joyful Name, Jesus, *Amen*

READ ON YOUR OWN

PSALM 144:15; PSALM 46:10 NASB; PSALM 46:1–2; PSALM 37:4 NLT

YOU SMILE ON ME

May the Lᴏʀᴅ smile on you
and be gracious to you.
—Numbers 6:25 NLT

Dear Jesus,

Would You help me to keep looking in the right direction today? There's a lot of beauty to see in Your creation and in Your people. When I look at these things—at *the things that are good, true, right, and beautiful*— I'm encouraged. You created me with the wonderful ability to enjoy beauty and goodness. These blessings make my soul sing, and they give me strength. They also make me smile.

But every day I also see things that are wrong and ugly. Sometimes people say mean, ugly things to me or to my friends. Help me know how to deal with these things without letting them take over my thoughts. Remind me to bring the ugliness to You and ask You to show me how *You* see it. Then I can leave it with You and go on with a lighter, happier heart.

This world is so broken with sin. Even though I want everything here to be perfect (including me!), I know it just can't be. Not in this life. But *You* are perfect and holy. Thank You for not giving up on me, Lord, even though I keep sinning. I praise You for staying by my side in this sinful world. You bless me by reminding me to look the *right* way—toward You and Your blessings. When I do, *You smile on me* and *fill me with joy*.

In Your perfect, holy Name, Jesus, *Amen*

READ ON YOUR OWN

PHILIPPIANS 4:8; NUMBERS 6:24–25 NLT; ACTS 2:28

YOUR FRIENDSHIP

Now we hope for the blessings God has for his children.
These blessings are kept for you in heaven. They cannot
be destroyed or be spoiled or lose their beauty.
—1 Peter 1:4

Dear Jesus,

I want to walk close beside You—trusting You and relying on You to help me. The friendship You offer me sparkles with so many precious promises from the Bible: You love me with a *perfect Love that will last forever*. You are always with me, every moment of my life. You know everything about me, and You've already paid for all my sins. I have an inheritance of *blessings that are being kept for me in heaven—they cannot be destroyed or be spoiled or lose their beauty*. You're guiding me through my life, and someday *You will take me into the glory* of heaven!

All these promises paint the same picture: You love me, and You created me to need You. So that must mean that needing You is just part of being human. Help me to look at this as a blessing. When I understand that needing You is actually a good thing, I can relax in Your loving Presence. I begin to see more and more clearly that You are always with me, guiding me step by step. Also, I learn to rely less on myself and more on You.

Help me live closer and closer to You, Lord, so that I can enjoy Your wonderful friendship. You've invited me to walk with You and trust You all through my life—and I love that! I also loving hearing You whisper: "Dear child, I am with you."

In Your wonderful Name, Jesus, *Amen*

READ ON YOUR OWN

JEREMIAH 31:3; EPHESIANS 1:7–8; 1 PETER 1:3–4; PSALM 73:24 NIV

SEPTEMBER

"I am the Lord your God.
I am holding your right hand.
And I tell you, 'Don't be afraid.
I will help you.'"

—Isaiah 41:13

FILLED UP WITH BLESSINGS

"In quietness and trust is your strength."
—Isaiah 30:15 NIV

Dear Jesus,

Please fill me all the way up with Your Love, Joy, and Peace! These are Glory-gifts that come from being in Your Presence. I'm like an empty *clay jar* that You created to fill up until I overflow with Your heavenly blessings. And I'm thankful that You've made me this way. I'm learning that feeling tired or weak doesn't stop me from being filled with Your Spirit. In fact, it's in those tougher times that You pour Your power into me the most—*giving me strength through Your Spirit*.

As we walk through this day together, help me trust You to give me the strength I need for each step. I won't waste my time or energy wondering if I can make it through today on my own. Instead, I can relax because I know that You're big enough and powerful enough to handle anything that comes my way.

Lord, You give me everything I need. The Bible tells me that *in quietness* (spending time alone with You) *and trust* (counting on You to take care of me) *is my strength*.

In Your powerful Name, Jesus, *Amen*

READ ON YOUR OWN

2 CORINTHIANS 4:7; EPHESIANS 3:16; ISAIAH 30:15 NIV

THANKS FOR THE TROUBLES?

"I am the vine, and you are the branches. If a person remains in me and I remain in him, then he produces much fruit. But without me he can do nothing."
—John 15:5

Dear Jesus,

When I run into a problem, my first thought is to run away from the difficulty. But You're teaching me that problems can be blessings when they help me grow in my faith. Please help me remember this the next time a problem pops into my life. Don't let me forget that I can trust You to bring something good out of it. Instead of worrying and getting stressed-out about problems, I want to be able to see them as a chance to trust You more.

I've started to think of those stress feelings as my very own, built-in alarm—waking me up to the fact that I need You. Thank You for always being by my side and for showing me how my struggles can teach me to turn to You for help.

This world likes to say, "You should learn to do everything on your own. Be independent!" That's just not possible, and it's not good either. Instead of trying to be completely independent, I want to learn to depend on You more and more.

It may sound crazy, but I'm learning to thank You for my troubles in this world. They help me see how much I need You. And they show me how wonderful it will be to live in a problem-free heaven with You forever!

In Your holy, awesome Name, Jesus, *Amen*

READ ON YOUR OWN

JOHN 15:5; 2 CORINTHIANS 4:7–8; EPHESIANS 5:20

YOU DON'T LET GO

"My grace is all you need. My power works best in weakness."
—2 Corinthians 12:9 NLT

Dear Jesus,

You are *my Strength*. You promise that You're always ready to help me and strengthen me—and this encourages me so much. On days when I'm feeling strong, I'm thankful for this promise. But on days when I'm feeling weak, that's when I grab on to Your promise like a life preserver. And that's when I'm *super*-thankful for Your help. I know I can call out to You at any time, *"Lord, save me!"* And You will!

I'm grateful that *You save me because of Your Love*—a Love that never ends. If I feel like I'm sinking under all my problems, I need to hold on to something that won't let me down, something I can trust with all my heart. That "something" is *You*! Your powerful Presence not only gives me strength, but it also holds me up and doesn't let go.

Because You're always near, I don't worry about those times when I'm feeling weak. In fact, the Bible tells me that *Your power works best in weakness*. I'm learning that Your power and my weakness fit together perfectly—like a hand in a glove. Please help me be thankful for my weaknesses and to trust in Your strength.

In Your strong Name, Jesus, *Amen*

READ ON YOUR OWN

PSALM 59:17; MATTHEW 14:30; PSALM 31:16; 2 CORINTHIANS 12:9 NLT

I WILL STILL BE GLAD

There may be no sheep in the pens.
There may be no cattle in the barns.
But I will still be glad in the Lord.
—Habakkuk 3:17–18

Dear Jesus,

When my world is looking dark and scary, that's when I need to come closer to You. I can do that by *pouring my heart out to You* and telling You all my troubles. I trust that You're listening and that You care. I feel safe when I remember how great and powerful You are—You're in control even when it looks like everything is falling apart.

Sometimes I really struggle with how broken and full of sadness this world is. The best thing I can do when I'm struggling is to spend time reading the Bible. That's where I'll find strength and courage and hope. I especially love this verse: *"But I will still be glad in the Lord. I will rejoice in God my Savior."* The prophet Habakkuk wrote these words when his nation was about to be invaded by a terrible enemy. Habakkuk's words remind me that no matter how bad things might get, I still have a good reason to be joyful: You are with me.

Thank You, Lord, for always listening to my troubles. Please help me to trust You and to find joy as You lead me through the hard times. Your ways are often a mystery to me, but I know You always do what's best. So *I will put my hope in You and praise You*. You make me strong!

In Your hopeful Name, Jesus, *Amen*

READ ON YOUR OWN

PSALM 62:8 NLT; HABAKKUK 3:17–19; PSALM 42:5

MY PRICELESS TREASURE

All things were made through Christ and for Christ.
—Colossians 1:16

Dear Jesus,

My life is a wonderful gift from You. So I open up my hands and my heart to receive this day of life—and I receive it gratefully! I love knowing that You're my Friend and Savior, but I also need to remember that You are my Creator. The Bible says that *all things were made through You and for You.* As I go through this day, help me see signs of Your loving Presence all along the way. And please teach my heart to listen as You whisper, *"I am with you, and I will protect you everywhere you go."*

On bright, happy days, I can talk to You about the many joys You've given me. Thanking You for them makes me even happier! On difficult days, I can hold tight to Your hand and trust You to keep Your promise that *You will help me.*

My life in this body is an amazing gift, but my spiritual life is a precious, never-ending treasure. Because I belong to You, I'll be able to live with You forever. You'll give me a wonderful new body that will never get sick or tired. Thank You for the priceless gift of salvation—*I am saved by grace because I believe!*

In Your saving Name, Jesus, *Amen*

READ ON YOUR OWN

COLOSSIANS 1:16; GENESIS 28:15; ISAIAH 41:13; EPHESIANS 2:8

A HABIT OF TRUST

Immediately the father cried out, "I do
believe! Help me to believe more!"
—Mark 9:24

Dear Jesus,

I'm trying to learn a new habit. Whatever happens to me today—good or not-so-good—I want to remember to pray, "I trust You, Jesus." It's not easy, especially when problems come along, but I know it will be worth it. Telling You that I trust You helps me believe that You are by my side in every situation. Sometimes I whisper these words of trust, and sometimes I speak them out loud. Lord, *I do believe! Help me to believe more!*

I like to spend time thinking about how trustworthy You are—I can always count on You. And I think about how wonderful You are! *Your unfailing Love* gives me so much joy, and *Your Power and Your Glory* amaze me. When I remember that You're in control, I can see everything that's happening through the Light of Your loving Presence. This helps me not to be so afraid. Problems become a chance to show that I trust You, no matter what. And as I learn to be more grateful for Your blessings, I realize that every good thing comes from Your hand.

This habit of declaring my trust in You keeps me close to You. And it makes our friendship stronger. I trust You, Jesus. Help me trust You more and more!

In Your faithful Name, Jesus, *Amen*

READ ON YOUR OWN

MARK 9:24; PSALM 143:8 NLT; PSALM 63:2 NLT; ISAIAH 40:10–11

THE LIGHT OF THE WORLD

O Lord, you are my lamp.
The Lord lights up my darkness.
—2 Samuel 22:29 NLT

Dear Jesus,

You are my lamp. You light up my darkness. You are the Light of the world. You're also the Light of my life, and I want to follow You. I need Your Light because I bump into some kind of darkness in this world every day. It might be someone I care about getting sick, another kid being bullied, or hurting a friend through my own selfishness. Even though there's so much darkness, I can *be brave* because I know *You have defeated the world.* Instead of thinking about my problems, I need to keep *You* in the center of my thoughts. Jesus, You light up the dark!

You've invited me to walk with You on *the path that goes toward peace.* That's what I want to do, but lots of other things try to steal my attention away from You. Some of those things are just silly—like TV shows or the little computer games I sometimes play. And then there are some things that I *have* to do, like homework and taking care of my pet. Please teach me how to think about You all the time, even while I'm doing other things.

When You're in the center of my thoughts, I can enjoy the peace of Your Presence—in tough times *and* in good times. As I pay attention to You, Jesus, You chase away the darkness with Your Light!

In Your bright, shining Name, Jesus, *Amen*

READ ON YOUR OWN

2 SAMUEL 22:29 NLT; JOHN 8:12; JOHN 16:33; LUKE 1:79

ENOUGH TROUBLE

*"I am the Alpha and the Omega, the Beginning and
the End. I will give free water from the spring of
the water of life to anyone who is thirsty."*
—Revelation 21:6

Dear Jesus,

You taught your disciples that *each day has enough trouble of its own.*
That means I'm probably going to have some trouble today—and every
day. Whether it's big or little, Lord, please help me stay calm when that
trouble comes along.

Problems may pop up and surprise me, but it's comforting to know
that *You* are never caught by surprise. You are *the Beginning and the End.*
You know everything that will ever happen! And best of all, You're always
with me. You comfort me and guide me through the toughest times.

Having *enough* trouble in my day can even be a blessing—it keeps
my attention on today. My brain likes to be busy. If I don't have enough to
think about today, then I might start worrying about tomorrow.

I'm learning that my troubles can help me live closer to You. As we
work together to take care of my problems, I'm seeing that I *can* stay
calm during tough times. But what matters the most is how much I enjoy
my closeness with You. Your friendship makes me so very, very happy!

In Your delightful Name, Jesus, *Amen*

READ ON YOUR OWN

MATTHEW 6:34; REVELATION 21:6; ROMANS 12:12

273

A WIDE PATH FOR ME

*You have made a wide path for my feet
to keep them from slipping.*
—Psalm 18:36 NLT

Dear Jesus,

You make a wide path for me to follow through my life and You *keep my feet from slipping* as I'm walking. That promise is so comforting! Because You are in control, I don't need to worry about what might happen or wonder if I can handle it.

Only *You* know what will happen in the future. And only You know exactly what I can handle. At any time, You can step in and change my situation to keep me safe. You might change it just a little, or You might change it a lot. You can even change this day I'm living in *today*—opening up the path I'm walking on right now.

What I'm seeing most of all is just how much You work in every part of my life. You sweep away lots of troubles to protect me. You help me make good decisions—showing me when to say yes and when to say no. And You cheer me up when I'm feeling down. The Bible says *You are a shield to those who trust You.* As I walk along my path with You, I'm learning that my job is to trust You, lean on You, and talk to You about everything.

I know You don't take away every problem, but I'm thankful for how You open up the path so I can walk without slipping or falling. This is just one of many ways that *You bless me and keep me* safe.

In Your blessed Name, Jesus, *Amen*

READ ON YOUR OWN

PSALM 18:36 NLT; PSALM 18:30; NUMBERS 6:24–26

MY SAVIOR AND FRIEND

"I am the One who is and was and is coming. I am the All-Powerful."
—Revelation 1:8

Dear Jesus,

Help me keep my eyes on You and think great thoughts about You. It's easy to get discouraged when my thoughts are full of less important things. Thinking too much about the news, my own troubles, or even the troubles of the people I care about—those can all make me lose my joy. It's true that this world is full of trouble, but that's not what I should be thinking of. Remind me that You are with me and *You have defeated the world.*

You're closer than the air I breathe. You are *King of kings and Lord of lords.* And You are also the God who loves me, saves me, and is my forever-Friend. In You I have everything I need!

Praising You is one of my favorite ways to remember that You're with me. It makes Your Light shine brighter in my world, and it pushes away the darkness and discouragement. I love to praise You by reading Your Word and singing songs from the Psalms. Filling my mind with the Bible's truth makes me stronger. Whenever troubles come my way, praise pulls me closer to You and reminds me to think about who You really are—My Savior and Friend who is the *All-Powerful* God!

In Your high and holy Name, Jesus, *Amen*

READ ON YOUR OWN

JOHN 16:33; REVELATION 19:16; REVELATION 1:8

NOT ONE SPECK

*"On that day you will know that I am in my Father. You
will know that you are in me and I am in you."*
—John 14:20

Dear Jesus,

The crazier this world gets, the more I need to pay attention to You. Help me remember that You are with me all the time and You've already won the greatest victory! The Bible tells me that *I am in You and You are in me*. That means I can look forward to an eternity of problem-free living with You in heaven. There won't be one speck of fear or one bit of worry in heaven. Instead, I will have perfect Peace and never-ending Love in Your Presence. Just thinking about this amazing future with You—*the King of Glory*—fills me with joy!

This *hope for the future* gives me strength and encourages me to keep following You through this sinful world. Whenever I start to worry about something I've seen, heard, or thought, I can bring that worry straight to You. No matter what's happening, *You* are the One who keeps me safe—not my friends, my stuff, or how popular I am. Help me keep turning to You and remembering who You are: my strong, glorious Savior and my forever-Friend. In You I am always safe and secure!

In Your all-powerful Name, Jesus, *Amen*

READ ON YOUR OWN

JOHN 14:20; PSALM 24:7 NLT; PROVERBS 23:18; JOHN 15:13

THE MOST IMPORTANT THING

"Only one thing is important. Mary has chosen the right thing, and it will never be taken away from her."
—Luke 10:42

Dear Jesus,

So many, many things try to steal my attention away from You. There are phones, video games, and noisy screens everywhere. This world is a very different place than it was when You gave this command: *"Be still and know that I am God."* But Your command is just as important today as it was when You spoke those words long ago. My soul needs quiet time with You. In the still, quiet hours of the night, dew falls on the flowers and grass, and it refreshes them. The same thing happens when I sit quietly with You and *think about You.* Your Presence refreshes my mind and heart.

As I go through the day, my mind can get stuck on things that don't really matter—like wondering what someone else thinks about me or whether I passed that test. Then my thoughts start spinning round and round, just like the spinning wheels of a car that's stuck in the mud. But as soon as I start talking with You about what's bothering me, my thoughts come unstuck. You help me sort out what's important and what is not. And You remind me that the most important thing is staying close to You.

Please put more and more of Your thoughts into my mind. Help me to keep talking to You, enjoying Your Presence.

In Your refreshing Name, Jesus, *Amen*

READ ON YOUR OWN

HEBREWS 3:1; PSALM 46:10; LUKE 10:39–42

I TRUST YOU, LORD

The ways of God are without fault.
The Lord's words are pure.
He is a shield to those who trust him.
—2 Samuel 22:31

Dear Jesus,

The Bible says that *You are a shield to everyone who trusts You.* Help me remember this precious promise when my world is feeling scary and unsafe. It's so comforting to know that You personally protect those who trust You. You're my safe place in the middle of trouble.

Finding my safety in You means that I need to *trust You* and *tell You all my problems.* No matter what's happening in my life, it's always the right time to say, "I trust You, Lord." Of course, I can't always stop and tell You all my troubles at that very second. I might be in the middle of a math test, a ball game, or a talk with a friend. But I can whisper, "I trust You"—or even just think it in my mind—and You'll hear it. Then, later, I can take time to tell You everything that's going on. Being able to talk to You whenever I need to is such a relief. It makes our relationship stronger, and it helps me figure out what to do.

Anytime I'm feeling worried or scared, I can turn to You and say, "Jesus, You are my Shield—I trust You to protect me."

In Your protecting Name, Jesus, *Amen*

READ ON YOUR OWN

2 SAMUEL 22:31; PSALM 46:1; PSALM 62:8

A LOVE THAT REACHES TO THE HEAVENS

Your love, O Lord, reaches to the heavens,
your faithfulness to the skies.
—Psalm 36:5 NIV

Dear Jesus,

You are the Friend I can trust completely—with all my heart. Instead of letting the things that are happening in this world spook me, I'm going to pour my energy into trusting You more and more. I'll look for all the ways You're working in the world. And I'll whisper Your precious Name, "Jesus." Because that tiny prayer instantly connects my heart and mind to You, like a phone call to my best friend. *You are close to everyone who prays to You.* Please wrap me up in Your arms and comfort me with Your Peace.

Help me remember that You are both loving and faithful. *Your Love reaches to the heavens,* and *Your faithfulness reaches to the skies.* This means that there's no end to Your Love. It lasts forever and never runs out! I'm thankful that You're *always* faithful, Lord. I can count on You, no matter what!

When I depend on my own strength and abilities, it doesn't work out so well—and it doesn't please You. Teach me to depend on You more and more. You're my Savior, who died and was raised to life so I could someday be with You in the *eternal glory* of heaven!

In Your awesome Name, Jesus, *Amen*

READ ON YOUR OWN

PSALM 145:18; PSALM 36:5 NIV; 2 CORINTHIANS 4:17

WAITING IS WORSHIP TOO

Those who trust in the Lord will find new strength.

—Isaiah 40:31 NLT

Dear Jesus,

Help me quit trying to make everything work out in a hurry—when *I* want it to. I can't control what happens or when it happens. I can only live today. So anytime an idea or something I want to do grabs my attention, help me remember to stop and ask You if it's part of Your plan for me today. If it's not, I can just leave it with You and trust You to take care of it. Then I can get busy again with what I need to do *today*. When I remember to live like this, my life is a lot happier and simpler. The Bible teaches that *there is a right time for everything*.

You've promised so many blessings to *those who trust in You*: *new strength*, hope, and the confidence that You're always near. Trusting You and waiting for Your perfect timing is actually a way for me to worship You. It shows that I'm depending on You and I'm ready to do Your will.

This world can be a really messy and confusing place. But I'm learning that living close to You makes my life simpler and less confusing. I praise You, Jesus, because *You have defeated the world*. Thank You for *telling me these things so that I can have peace in You*.

In Your wonderful Name, Jesus, *Amen*

READ ON YOUR OWN

ECCLESIASTES 3:1–2; ISAIAH 40:30–31 NLT; JOHN 16:33

AS BRIGHT AS THE SUN

The way of the good person is like the light of dawn.
It grows brighter and brighter until it is full daylight.

—Proverbs 4:18

Dear Jesus,

When I'm struggling and things are especially tough, it's easy for me to think that they'll never get better. The longer I wrestle with a problem, the more I feel this way. It gets harder and harder to imagine being happy again. Sometimes I think I just might give up—and give in to being miserable. Then I remember that You're always right beside me, Jesus. Help me hold on tight to You and trust that You are able to *light up my darkness.*

Instead of thinking about everything that's going wrong, I'm going to think about *You*—remembering that *You are always with me. You are holding my hand* and encouraging me to *live by what I believe* as I walk through this dark, tough time. Once I start looking at my life through eyes of faith, it's easier to see that brighter times *are* coming! That's something wonderful to praise You for!

As I worship You in my dark and difficult times, You show me *the first light of dawn* on the path ahead. Please help me keep following that path—Your path for me. Little by little, that dim light will shine *brighter and brighter*, until it's as bright as the sun!

In Your amazing Name, Jesus, *Amen*

READ ON YOUR OWN

PSALM 18:28 NLT; PSALM 73:23; 2 CORINTHIANS 5:7 NLT; PROVERBS 4:18

YOU ARE STRONG ENOUGH

Give your worries to the Lord.
He will take care of you.
He will never let good people down.
—Psalm 55:22

Dear Jesus,

I've been carrying around all my worries and struggles, and it's wearing me out! My muscles aren't strong enough to handle these heavy loads. But the Bible says that I can *give my worries to You*, and *You will take care of me*. Please help me hand over my burdens to You, Lord, so that You can carry them—just like I would let my mom or dad carry my heavy backpack for me.

Whenever I realize that something is weighing me down, I need to figure out if it's really my problem or if it's someone else's. If it is someone else's problem, I can just let it go. If it's *my* problem, I can talk to You about it and ask You to show me what You want me to do.

Too often, though, I hold on to my worries and struggles until they're all I'm thinking about. Please help me remember to bring my load of worries to You *before* I get all worn out. Leaving them with You makes my heart feel so much lighter—helping me enjoy Your Presence more and more.

Lord, You've promised *to take care of me. You will use Your wonderful riches to give me everything I need*. Thank You for loving me and taking such good care of me!

In Your magnificent Name, Jesus, *Amen*

READ ON YOUR OWN

PSALM 55:22; ISAIAH 9:6; PHILIPPIANS 4:19

YOU SHARE YOUR JOY WITH ME

Great is his faithfulness;
his mercies begin afresh each morning.
—Lamentations 3:23 NLT

Dear Jesus,

Help me to *trust You and not be afraid.* I don't want to ever forget that *You are my Strength and my Song.* I feel happy and safe when I think about what it means to have You as my Strength. You made the world and everything else in the whole universe—and You did it all just by speaking. There's no end to Your power! Every time I have to face things I'm afraid of or things I'm not strong enough to do, I know I can count on You and Your power to help me.

You've been showing me that trying to fight my fears doesn't really work. It just makes me think about them even more! Instead, I need to think about *You* and *Your faithfulness* to me. Because when I choose to *trust You,* there's no limit to how much strength You can pour into me.

I'm so thankful that You are my Song and You share Your Joy with me. I love walking along *the path of life* with You, Jesus! Because when I'm living close to You, *You fill me with joy and pleasure.* This journey that we're on is leading me toward my home in heaven—and I'll happily sing Your song with You as we're walking along together.

In Your joyful Name, Jesus, *Amen*

READ ON YOUR OWN

ISAIAH 12:2–3 NLT; PSALM 56:3;
LAMENTATIONS 3:22–23 NLT; PSALM 16:11 NIV

A BEAUTIFUL PICTURE

I am guiding you in wisdom.
And I am leading you to do what is right.
—Proverbs 4:11

Dear Jesus,

You are guiding me wisely and leading me to do what is right. But there are still times when I get confused and really don't know what to do. Some days I think I've done the right thing, but it turns out all wrong. Then I remember that even though You did *everything* the way it should have been done—You did everything perfectly right—many of the people around You still chose to do wrong. So I know You understand what I'm feeling.

Please help me to trust You no matter what. It's only when I'm trusting You that I can find the right path to follow. As I walk through this day, I'll face all kinds of things—some happy and some sad, some right and some wrong, some big and some small. I believe that You'll take all those things and work them into *Your good plan* for my life.

Right now, I can only see a little bit of the big picture of my life. It's like looking at just a few pieces of a giant picture puzzle. By themselves, those pieces don't make sense. But I'm learning to *live by what I believe, not by what I can see.* I'm trusting that You *are* leading me along the right path. And someday all the pieces will fit together into a beautiful picture! Thank You, Lord!

In Your great Name, Jesus, *Amen*

READ ON YOUR OWN

PROVERBS 4:11; ROMANS 8:28; PROVERBS 20:24; 2 CORINTHIANS 5:7

TO KNOW YOU

"This is the way to have eternal life—to know you, the only true God, and Jesus Christ, the one you sent to earth."
—John 17:3 NLT

Dear Jesus,

I come to You today looking for rest. I really, really need to take a break because my mind has been way too busy judging everyone and everything around me. Now it's almost a habit—where I'm judging what someone is wearing, what my friend says, what he doesn't say, this thing that happened . . . even the weather! But the Bible tells me that I'm supposed to be busy *knowing You* and following You. When I start acting like I'm the judge, it's like I'm trying to take over Your job. Please forgive me, Jesus. Help me turn away from this sinful way of thinking and keep turning to You. I want to think about You more and more—enjoying Your loving Presence.

Teach me to live like a sheep with its Shepherd, a servant with the King, and a lump of clay with the Potter. Instead of letting my opinions and attitudes shape me, I want *You* to shape my life. Help me trust You to do whatever You want with me and to thank You for it. You invite me to come to You at any time—but not as Your equal. There is no one else like You! Only You are the *King of kings*. My heart is happiest when I'm holding tight to Your hand and worshiping You as we walk along together.

In Your glorious Name, Jesus, *Amen*

READ ON YOUR OWN

MATTHEW 7:1; JOHN 17:3 NLT; ROMANS 9:20–21; REVELATION 19:16

YOU ARE ENOUGH

She will give birth to a son. You will name the son Jesus. Give
him that name because he will save his people from their sins.
—Matthew 1:21

Dear Jesus,

You are *Immanuel. This name means "God is with us."* And this name of Yours tells me that You *are* enough—You're all I need!

That's pretty easy to believe when things in my life are going just the way I want. But when I run into tough times—especially when the problems show up one right after the other—I sometimes start to wonder if You really *are* taking care of me. Before I know it, my mind is spinning, spinning, spinning while I try to figure out how *I* can make things better. Once my brain gets going, it's hard to stop. So many plans and possibilities zoom through my mind that I end up feeling tired and even more confused.

Instead of thinking about my problems so much, I need to remember that *You are always with me.* Knowing that You're ready to help me through even the biggest problems is something I can be thankful for, no matter what's happening. Of course, I also have to try my best to make good and wise choices. But even though I mess up sometimes, I know You'll see me through as long as I keep turning to You for help. I choose to *be joyful and glad, because You are my Savior*—You are the God who saves me.

In Your saving Name, Jesus, *Amen*

READ ON YOUR OWN

MATTHEW 1:21–23; MATTHEW 28:20; HABAKKUK 3:17–18 GNT

YOUR LOVE CHASES ME

Mary hid these things in her heart; she
continued to think about them.
—Luke 2:19

Dear Jesus,

Your Love chases after me every day of my life! I just need to remember to look for signs of Your Love and Your Presence in my life today.

You show Yourself to me in so many ways. You're in the Bible verse that pops into my mind just when I need it. You're in the people who speak kind and helpful words to me. You're in the good things that happen by "accident"—things that are actually part of Your perfect plan. I see You at work in the natural world all around me: in the blooming flowers and the leafy trees and the busy ants and the jumping squirrels. Lord, Your Love is alive and active. It happily looks for me and finds me (kind of like a game of Hide and Seek), and it leaps into my life! Please open the eyes of my heart to see all the big *and* the small ways You bless me.

I want to pay extra-close attention to the different ways You show up in my life—*thinking about* what You do and storing up those thoughts in my heart like gold coins in a treasure chest. I'm going to start writing down what I notice too, so I can enjoy Your gifts again and again. These signs of Your Presence keep me strong and ready to face whatever trouble might be coming. Help me remember that *nothing in the whole world will ever be able to separate me from Your Love!*

In Your wonderful Name, Jesus, *Amen*

READ ON YOUR OWN

PSALM 23:6 THE MESSAGE; PSALM 119:11; LUKE 2:19; ROMANS 8:39

LORD, YOU'RE WAITING TOO

The Lord wants to show his mercy to you.
He wants to rise and comfort you.
—Isaiah 30:18

Dear Jesus,

I'm grateful that *Your mercies never stop. They are new every morning.* I can begin each day with confidence because I know that Your endless supply of blessings is waiting for me—even if I messed up yesterday or things didn't go how I planned.

I know that You hear all my prayers. Not a single one slips by You. This helps me wait for Your answers and not give up. While I sit in Your Presence, help me soak up Your never-ending Love and mercy like a tree planted near a river that never runs out of water. These blessings from You keep my spirit healthy. I don't have to worry, because You always take care of me.

Even though You haven't answered some of my prayers yet, I trust that You know what You're doing and You are faithful. You keep all Your promises in Your own perfect way and Your own perfect timing. If I get tired of waiting, please remind me that *You* are waiting too—waiting to *show me Your mercy and comfort.* You wait for just the right time to bless me with all the things You've lovingly prepared for me. While I'm spending time with You, I like to remember Your promise that *everyone who waits for Your help will be happy.*

In Your faithful Name, Jesus, *Amen*

READ ON YOUR OWN

LAMENTATIONS 3:22–24; JOHN 14:27; ISAIAH 30:18

THANK YOU FOR EVERYTHING

Always give thanks to God the Father for everything,
in the name of our Lord Jesus Christ.
—Ephesians 5:20

Dear Jesus,

Please help me to soak up *Your Peace* like a sponge—all the way through to the inside of my heart. As I sit quietly in the warm Light of Your Presence, I want to feel more and more of Your Peace. This isn't something I can do on my own by trying harder. All I have to do is open my heart and receive Your Peace as a gift from You to me.

It seems like everywhere I turn, people are talking about growing up and learning to be independent. But the truth is, no matter how old I get, I'll always need to depend on You. That's something I've learned from my troubles, Lord. I'm not strong enough to get through the hard stuff by myself! In those difficult times, You pull me closer and closer, pointing out little surprise blessings—one after another—like seashells in the sand.

You've been teaching me to thank You for my tough times. That's really hard for me to do, Jesus. But I'm learning that when I trust You enough to thank You for *everything*, that's when You do Your best work in me.

I'm starting to see that needing You all the time is a wonderful gift—it helps me know that You are always here for me!

In Your perfect Name, Jesus, *Amen*

READ ON YOUR OWN

JOHN 14:27; ISAIAH 58:11; EPHESIANS 5:20

TRULY FREE

"If the Son makes you free, then you will be truly free."
—John 8:36

Dear Jesus,

I'm tired from carrying around all the mistakes I made yesterday. I wish I could go back and do things differently—erasing my mistakes with a great big eraser and starting over. But I can't change the past and I can't undo those mistakes.

I know that You can do anything and everything, Lord. But even *You* don't choose to go back and change the past. So I don't want to waste my time wishing that things had been different. Instead, I ask You to forgive me and help me learn from my mistakes so I can "write" a better page in my life today.

When I keep thinking about all the things I've done wrong, it's like I'm dragging around all those mistakes on heavy chains that are wrapped around my ankles. They're so heavy I feel like I can hardly move. That's when I like to imagine You coming to my rescue and cutting off those chains! You came to this world to rescue and *set free* everyone who *believes in You.* So I want to walk in the truth that *I am truly free.*

Lord, I'm so happy that You bring good things out of my messes—forgiving me and leading me along new paths. As I talk to You about my mistakes, help me to *learn from You.* Please show me the changes You want me to make and *lead me on the paths that are right.*

In Your forgiving Name, Jesus, *Amen*

READ ON YOUR OWN

MATTHEW 11:28–29; JOHN 8:36; JOHN 3:16; PSALM 23:3

A KIND OF LADDER

"May the Lord bless you and keep you."
—Numbers 6:24

Dear Jesus,

Help me to see my problems as a chance to look at things through Your eyes. When everything is going my way, it's easy to sleepwalk through my days—just doing what I always do. But when I bump into a problem that blocks my way, suddenly I wake up and pay attention.

You're showing me that when I run into something I can't fix right away, You're giving me a choice. I can either get angry and start feeling sorry for myself—which makes me feel much worse—or I can choose to see this problem as a kind of ladder. It's a ladder that lets me "climb" up and see my life the way You do. Looking at things from high up on the ladder, I'm able to see that even huge problems aren't as big as I thought they were. Compared to Your power, the biggest problem is just *a small trouble* that will only last a short time.

Once I can see my troubles as small things that won't last forever, I'm able to turn my back on them and turn to You, Jesus. As I'm paying attention to You, *the Light of Your Presence* shines on me—*blessing me and keeping me* close to You. My heart is never happier than when I'm spending time with You.

In Your brightly shining Name, Jesus, *Amen*

READ ON YOUR OWN

2 CORINTHIANS 4:17–18; PSALM 89:15; NUMBERS 6:24–25

WHERE YOU ARE

*My whole being thirsts for you, like a man in a
dry, empty land where there is no water.*
—Psalm 63:1

Dear Jesus,

There are times when my thoughts get stuck—kind of like a shoe gets stuck in the mud. The problem is, my thoughts usually get stuck on something that isn't really all that important. Please help me pull those thoughts out of "the mud" so I can think more about You, Jesus.

When my mind isn't busy, I often start thinking about the future. I'll plan and plan, trying to figure out how to make everything go *my* way. But I'm really just wasting time. First of all, I can't control the future. Plus, I usually end up changing my mind anyway—sometimes more than once in the same day! I know there's a time to make plans, but it's not *all* the time! In fact, it's not even most of the time.

I want to live *right now*, in the present. Because that's where You are. As I spend time in Your Presence, Your Love soaks in and I'm able to relax. You help me set aside my problems and think about You and Your Love instead. *My whole being thirsts for You*, but usually I don't realize what I'm really thirsty for. So, I ask You to keep reminding me that I'm thirsty for *You*, Lord.

Please *lead me beside peaceful streams*, where I can rest and enjoy Your Presence. Thank You for loving me so very, very much!

In Your loving Name, Jesus, *Amen*

READ ON YOUR OWN

EPHESIANS 3:16–18; PSALM 63:1; PSALM 23:2–3 NLT

JOY AND HOPE

Be joyful because you have hope.
—Romans 12:12

Dear Jesus,

You are the Lord of my life, and I trust You. I really do! But sometimes, when You're telling me "No" or "Not now," it seems like You're holding me back and holding me down. To be honest, I don't like that feeling. It's uncomfortable to feel like I have no control. Part of me wants to break free and try to take control. The other part of me knows that You always do what's best. And feeling so uncomfortable can wake me up and remind me that *You* are in charge of my life.

Anytime I'm facing something that makes me sad or mad or scared, I have to decide: Will I grumble and complain and be upset with You? Or will I come closer to You through praying and singing and reading my Bible? The more I choose being close and trusting You, the more I find hope in *Your unfailing Love.*

Day after day, You're teaching me to *be joyful* while I wait in Your Presence. And I'm learning that I *can* be happy, because *being with You* is so wonderful. Help me to keep trusting You, Lord, believing that *You will lift me up when the right time comes.* Until then, I'll *give all my worries to You* because *You care for me*—You're taking good care of me!

In Your powerful Name, Jesus, *Amen*

READ ON YOUR OWN

PSALM 33:22 NLT; ROMANS 12:12; PSALM 16:11; 1 PETER 5:6–7

YOU'RE ALWAYS DOING SOMETHING NEW

"Look at the new thing I am going to do.
It is already happening. Don't you see it?"
—Isaiah 43:19

Dear Jesus,

I come to You with a heart that's saying, "Thank You! Thank You! Thank You!" You've filled my life with so many blessings. A thankful heart helps me see how much You love me. It also makes me feel even happier that You are my Friend. *Nothing in the whole world will ever be able to separate me from Your Love.* Nothing! Your promise to always be with me helps me feel safe and secure. Whenever I start to worry, please remind me that You are keeping me safe. I can trust You completely.

I'm learning that I'll never be in control of everything that happens in my life, but that's okay. Because *You* are in complete control—100 percent. I can *trust You* to do what's best for me.

You use the tough times to teach me to search for You and know You better. Help me, Lord, to hold tight to You instead of always trying to do things the old, easy, comfortable way. I want to live my life as the big, wonderful adventure it is—an adventure that I share with You, my forever-Friend. You're always doing something new! Help me to keep my eyes wide open and be on the lookout for everything You're doing in my life.

In Your marvelous Name, Jesus, *Amen*

READ ON YOUR OWN

ROMANS 8:38–39; PSALM 56:3–4; ISAIAH 43:19

MY SAFE PLACE

He is my shield and my saving strength, my high tower.
—Psalm 18:2

Dear Jesus,

You are the One I can trust completely! There are some people I trust *a lot*, but they make mistakes—and sometimes those mistakes hurt me. And this world, Lord . . . it's crazy and always changing. I never know what's going to happen! That's why You're the only One I can trust perfectly. You never change! *You are my Rock. I can run to You for safety.*

Because You're my safe place, I can feel sure about You no matter what's going on. Every time anything new happens—I make the swim team, or my friend gets sick, or my family moves to a different place—my first thought is to try to take charge. I want to do *something* that will make me feel a little less scared and a little more in control. But You're teaching me to relax and let You take charge. *You are my Protection and my Strength*, and You always go with me, wherever I go. Please help me to face life's changes—even the ones I didn't want to happen—without fear.

Instead of letting my worry-thoughts run around in my mind, I need to lasso them and bring them to You in my prayers. When I start to feel worried or afraid, I can pray, "I trust You, Jesus!" As I bring my troubled thoughts to You, You calm my fears and give me Your Peace. The Bible promises that *if I trust You, I will be safe.*

In Your strong Name, Jesus, *Amen*

READ ON YOUR OWN

PSALM 18:2; PSALM 46:1–2; 2 CORINTHIANS 10:5; PROVERBS 29:25

OCTOBER

I pray that the God who gives hope will fill you with much joy and peace while you trust in him. Then your hope will overflow by the power of the Holy Spirit.

—Romans 15:13

YOU ARE MY JOY

Be full of joy in the Lord always. I will say again, be full of joy.
—Philippians 4:4

Dear Jesus,

You are my Joy! Every time I think, whisper, or say these four words out loud, Your Light shines into my life. Because You're always with me, *the joy of Your Presence* can be mine at any time. Even if I've messed up or I'm feeling worried about something, I can open my heart to You by saying, "I love You, Jesus!" I like to think about all the ways You love me and all that You've done for me. Those thoughts fill me with *joy in You*, my Savior.

As one of Your followers, I know You've given me the power to rise above the hard times by sending Your Spirit—the Holy Spirit—to live inside of me. He is my Helper, and He has unlimited power. You've also given me hope for the future by promising that *You will come back* to this earth one day. *Then You will take me to be with You so that I can be where You are*—forever!

Whenever my day looks dark, I need to remember that You are *the Light of the world*. Your Light brightens my day like the sun popping out from behind the clouds after a stormy, rainy morning. As I relax with You, I can almost hear You whispering, "Dear child, I am your Joy."

In Your beautiful Name, Jesus, *Amen*

READ ON YOUR OWN

PSALM 21:6 NIV; PHILIPPIANS 4:4; JOHN 14:3; JOHN 8:12

THE MOST WONDERFUL MAP

Guide me in your truth.
Teach me, my God, my Savior.
I trust you all day long.
—Psalm 25:5

Dear Jesus,

You will be my Guide from now on! This promise fills me with so much joy and peace—because I know that You're going to lead me through every day of my life, including today. I can always count on You. Because You are God, You've already gone ahead of me into the future and prepared a path for me. At the same time, You stay close beside me. *You hold my hand. You guide me with Your advice. And later You will receive me into heaven.*

It's not always easy for me to make decisions, so I sometimes depend on other people to help me. Some people give good advice, but others don't. Only *You* give the perfect advice every time. I know I can trust You to lead me wisely. *You are always with me. You guide me in Your truth, teaching me* and showing me everything I need to make good decisions. Please help me to *trust You all day long.*

As I walk through my life with You, I'm thankful for the wonderful map You've given me: the Bible. *Your Word is like a lamp for my feet and a light for my path.* Help me to follow this Light and follow You, Jesus. You know the very best way for me to go!

In Your guiding Name, Jesus, *Amen*

READ ON YOUR OWN

PSALM 48:14; PSALM 73:23–24; PSALM 25:5; PSALM 119:105

NOT GUILTY!

He is so rich in kindness and grace that he purchased our
freedom with the blood of his Son and forgave our sins.
—Ephesians 1:7 NLT

Dear Jesus,

Help me remember that I am *not* in a courtroom, being judged. Your Word promises that once I trust You as my Savior, I'm forgiven. *I am not judged guilty* in the courts of heaven. Thank You so much for dying on the cross and taking the punishment for all my sins! When I remember what You've done for me, I can live happy and full of joy. It's like stepping outside and breathing fresh air again after being stuck indoors for a few days! Help me relax like that in Your Love and to stop feeling guilty for the things I've done wrong.

Of course, that doesn't mean I can just keep on sinning either. I need to keep trying to do what's right. But I still sin and make mistakes, and then I start feeling guilty again. Help me believe that Your death on the cross really does *make me free*, Jesus. You paid the full price for my sins, so I don't need to be afraid—I am *truly free.*

I'm learning that the closer I live to You, the easier it is to see how You want me to live. And this helps me breathe in Your Joy and Peace more and more. I feel so blessed by the forgiveness and kindness *You have showered on me.* Please keep working in my heart, Lord. Teach me to be thankful for all You've done. I want my heart to *overflow with thankfulness*!

In Your loving Name, Jesus, *Amen*

READ ON YOUR OWN

ROMANS 8:1; JOHN 8:36; EPHESIANS 1:7–8 NLT; COLOSSIANS 2:6–7 NLT

BUILDING ON THE ROCK

*I keep my eyes always on the L*ORD*.*
He is at my right hand.
So I will always be secure.
—Psalm 16:8 NIRV

Dear Jesus,

You are the One I'm building my life on. You are *my Rock*—and not even the fiercest, strongest storms will ever shake You. I praise You, mighty Lord!

Without You, there's nothing solid to build my life on. That's because everything else in this world changes—even the good things. I can try to build my life on great friends or good grades or the cool stuff I have. But none of those things lasts forever. It's like trying to make a sand-castle right next to the ocean, where it will be washed away by the waves. Without You, Jesus, *everything is "completely meaningless"* in the end. But because You're my Savior and You live forever, my life has meaning—it makes sense. I can build my life on the solid Rock of Your Presence.

I've found that if *I keep my eyes on You*, I can walk through my days with less and less fear. You help me know which way to go and what to do. You're the Guide who is always with me. When I look up ahead, imagining the path of my future, I know that You are *there* too. I can almost see You waving to me. You are guiding me step by step, all the way home to heaven!

In Your mighty Name, Jesus, *Amen*

READ ON YOUR OWN

2 SAMUEL 22:47; ECCLESIASTES 1:2 NLT; PSALM 40:2; PSALM 16:8 NIRV

YOUR WAYS ARE A MYSTERY

I will wait for God to save me.
My God will hear me.
—Micah 7:7

Dear Jesus,

The Bible teaches me that *You care for me*—You are taking care of me! But when my struggles get worse instead of better, it's easy to feel like You're letting me down. Sometimes I start to wonder if You really do care that I'm going through such a tough time. I know You have the power to fix everything, Lord. But You don't change the things I really, really want You to change, and that's hard for me.

Anytime I start thinking that way, please calm me down. Teach me to *be still* in Your Presence instead of trying to force everything to be the way I want it. More than anything, I just want to fall back into Your strong arms with a big sigh of relief and let You hold me close. Even though there are so many things I don't understand, I can enjoy being in Your Presence. I can rest, knowing that You won't ever quit loving me.

Your ways are often a mystery to me, and I can't figure them out. But I do know this: Your Love is wonderful, and it never, ever ends. So *I will look to You for help. I will wait for You to save me*. Because You are my God, and *You hear me* when I call to You.

In Your saving Name, Jesus, *Amen*

READ ON YOUR OWN

1 PETER 5:6–7; PSALM 46:10; EXODUS 33:14; MICAH 7:7

I'LL HOLD ON TO HOPE

I pray that you will have greater understanding in your heart.
Then you will know the hope that God has chosen to give us.
—Ephesians 1:18

Dear Jesus,

Help me to *be joyful because I have hope* in You. Sometimes my problems and the troubles of this world make it hard to be joyful. But I'm learning that one of the best ways to find joy is to hope in You and Your promises.

I'd really like to learn more about this *hope that You have chosen to give me.* The Bible calls it the hope of *rich and glorious blessings You have promised to Your people.* When I decided to believe in You, it's like You put my name on those beautiful blessings and said: "Here. These belong to you, because you're in My family now. And you belong to Me forever." This is what I need to remember on those days when troubles are pulling me down. Help me hold on to hope with everything I've got! Your hope—Your promises—will give me strength to get through my problems and find joy in the middle of them.

The hope I have in You is like a hot-air balloon for my heart. I climb into the basket under the balloon by trusting You. This lifts me high above my troubles and fills my heart with joy. From up high, I can see that my troubles aren't so big, and they won't last forever. I just need to trust You and believe that You won't ever let me down.

I do believe, Jesus. *Help me to believe and trust You more!*

In Your holy Name, Jesus, *Amen*

READ ON YOUR OWN

ROMANS 12:12; EPHESIANS 1:18; PROVERBS 23:18; MARK 9:24

READY FOR THE ADVENTURE!

*Yes, I am sure that nothing can separate
us from the love God has for us.*
—Romans 8:38

Dear Jesus,

I'm ready for the adventure of today! I'm ready to walk boldly along the path of my life—trusting You, the Friend who is always with me. I can be brave and confident because Your Presence goes with me every step of the way—today, tomorrow, and forever.

Help me not to worry or be afraid. Those feelings are like robbers who steal my joy. Teach me to trust that You'll help me face any problems that come into my life. Sometimes I start worrying about what might happen or what could go wrong. The next thing I know, I'm trying to figure out how to fix problems that haven't even happened yet—and problems that might *never* happen! But You're teaching me to *look only to You. You are the One who began my faith, and You make my faith perfect.* When I keep my eyes on You, Jesus, so many of those problems I've been worrying about just disappear.

Whenever I start to feel afraid, please remind me that *You are holding my hand* and *You will help me.* The Bible promises that *nothing above me, nothing below me, or anything else in the whole world will ever be able to separate me from Your loving Presence.*

In Your glorious Name, Jesus, *Amen*

READ ON YOUR OWN

PSALM 48:14; HEBREWS 12:2; ISAIAH 41:13; ROMANS 8:38–39

TALKING TO YOU

You are my God, and I will thank you.
You are my God, and I will praise your greatness.
—Psalm 118:28

Dear Jesus,

Help me not to think of prayer as a chore. Instead, I want to see it as a chance to talk with the One I love most of all—*You*! When *I delight in You*, we have the sweetest conversations. And that makes me want to talk with You more and more!

An easy way to start talking to You is to thank You for being my Savior, my God, and my Friend. Thanking You helps me connect to You, kind of like calling You on the phone. Because You answer my "call" every time, I know I can pray and talk to You about all kinds of things.

There's nothing I can't share with You. That's because You understand me completely, and You already know everything that's happening in my life. You loved me so much that You paid the price for my sins on the cross. Because You died for me, I can trust that You will always do what's best for me. I can *pour out my heart to You,* Jesus. *You are my refuge*—my safe place.

The Bible gives me so many great promises I can hold on to. Some of my favorites are: *You delight in me* and You love me with a perfect Love that never ends. Please wrap Your arms around me as I rest here with You. Help me believe that I really am Your dearly loved child. I know You'll never let me go, and that fills me with joy!

In Your joyful Name, Jesus, *Amen*

READ ON YOUR OWN

PSALM 37:4 NLT; ZEPHANIAH 3:17 NLT; PSALM 118:28; PSALM 62:8 NLT

YOU HELP ME SEE WHAT IS TRUE

"You will know the truth. And the truth will make you free."
—John 8:32

Dear Jesus,

You understand me so much better than I understand myself. So I can come to You with my problems and worries, and You give me the perfect advice. As I spend time with You in the Light of Your Love, I can see myself the way I really am: beautifully dressed in Your perfect goodness. I know I will still have struggles in this world. But I'm grateful that You love me just as much on my not-so-good days as on my good days. Your Word promises that *nothing in the whole world will ever be able to separate me from Your Love!*

Because You're so wise, You help me see what is true and live the right way. I can be totally honest with You about my struggles and fears, and You'll help me make good choices. The Bible says that *knowing the truth will make me free.* You *are* the truth, Jesus, and You always know what's best for me. Thank You for working in my heart to set me free from my sins and shame.

Lord, You're teaching me to *delight in You* more than anything else. You really are the One my heart wants the most! Please keep me close to You—reminding me often of Your Love for me and Your Presence with me.

In Your wise Name, Jesus, *Amen*

READ ON YOUR OWN

ISAIAH 9:6; ROMANS 8:39; JOHN 8:32; PSALM 37:4 NLT

NO MORE TEARS

He will wipe away every tear from their eyes. There will be no more death, sadness, crying, or pain. All the old ways are gone.
—Revelation 21:4

Dear Jesus,

You know about every single one of my troubles. *You have collected all my tears in Your bottle.* So please help me not to be afraid of tears—or the troubles that cause them. I know You can use even my problems for good. You're teaching me to be comforted by the fact that You're in control. And I'm learning to trust that You know exactly what You're doing!

You can see all times and all places—all at the same time! That means Your ways of doing things in this world are so much bigger and better than I could ever understand. If I could see everything You see, I would be amazed at how perfectly You work everything out. Right now, though, *I see things imperfectly, like puzzling reflections in a mirror.* Life in this world seems like a mystery sometimes. Jesus, please help me to trust You when I'm feeling confused.

The fact that You collect all my tears in Your bottle shows me how much You love me. And the Bible promises that someday *You will wipe away every tear from my eyes. There will be no more death, sadness, crying, or pain.* There will be joy, joy, and *more* joy waiting there for me! That's how wonderful heaven will be!

In Your amazing Name, Jesus, *Amen*

READ ON YOUR OWN

PSALM 56:8 NLT; 1 CORINTHIANS 13:12 NLT; REVELATION 21:4

GET TO, NOT *HAVE* TO

In all the work you are doing, work the best you can. Work
as if you were working for the Lord, not for men.

—Colossians 3:23

Dear Jesus,

When I don't feel like doing the task I need to do, help me see it as
an opportunity instead of a yucky chore. You're teaching me to change
the way I think about things. Instead of thinking, "I *have* to" do this, I can
choose to think, "I *get* to" do it. This makes a huge difference in the way
I feel. It helps me to be more grateful. I still don't love cleaning up the
dishes or making my bed, but now I can see that I'm blessed to have
plates to eat off of and a bed to sleep in.

I know this new way of thinking is not a magic trick. I still have to
do the work, but I can do it with a smile—instead of a frown—by telling
myself, "I *get* to."

I'm also learning that it's important to stick with a job and keep working. Some things take more time—especially bigger tasks, like learning
multiplication tables or helping to clean out the garage. If I get tired or
feel like giving up, I need to remind myself: "I *get* to do this!" And I can be
thankful that I'm *able* to do the things I need to do. So I thank You, Jesus,
for giving me the muscles and the smarts to do these things.

Thankfulness clears away those "I have to" thoughts and pulls me
closer to You. *In all the work I do*, I want to *do the best I can*. I want *to work*
as if I'm working for You.

In Your wonderful Name, Jesus, *Amen*

READ ON YOUR OWN

COLOSSIANS 4:2; PHILIPPIANS 4:13; COLOSSIANS 3:23

SAY "NO!" TO WORRY

The LORD your God is with you;
the mighty One will save you.
—Zephaniah 3:17 NCV

Dear Jesus,

Teach me how to live in this moment, right now. I don't want to *worry about tomorrow*. Instead, I want to focus on Your Presence with me today—here and now. I want my life to be about getting closer and closer to You. Maybe that's easy for other kids, but it's not so easy for me. It seems like I usually slip into planning and worrying kinds of thoughts.

Please help me say "No!" to these worry-thoughts. This world I live in is full of sin and struggles. That means I always have plenty of things I could get worried about. But the Bible tells me that *each day has enough trouble of its own*. You know exactly how much trouble I'll face today, and You know exactly how much I can handle. Plus, You're always with me—ready to step in and make me stronger by cheering me up and comforting me.

I've found that my life is so much better when I'm walking close to You! That's why I need to keep "catching" my thoughts and bringing them back to You whenever they wander away. I can run into Your arms with a smile on my face and joy in my heart. Because I know You love me so much that *You delight in me and rejoice over me with singing.*

In Your delightful Name, Jesus, *Amen*

READ ON YOUR OWN

MATTHEW 6:34; ISAIAH 41:10; JOHN 10:10; ZEPHANIAH 3:17 NIV

YOUR LOVE IS BIGGER!

"See, I have written your name on my hand."
—Isaiah 49:16

Dear Jesus,

As I come into Your loving Presence, I ask You to lead me through this day, one step at a time. I know that You only shine Your Light into one day at a time—and that day is today. If I try to look ahead into the future, it just looks dark. *Your Face shines on me* only in the present—not the past or the future. *Right now* is where I can find Your perfect, never-ending Love, Jesus.

Your Love for me is even greater than the love of the best mom or dad in the whole world. Good moms and dads love their kids so much that they think about them a lot every day—and they never just forget about them. But Your amazing Love is so much bigger and better than that! The Bible tells me that *You have written my name on Your hand*. That shows how precious I am to You, Lord. You will never, ever forget me!

I really want to *know Your Love*—even though it's much too great for me to ever *fully know* or understand it. But that's my goal anyway. I admit that it's a huge goal. It's so big that I'm going to need the help and power of Your Holy Spirit. Please fill me up with Your wonderful Love, Lord. And help me to love You back with my whole heart!

In Your holy Name, Jesus, *Amen*

READ ON YOUR OWN

NUMBERS 6:25 NIV; ISAIAH 49:15–16; EPHESIANS 3:19 GNT

THE BATTLE FOR MY THOUGHTS

Control yourselves and be careful! The devil is your enemy. And
he goes around like a roaring lion looking for someone to eat.

—1 Peter 5:8

Dear Jesus,

There's a huge battle going on right this very minute—a battle for my thoughts. Heaven and earth meet up in my brain, which means that even though I *want* to think good and heavenly thoughts, sometimes not-so-good thoughts from this sinful world sneak in!

Thank You, Lord, for creating me with the ability to think good thoughts about good things. Once I shut out all the noise of this world and turn my thoughts toward You, it's like I'm *sitting with You in the heavens*. This is an amazing blessing—but it's only for those who *believe in You* and belong to You. You created me to want to spend time with You. As I think about You and Your Word, You fill my mind with *life and peace*.

This world is always trying to pull my thoughts back down to the things that are happening all around me. And a lot of those things aren't good, like lies and selfishness and bragging. Please keep me alert to the battle for my mind that is constantly being fought. Remind me to keep talking to You, Jesus. And guide my thoughts away from worry and back to You.

Lord, I really want to win this battle for control of my mind—today and every day. Someday I'll enjoy the peace and trouble-free life of heaven, and that will be awesome!

In Your powerful Name, Jesus, *Amen*

READ ON YOUR OWN

EPHESIANS 2:6; JOHN 3:16; ROMANS 8:6; 1 PETER 5:8

THE GREATEST KING OF ALL!

God is the blessed and only Ruler. He is the greatest
King of all. He is the most powerful Lord of all.
—1 Timothy 6:15 NIRV

Dear Jesus,

I come to You, wanting to rest in Your Presence. Spending time with You cheers me up and gives me more energy. I'm amazed that I get to sit and talk with You—the Creator of the universe! And I get to do that anytime and anywhere, even just sitting in my own room!

The kings and presidents that rule this world would never let just *anyone* come to see them. Ordinary, everyday people almost never get to talk to them. Even other leaders have to make special appointments and get permission. I'm so happy and thankful that *You*, the King of the whole universe, will talk to me anytime.

Please help me remember that You are always with me—no matter what's happening. *Nothing* can separate me from Your loving Presence! When You cried out from the cross, *"It is finished!"* the curtain in the Temple *was torn into two pieces, from the top to the bottom.* That opened up the way for me to talk to You face to Face. I don't have to get permission or make an appointment or wait in line. Nobody is standing between You and me, saying, "No, no, you can't talk to Him right now. He's busy." How awesome it is that You, *the greatest King of all*, are always ready to listen to me! You're my best Friend forever!

In Your royal Name, Jesus, *Amen*

READ ON YOUR OWN

COLOSSIANS 1:16; JOHN 19:30; MATTHEW 27:50–51 NCV; 1 TIMOTHY 6:15 NIRV

THE CREATOR OF EVERYTHING

In the beginning God created the heavens and the earth.

—Genesis 1:1 NIV

Dear Jesus,

You are with me all the time—when I'm playing, doing homework, or talking to friends. There's not one second of the day that You aren't here beside me. That makes it easier to know what to do and which way to go. Instead of wondering what's coming in the future or worrying about what I should do if *this* thing or *that* thing happens, I can just talk to You. Because You're right here! Whenever I need to make a choice, I can trust You to show me what to do.

Sometimes, though, I start thinking about decisions I might have to make in the future—and then I miss the ones that I need to make right now. I just go through my day without really thinking about what I'm doing. When I live like this, my life starts to feel boring. Everything follows the same old routines. There's nothing new or exciting. It's like I'm sleepwalking through my day!

But *You* are the most creative Being ever! You created the whole universe! And You don't want me to lead a dull, boring life. Instead, You lead me to new adventures, showing me exciting things and teaching me all kinds of things I didn't know. Help me to follow You wherever You want me to go!

In Your wonderful Name, Jesus, *Amen*

READ ON YOUR OWN

PSALM 32:8; GENESIS 1:1 NIV; ISAIAH 58:11

A BETTER WAY

You give peace to those who trust you.

—Isaiah 26:3

Dear Jesus,

So often I look for safety and security in the wrong place—in the things of this world. I make lists of everything I need to have so I can feel safe: friends, family, good grades, and the stuff that will help me fit in. My goal is to get all those things and make sure that I keep them. Then I can relax—at least, that's what I tell myself. The problem is, even when I finally get all those things, I still can't relax. Because then I'm worried about keeping them! The harder I try to have everything I think I need, the worse I feel.

You're teaching me that there's a better way to feel safe and secure. Instead of trying to check everything off my list, I need to *think about You*—and keep on thinking about You. *You* are the reason I can feel safe, because You're always with me. The Bible says You will *give true peace to those who trust You and depend on You*. Talking to You also helps me sort out what's important and what doesn't really matter so much.

Lord, please teach me not to *focus on the things that I can see*—this world and all its stuff—*but on the things I cannot see*: Your Love and Your Presence.

In Your amazing Name, Jesus, *Amen*

READ ON YOUR OWN

HEBREWS 3:1; ISAIAH 26:3; 2 CORINTHIANS 4:18 CEB

LOOKING FOR YOU

"My sheep listen to my voice. I know them, and they follow me."
—John 10:27

Dear Jesus,

I am always with You—in Your Presence. And *being with You fills me with joy*! That means I can have joy no matter what's happening around me. As I walk through this day, I'm going to be looking for signs of Your Presence. Even though I can't see Your Face the way I can see a friend's face, I *know* You're here with me.

Sometimes I see You working in big ways. Wonderful things seem to "just happen," but I know they are really Your work. Other times I see You in smaller ways—like a butterfly floating by or a hug from a friend when I need it most. The more I look for You, the more I find You. So please help me keep my eyes wide open—looking for You in the big and little things that happen today. I don't want to miss a single glimpse of You.

I want to fill my mind and heart with Your words in the Bible. That's where You speak to me most clearly. Your promises soak into my thoughts and bring me close to You. I love to hear You telling me through Your Word: *"Listen to My voice. I know you, and you follow Me. I give you eternal life. No person can steal you out of My hand."*

In Your all-powerful Name, Jesus, *Amen*

READ ON YOUR OWN

PSALM 16:11; JEREMIAH 29:13; JOHN 10:27–28

MOUNTAIN CLIMBING

The Lord God gives me my strength.
—Habakkuk 3:19

Dear Jesus,

You give me my strength. You lead me safely on the steep mountains. This life is an adventure, and I can live every moment in the beauty and glory of Your Presence. But I admit, Lord, that sometimes I get tired. I look up ahead on our path and all I see are steep, steep mountains that I can't climb by myself. But then I remember that *I am always with You,* Lord. *You hold my hand, and You guide me,* and You help me climb those mountains.

My journey with You isn't always easy. Some days I feel like I'm hiking through thorny bushes in a dark forest. Sometimes the trail we're walking on looks so difficult that it seems impossible to keep going. But I'm learning that You help me do the impossible, *and* You give me joy even during the toughest times. So I'll be watching for all the little joy-gifts You've placed along my path. No matter how many of those joy-gifts there might be, none of them can compare to *You,* the Friend I love most of all. You're the greatest treasure I could ever find!

When I stop and look back at where my journey first started, I can see how far I've already come. As I take time to relax with You, I sense the glory of Your Presence all around me—and that makes me love You even more!

In Your glorious Name, Jesus, *Amen*

READ ON YOUR OWN

HABAKKUK 3:19; PSALM 73:23–24; HEBREWS 1:3

SEEING YOU BETTER

If I rise with the sun in the east,
and settle in the west beyond the sea,
even there you would guide me.
With your right hand you would hold me.
—Psalm 139:9–10

Dear Jesus,

I want to make *You* the center of my search for safety and security. I've been trying to make my world feel safe with all *my* ideas and plans, but that's never enough. Then I start wishing I could know everything that's going to happen and what I need to do about it. That's impossible too! It's also not good for me. If I'm going to grow in my faith, I need to learn to trust You more and more, especially when I'm feeling scared or worried. Instead of trying to take control and make everything turn out just right, the best thing I can do is hold on tight to Your hand and depend on You to take care of me.

Another thing I sometimes wish for is that I'd never have another problem. But You're showing me that problems can actually help me see You better. My troubles may make things seem dark, but that's when Your Light shines the brightest, encouraging me and comforting me.

Please help me see my problems as *an opportunity for great joy*. No matter what's happening—even if I'm feeling sad or lonely or confused—I always have a reason for joy. You've promised that I have a problem-free future with You waiting for me in heaven!

In Your joyful Name, Jesus, *Amen*

READ ON YOUR OWN

PSALM 139:9–10; JAMES 1:2 NLT; PHILIPPIANS 4:4

WRAPPED UP IN YOUR LOVE

*All praise to God, the Father of our Lord Jesus Christ. God
is our merciful Father and the source of all comfort.*
—2 Corinthians 1:3 NLT

Dear Jesus,

I'm coming to You today for help and comfort. You're my best Friend, Jesus, and I'm so glad I get to walk with You through this day. I know You're always right by my side. Just saying Your Name instantly reminds me that Your Presence is with me. You've never let me down in the past, Lord, so I can trust You to help me today. I'm learning how much I need Your help *all* the time—with the big things in life *and* the little things too.

Every time I need comfort, You wrap me up in Your strong, loving arms. That makes me feel so much better! And then I'm able to *comfort others—the same way You comfort me*. That's like getting two blessings in one! While I'm comforting someone else with Your comfort, some of that blessing soaks into me.

It's such an amazing gift to have a Friend who is always with me. The more I turn to You, the more I learn how faithful, loving, and powerful You are. No matter what tough things may happen in my life, I know that *nothing will ever be able to separate me from Your Love and Presence*.

In Your comforting Name, Jesus, *Amen*

READ ON YOUR OWN

PSALM 105:4; PSALM 34:5; 2 CORINTHIANS 1:3–4 NLT; ROMANS 8:38–39

THE GIFT OF YOUR PRESENCE

Let everyone who trusts you be happy.
Let them sing glad songs forever.
—Psalm 5:11

Dear Jesus,

I always have a reason to dance and sing and celebrate—because You're always with me! You give me this wonderful gift of Your Presence, and my praise is one of the gifts I can give back to You.

You're teaching me that praising You and enjoying Your Presence is *much* more important than trying to make everything go my way. But it's still so tempting to try to take control. Help me to stop trying so hard to be in control. It's not possible anyway, and it's an insult to *Your great faithfulness* to me.

You've laid out a path for each of Your children to follow, and my path is different from everyone else's. So it's important for me to listen to You—through Your words in the Bible and through prayer. Then I'll know the right path to take.

Please help me get ready for this day and for everything that lies ahead. Because You're always with me, I don't have to be afraid of what might happen. I'm safe as long as I hold tight to You and trust You while we're walking along together. Thank You, Lord, for the precious blessing of Your Presence. Please also *bless me with Your Peace*.

In Your holy Name, Jesus, *Amen*

READ ON YOUR OWN

PSALM 5:11; LAMENTATIONS 3:22–23 NLT; JUDE 24–25; PSALM 29:11

I JUST WANT TO WORSHIP!

We are receiving a kingdom that can't be shaken. So let us be thankful. Then we can worship God in a way that pleases him. Let us worship him with deep respect and wonder.

—Hebrews 12:28 NIRV

Dear Jesus,

Because You are full of grace and truth, I have received one gift after another from You. As I think about Your amazing gift of salvation, I just want to praise and worship You! *I have been saved by grace because I believe* in You! It's a gift that You paid for with Your own blood. *I didn't do anything to save myself.* All I had to do was just receive this priceless gift and believe—and You even helped me believe! Thank You for giving me such an amazing treasure!

Since becoming Your child, I'm seeing that Your grace is filled with many different blessings. My guilty feelings melt away in the warm Light of Your forgiveness. Now that I'm Your child, my life has meaning and purpose. I have reasons for getting up in the morning, and I have goals for my day. My relationships with family, friends, and even the new people I meet are better now—because I can offer them the love and grace You give to me.

Lord, please remind me to spend time thinking about all Your blessings in my life and thanking You for each one. This attitude protects my heart—keeping out the "weeds" of unthankfulness that can grow so fast. Help me to *be thankful* always!

In Your priceless Name, Jesus, *Amen*

READ ON YOUR OWN

JOHN 1:16 NCV; EPHESIANS 2:8–9; JOHN 1:12; HEBREWS 12:28 NIRV

WITH YOUR HELP

With your help I can attack an army.
With God's help I can jump over a wall.
—Psalm 18:29

Dear Jesus,

The Bible promises that You are both with me and *for me*. When I decide to do something that You've planned for me to do, nothing can stop me! So I won't give up, no matter how many hard things I bump into along the way.

I know there will be lots of ups and downs as I'm walking on my path with You. There will be good days and not-so-good days. But *with Your help*, I can handle any difficulty—I can get past anything that's blocking my way. You are my *ever-present Help* and You are all-powerful! These truths about You give me the courage I need to keep going.

Something I'm learning is that a lot of my stress comes from trying to make things happen when *I* want them to. But You're in charge of time, and everything will happen in Your perfect timing. Even though I'm not so good at waiting, I really do want to stay close to You and do everything *Your* way. Please lead me step by step along the path You've planned for me. Show me where You want me to go—and how fast I should go. Instead of running ahead of You toward my goal, I want to stay close to You. Help me trust You to get me there at just the right time. As I slow down, I can really enjoy this adventure with You!

In Your awesome Name, Jesus, *Amen*

READ ON YOUR OWN

ROMANS 8:31; PSALM 18:29; PSALM 46:1; LUKE 1:37

THE BEST WAY TO LIVE

Those who know the Lord trust him.
He will not leave those who come to him.
—Psalm 9:10

Dear Jesus,

I want to walk with You along a path of trust—and keep talking to You as we're walking together. That's the best way to live! When I try to go my own way instead of trusting You, that's when I end up on the wrong path. I'm thankful that You're powerful enough to take that wrong path and turn it into a way back to You. But I can lose a lot of time and waste a lot of energy on those wrong paths. So as soon as I realize that I've wandered away from You, I need to whisper, "I trust You, Jesus." This little prayer helps me turn to You and get back on the right path.

The more I trust in the things of this world—like being popular, being smart, or being good at sports—the harder it is for me to remember that You are with me. Worries and fears start to fill up my thoughts. They pull me farther and farther away from Your Presence. To stay close to You, I need to keep telling You, "I trust You." It's okay for me to say that prayer as often as I need reminding! This small act of faith keeps me walking with You, step after step. Help me *trust You with all my heart. Show me which path to take.*

In Your dependable Name, Jesus, *Amen*

READ ON YOUR OWN

ISAIAH 26:4; PSALM 9:10; PSALM 25:4; PROVERBS 3:5–6 NLT

YOUR PLANS ARE BETTER!

"Just as the heavens are higher than the earth,
so are my ways higher than your ways.
And my thoughts are higher than your thoughts."
—Isaiah 55:9

Dear Jesus,

When things don't go my way, I often get upset—and I say or do hurtful things. Anytime I'm starting to get all bothered and upset, please help me stop what I'm doing and *come to You*. Remind me to spend a few minutes just enjoying Your Presence. Then, as I *talk with You* about what's bothering me, You help me see things the way You see them. You show me what's really important. And You help me know what to do next. Before I know it, I'm able to move on—trusting You and staying close to You.

I confess that I usually get upset because I want to be in control. I plan out my day, and then I expect others to follow my plans and not mess things up. That's exactly when I need to remember that *You* are in control. And *just as the heavens are higher than the earth, so are Your ways higher than my ways*. Help me not to get mad or grumble when things don't go how I'd planned. Please use those times to remind me that You are God and I'm Your much-loved follower. Help me to *trust in Your unfailing Love*.

Lord, teach me to cheerfully set aside my plans—because Your plans are amazingly wise, and they're always so much better than mine!

In Your wise, wonderful Name, Jesus, *Amen*

READ ON YOUR OWN

PSALM 27:8 NLT; ISAIAH 55:9; 2 SAMUEL 22:31; PSALM 13:5 NLT

I'LL BRING MY PROBLEMS TO YOU

"None of you can add any time to your life by worrying about it. If you cannot do even the little things, then why worry about the big things?"
—Luke 12:25–26

Dear Jesus,

When problems come along, help me not to think about them too long or too hard. Because I can get stuck in those troubling thoughts and forget about You. I try to figure out how I can solve a problem as fast as possible. It's like my mind gets ready for a tough battle, and my body gets all tense and worried. Unless I win the battle by solving the problem right away, I end up feeling defeated and upset with myself.

You are showing me that there's a better way! When a problem starts to take over my thoughts, I need to bring it to You. Please remind me to talk to You about it and look at it *in the Light of Your Presence*. This helps me see the problem the way You see it. Sometimes I even have to laugh at myself for thinking my problem was so huge and terrible when it wasn't really a big deal at all!

I know *I will have trouble in this world*. But what matters the most is that I'll always have *You* with me. And You'll give me everything I need to handle every problem that comes into my life. Help me remember to bring my troubles to You so I can see them the way You do—in Your brilliant Light.

In Your shining Name, Jesus, *Amen*

READ ON YOUR OWN

LUKE 12:25–26; PSALM 89:15; JOHN 16:33

WIDE AND LONG, HIGH AND DEEP

I pray that Christ will live in your hearts because of your faith. I pray that your life will be strong in love and be built on love.

—Ephesians 3:17

Dear Jesus,

The way You love me is awesome! Your Love never lets go of me! In this world I don't ever know what's going to happen. I feel unsafe sometimes. And when I look around me, I see people breaking their promises more often than I can count.

But Your promise to love me is a promise that will *never* be broken, and I'm so grateful. *The mountains may move, and the hills may disappear, but even then Your faithful Love for me will remain.* Moving mountains and disappearing hills sound terrible! But no matter *what* is happening, Your Love won't move away from me or disappear. I can build my whole life on that wonderful truth!

Jesus, it's hard for me to understand just how much You love me. Please *give me strength through Your Spirit.* Help me to *understand how wide and how long and how high and how deep Your Love is.* Thank You that Your amazing Love is for *me!* Lord, I want to really *know this Love that is greater than any person can ever know!*

I ask You to set me free from the prison of lies that I've believed about myself. Help me to see myself the way You see me: wrapped up in *Your coat of goodness* and shining with Your Love.

In Your great Name, Jesus, *Amen*

READ ON YOUR OWN

ISAIAH 54:10 NLT; EPHESIANS 3:16–19; ISAIAH 61:10

A PROMISE FOR ME

Let us run the race that is before us and never give
up. . . . We should remove the sin that so easily catches us.
—Hebrews 12:1

Dear Jesus,

Help me remember that You are with me as I walk step by step through this day. Your Presence with me is a precious promise that comforts me and makes me feel safe. After You died on the cross and then rose up from the grave, You told Your followers: *"You can be sure that I will be with you always. I will continue with you until the end of the world."* That promise is for *all* Your followers. So, my decision to follow You means that Your promise is for me too!

While I've been walking with You, I've seen that Your Presence is a powerful and important protection. There are lots of dangers on the path through my life. Some are invisible, like feeling sorry for myself. Pride, selfishness, and stubbornness are big problems too. Then there are the things I can see and hear that try to pull my attention away from You. If I take my eyes off of You and follow someone else, that's when I'm in real danger. Even good friends can lead me down the wrong path if I let them be more important than You.

Thank You for showing me that the way to stay on *the path of life* is to keep paying attention to You, Jesus. Your Love and Presence are always with me—always protecting me. I feel happy and safe when I remember that You're taking such good care of me.

In Your protecting Name, Jesus, *Amen*

READ ON YOUR OWN

MATTHEW 28:20; HEBREWS 12:1; PSALM 16:11 NIV

I CAN RUN TO YOU

The person who trusts in himself is foolish.
But the person who lives wisely will be kept safe.
—Proverbs 28:26

Dear Jesus,

I know that You're the One who keeps me safe. But sometimes I get so busy thinking and planning that I forget. Worry grows inside me, and my thoughts start spinning round and round. I search for answers and try to figure out a way to feel safe. And the whole time, *You are right here with me, holding my hand*! Help me remember that Your Presence is with me all the time.

Instead of being foolish and *trusting in myself*, I want to *live wisely* and trust You to keep me safe. You're teaching me that being wise means trusting You more than I trust myself or anyone else. I can tell You about my problems because You're always ready to *guide me with Your advice* and help me *do what is right*.

I'm grateful that I can bring every one of my worries, fears, and troubles to You. Sometimes, though, my thoughts and feelings get all tangled up in my mind—and I get confused. That's when it really helps me to write down my prayers so I can think more clearly.

As I wait in Your Presence, please show me the way You want me to go. And guide my thoughts—help me to keep thinking about You and Your Word. Just whispering Your Name, "Jesus," keeps my attention on You. *You are like a strong tower. I can run to You for safety*.

In Your strong Name, Jesus, *Amen*

READ ON YOUR OWN

PSALM 73:23–24; PROVERBS 28:26; PROVERBS 18:10

GROWING IN YOU

You will make me happy forever at your right hand.
—Psalm 16:11 NIRV

Dear Jesus,

When I am with You, You fill me with joy, true peace, and *unfailing love.* I love walking with You along the path of life because I get to enjoy Your company every step of the way. I'm thankful that You are always by my side, offering me the joy of Your Presence.

You promise to give me *true peace* as I *trust You* and *depend on You.* Please help me to keep talking to You—with words that I say out loud, with my thoughts, and with songs of praise. This helps me trust You even more.

When I spend time studying the Bible, it soaks into my mind. This changes the way I think and the way I live. As I think about who You are—how good and wonderful You are—Your Light shines into my heart and *blesses me with peace.*

Lord, I want to grow in Your Presence *like an olive tree growing in the house of God.* As the sunlight of Your Presence shines on me, it feeds my soul and helps me grow to be more like You—full of love, joy, peace, and kindness. And the more *I trust in Your unfailing Love*, the more I realize how safe and secure I am in You!

In Your loving Name, Jesus, *Amen*

READ ON YOUR OWN

PSALM 16:11 NIRV; ISAIAH 26:3; PSALM 29:11; PSALM 52:8 NLT

NOVEMBER

Let us come to him with thanksgiving.
Let us sing psalms of praise to him.

—Psalm 95:2 NLT

THE AMAZING GIFT OF GRACE

"God gave his Son so that whoever believes in him may not be lost, but have eternal life."
—John 3:16

Dear Jesus,

Thank You for the wonderful, amazing, glorious gift of grace! The Bible teaches me that *I have been saved by grace because I believe* in You. That's what faith is all about—believing in You, trusting You as my Savior. *I didn't save myself. It's a gift from You.* You even help me have the faith to believe in You! I have the never-ending blessing of *eternal life* because You died on the cross for me. Help me receive these gifts with a happy heart and be grateful for them every day. I can never thank You enough for Your grace.

I want to take time to think about how awesome it is that You've forgiven all my sins. Believing in You was the first step on my journey to living in heaven with You. One day, this old, troubled world will be gone and there will be *a new heaven and a new earth*. You've promised that I'll have a home there forever—with You! *That* gives me a great reason for joy every day.

As I walk with You today, I'll try to remember to keep thanking You for the priceless gift of grace. And as I thank You, I pray that You'll help me see all the other gifts You give me. Then I'll have even more reasons to praise You!

In Your amazing Name, Jesus, *Amen*

READ ON YOUR OWN

EPHESIANS 2:8–9; JOHN 3:16; MATTHEW 10:28; REVELATION 21:1

PATIENT WHEN TROUBLE COMES

Pray at all times.
—Romans 12:12

Dear Jesus,

Thank You for taking the punishment for all my sins. And thank You for wrapping me up in Your own perfect goodness. You're the reason that I'm so *joyful—I have hope* because You died for me. I know that I'm on my way to heaven, and I'll get to live with You there forever. Nothing can take that hope away from me, and *no one can snatch me out of Your hand*. With You, I am safe and secure forever!

The Bible teaches me to *pray at all times*. That means I need to keep talking to You all day long—especially when I'm struggling with lots of problems. But on those tough days, it's sometimes harder for me to remember to pray. I get so tired and stressed-out. That's why I'm thankful for Your Holy Spirit, who lives inside me. I can ask Him to *control my thinking* and help me. Your Spirit gives me strength, guides my thoughts, and helps me pray when I don't know what to say. I'm learning that my prayers don't have to be fancy or full of big words. I can just talk to You straight from my heart.

Lord, please remind me to keep talking to You on those tough days most of all. Then I can *be patient when trouble comes* as I wait with You.

In Your hope-filled Name, Jesus, *Amen*

READ ON YOUR OWN

ROMANS 12:12; JOHN 10:28; ROMANS 8:6

CALM AND CONFIDENT

They do not fear bad news;
they confidently trust the Lord to care for them.
—Psalm 112:7 NLT

Dear Jesus,

Please teach me to think about You and trust You as I go step by step through each day. I have to admit that too many things can pull my attention away from You. Especially all the sights and sounds of this world. Some days I get so distracted that I feel like I'm riding a roller coaster up and down—and the whole time, I'm looking here, there, and everywhere. But I don't want other things controlling my thinking. I want my attention to be on *You*! I know it's possible to be aware of Your Presence no matter what's happening around me. That's the way I want to live every day.

Help me not to let surprises trip me up. Instead of getting upset or worried when problems come my way, I want to be calm and confident—remembering that *You are with me*. As soon as something grabs my attention, please remind me to talk with You about it. I can share my joys and my sadness with You, Jesus. I know You'll help me figure out what to do with the good things *and* the not-so-good things.

Lord, I ask You to live in me and to work in me more and more each day. And please work through me too. I want to shine Your Light and Your Peace into this troubled world.

In Your peaceful Name, Jesus, *Amen*

READ ON YOUR OWN

PSALM 112:7 NLT; ISAIAH 41:10; PSALM 46:1–2;
1 THESSALONIANS 5:16–17

YOU CARRY MY HEAVY LOAD

God, my strength, I will sing praises to you.
God, my protection, you are the God who loves me.
—Psalm 59:17

Dear Jesus,

As I think about everything I need to do today, what I need most is to trust You enough to lean on You. Everyone leans on something: Sometimes it's their own body's strength and muscles. Or their smarts. Or their beauty or money. Or being popular. And it seems like just about everybody leans on family or friends.

All these things are gifts from You. I want to enjoy them and be grateful for them. But depending on them is risky. Every single one of them can let me down. My muscles might not be strong enough to do some jobs. I won't understand every question in class. Money can disappear, friends move away, and even family members don't always keep their promises.

When I have a problem I can't fix on my own, it starts to be all I can think about. Pretty soon I'm worrying about how to make it through the day. It's such a waste of time and energy! Worst of all, it pulls me away from You, Lord. Whenever this happens, please open my eyes to see *You* right in the middle of my trouble. Help me to "see" that You're standing beside me, ready to help as soon as I ask. Instead of pretending that I'm stronger than I really am, I can lean on You. When I do, You *carry my heavy load* for me and show me what to do. *I sing praises to You for being my Strength!*

In Your wonderful Name, Jesus, *Amen*

READ ON YOUR OWN

PROVERBS 3:5 ESV; PSALM 68:19 NIRV; PSALM 59:17

BUSY DOING GOOD

Do not let evil defeat you. Defeat evil by doing good.
—Romans 12:21

Dear Jesus,

Help me *not to let evil defeat me*. Instead, help me to *defeat evil with good*. Sometimes it seems like most of the things that are happening in this world are bad and ugly things. I hear about fighting and wars. Some people even *call good things bad and bad things good*. All this can be scary *if* I forget to keep talking to You. But as soon as I start talking to You, I feel better—I feel comforted. You understand everything, Lord. You know all the sinful things that are going on in *people's minds* and hearts. None of this evil surprises You!

Instead of being upset by the darkness around me, I want to shine even brighter with Your Light. When it looks like evil is winning, that's when I need to try harder than ever to do something good! Sometimes that means standing up to evil—like defending someone who's being made fun of. Other times, it means just trying to do all the kind and helpful things I can.

Please teach me to stop worrying about the bad things that are happening in this world. Instead, I want to be busy *doing the good things You planned for me to do long ago*.

In Your powerful Name, Jesus, *Amen*

READ ON YOUR OWN

ROMANS 12:21; ISAIAH 5:20; JEREMIAH 17:9; EPHESIANS 2:10 NLT

THE BEST LIFE

The Lord hears good people when they cry out to him.
He saves them from all their troubles.
—Psalm 34:17

Dear Jesus,

Help me to live the best life I can—by depending on You all the time. I used to think that the best life meant winning—never making a mistake, never flubbing up my words, always getting good grades and being the one to make people laugh. But trying to win at everything with my own strength hasn't worked. It's too easy to end up going my own way, forgetting about You. Just asking You to bless whatever I've decided to do isn't really depending on You either. I'm seeing that I need to come to You with an open mind and heart and say, "Please show me what *You* want me to do, Jesus."

Sometimes You give me a dream that seems completely impossible. And if I tried to do it by myself, it *would* be impossible! But when I really depend on You, the impossible becomes completely possible.

Living this life with You is a walk of faith, and only You know which is the best way for me to go. So I need to learn to keep trusting You. That doesn't mean I'll never make another mistake or have another problem. But I know that You'll use my failures to grow my faith and teach me to depend on You even more. Thank You for being so trustworthy!

In Your dependable Name, Jesus, *Amen*

READ ON YOUR OWN

PSALM 34:17–18; 2 CORINTHIANS 5:7; PHILIPPIANS 4:13

THE MOST IMPORTANT THING ABOUT MY FUTURE

"Don't worry about the food you need to live. Don't worry about the clothes you need for your body."
—Luke 12:22

Dear Jesus,

As I sit quietly with You, my fears and worries are bubbling up in my mind like boiling water on a hot stove. Most of those worry-bubbles pop and then disappear in the Light of Your Presence. However, some of my fears just keep on bubbling up inside me. Mostly they're worries about what might happen in the future. My thoughts zoom ahead to tomorrow, next week, next month, or even next year. I start imagining how big my future troubles will be. Then I start worrying that I won't be able to handle those troubles! But in those fear-filled moments, I'm forgetting the most important thing about my future: I don't have to handle anything on my own. You'll be in it with me. And You promise that *You will never leave me or forget me.*

The next time a worry about the future attacks me, help me capture it and bring it to You. Remind me that You are with me now, and You'll be with me then. With that truth in my mind, I know I can handle even the toughest troubles—because You are right by my side all the time.

Please teach me to keep my thoughts in this present moment. That's where I can find You and enjoy Your Peace.

In Your comforting Name, Jesus, *Amen*

READ ON YOUR OWN

LUKE 12:22–23; DEUTERONOMY 31:6; 2 CORINTHIANS 10:5

THE MASTER OF TIME

God is our protection.

—Psalm 62:8

Dear Jesus,

My life is in Your hands. And Your hands are able to take care of me and every need I will ever have. You're always watching over me, so please help me relax. I can trust You to do what's best for me. All those "what-ifs" and "whens" that spin around in my thoughts—I can leave those in Your hands and totally trust You to take care of me.

I realize that I can't control time—not even a little bit—but sometimes I *wish* I could! When I'm looking forward to something in the future, like my birthday, I want to fast-forward to that wonderful day. But just because I want to skip ahead doesn't change the fact that I have to wait. When I'm hurting and struggling through tough times, I want to make everything speed up so I can get through those hard times quickly. But, again, I just have to wait.

Lord, help me to accept my waiting times instead of fighting against them. And help me remember that I don't have to wait alone. I can relax because I know that You are with me, and You're the Master of time. As I *tell You all my problems,* I can *trust You* to understand my struggles perfectly. Thank You for *loving me with a Love that will last forever*!

In Your perfect Name, Jesus, *Amen*

READ ON YOUR OWN

PSALM 31:14–15; PSALM 62:8; JEREMIAH 31:3

MY HOPE IS IN YOU

We are glad because of him;
we trust in his holy name.
—Psalm 33:21 GNT

Dear Jesus,

You're training me to follow You on this path of adventures called "Life." The trail that I'm walking on with You is sometimes tough and challenging. There are days when You lead me to places I don't want to go. Please help me remember that You know what You're doing, so this path is the perfect one for me. When I keep my attention on You, following where You lead, I can hear You whisper in my mind, "Trust Me, my dearly loved child."

Today I feel like I'm hiking through a thick jungle. I can't see what's up ahead of me or behind me or what's off to the side. So, I'm going to hold tight to Your hand as I walk through this shadowy darkness. Even though I have no idea where I'm going, I know that You're right here beside me, Jesus. Your Presence with me is rock-solid truth. I'm trusting that You're in full control of this situation. You've got this!

Even when I'm surrounded by a jungle of trouble, I need to quit worrying about how I'll get out of this mess. Instead of focusing on my problems, I want to focus on enjoying You and *looking to You for help*. From this point on, I'm going to talk to You, *put my hope in You*—and watch to see what You will do. *You are my Protector and my Help*!

In Your protecting Name, Jesus, *Amen*

READ ON YOUR OWN

ISAIAH 50:10; PSALM 33:20–21 GNT; MICAH 7:7

A PEEK INTO HEAVEN

Praise be to the God and Father of our Lord Jesus Christ. In Christ, God has given us every spiritual blessing in heaven.
—Ephesians 1:3

Dear Jesus,

You've been showing me that a thankful attitude opens "windows" of heaven—and that Your blessings come pouring through those windows like a burst of sunshine after a storm. When I look up to You with a grateful heart, it's like getting a little peek into heaven. Even though I cannot live in heaven yet, I can enjoy little tastes of how wonderful my future home will be. These tiny tastes of glorious wonders give me hope and fill me with joy.

Being thankful also opens my eyes to see more reasons I have to be grateful. Then that helps me see even *more* things to thank You for, which makes me more thankful, which . . . It's like a never-ending circle of blessings and grateful joy!

I realize that being thankful isn't a magic formula, though. I can't just say, "I want more blessings, so I'll thank the Lord for something." Instead, thankfulness is a way to tell You how much I love You and trust You. You've been training me to be thankful even in the middle of my troubles—without pretending that everything's okay. No matter what's happening, I can *be joyful in You, my Savior*. I'm grateful that *You are my Protection and my Strength. You always help me in times of trouble.* Thank You, Lord!

In Your strong Name, Jesus, *Amen*

READ ON YOUR OWN

EPHESIANS 1:3; HABAKKUK 3:17–18 NIV; PSALM 46:1

I WILL FOLLOW YOU

*"The sheep listen to the voice of the shepherd. He calls his
own sheep, using their names, and he leads them out."*

—John 10:3

Dear Jesus,

You call me by name and You lead me. You know me—every single detail about me! I'm never just another kid to You. You work in my life in the most wonderful ways. I love to hear You whisper in my heart: "My dearly loved child, *follow Me*."

After You rose up out of that tomb, Mary Magdalene saw You. But she thought You were the gardener. You said just one word to her: *"Mary!"* And when she heard You call her name, she instantly knew who You were! *Mary cried out, "Rabboni!" (which is Hebrew for "Teacher").*

Because You are my Savior, Jesus, You also call *my* name. You whisper it deep down in my spirit. When I read the Bible, You speak to *me* through all that it says. You remind me that You love me and that I am blessed.

I especially love these beautiful words of blessing: *I called you out of darkness into My wonderful Light,* and *I love you with a Love that will last forever.* These Bible verses help me know how very, very much You love me. And these truths will never change—they give me a solid rock to build my life on. Help me follow You joyfully, Lord. I can't wait to *tell about the wonderful things You have done* for me!

In Your magnificent Name, Jesus, *Amen*

READ ON YOUR OWN

JOHN 10:3, 27; JOHN 20:16 NLT; 1 PETER 2:9; JEREMIAH 31:3

HIDDEN TREASURE

You always gave him blessings.
You made him glad because you were with him.
—Psalm 21:6

Dear Jesus,

You've been teaching me something really cool! You're teaching me that I can always be glad no matter what's happening in my life. *I can be glad because You are with me.*

Some days are like walking on a beautiful path that has joy scattered around everywhere—sparkling like diamonds in the sunshine. On those bright, cheerful days, being happy is as easy for me as breathing. But other days are dark and gloomy, and the path is hard to follow. All I see are dull, gray rocks of troubles. They stub my toes and trip my feet. On those gray days, I have to search for joy like I'm searching for a *hidden treasure*.

Help me remember that even a gray day doesn't just happen. You've created it, so it's *not* a mistake. And You're with me in every second of it—from morning till night. Even when I forget about You for a little while, You are still here. You never forget about *me*!

I'm thankful that I can talk to You about whatever is on my mind. You understand me perfectly, and You know exactly what's happening in my life. I'm learning that when I keep talking to You, my day begins to brighten and I start to cheer up. Because You are with me, even the darkest, grayest day can be a glad day!

In Your joyful Name, Jesus, *Amen*

READ ON YOUR OWN

PSALM 21:6; PROVERBS 2:4; COLOSSIANS 1:16

THE WAY YOU SEE ME

Those who go to him for help are happy.
They are never disgraced.
—Psalm 34:5

Dear Jesus,

I want to learn more about the riches of Your gift of salvation, including the joy of feeling loved perfectly and forever! But I often judge myself based on things that don't really matter—things like how I look, what I'm feeling, or how well I do in school or at a game.

If I look in the mirror and like what I see, I feel more worthy of Your Love. When everything in my life is going just the way I want and I think I'm doing everything right, it's easier to believe I'm Your dearly loved child. But when I've messed up or I'm just plain tired, I don't feel as loved. Sometimes I even forget about You, and then I feel like I have to figure out how to make things better all by myself.

Instead of trying to fix myself and everything else, help me to *fix my thoughts on You*, Jesus. That means I need to pay really close attention to You and what You say. You're the One who loves me all the time—even when I mess up. And because You've saved me from my sins, You don't focus on my mistakes. I'm so thankful that You see me wrapped up in *Your goodness* and shining in Your perfect Love!

In Your holy Name, Jesus, *Amen*

READ ON YOUR OWN

EPHESIANS 2:8–9; HEBREWS 3:1 NIV; PSALM 89:16; PSALM 34:5

A PATH FOR ME TO FOLLOW

Jesus said to her, "Didn't I tell you that if you believed, you would see the glory of God?"
—John 11:40

Dear Jesus,

I know You have a plan for my life and a path You want me to follow. But sometimes that path seems completely blocked. Big boulders of trouble are in the way, and I can't move forward at all. Other times, the path is covered with smaller rocks and obstacles—so I have to walk very slowly. Then, when the time is right, You suddenly clear away all the things that were blocking my path, and I can walk or run as fast as I want to. It's not because of anything I've done. It's because of *You*—doing so easily the things *I* can't do at all. I love getting to see these little glimpses of *Your Power and Glory* at work. You're amazing, Lord!

As I keep traveling down this path that You've planned for me, I'm going to count on Your strength to keep me going. Please help me stay alert—and be on the lookout for Your miracles. Not everyone can see Your miracles. Only those who believe and trust in You are able to clearly see these wonderful things You do. *Living by what I believe, not just what I can see*, keeps me close to You. And when I'm close to You, that's when I have the best view of all the awesome things You do!

In Your glorious Name, Jesus, *Amen*

READ ON YOUR OWN

PSALM 63:2 NLT; 2 CORINTHIANS 12:9; 2 CORINTHIANS 5:7; JOHN 11:40

YOU NEVER LEAVE ME

"I will not forget you."
—Isaiah 49:15

Dear Jesus,

I love to hear You whisper these comforting words to my heart: *"Nothing can separate You from My Love."* As I sit with You, relaxing in Your Presence, this holy promise soaks into my mind, my heart, and my soul. Whenever I start to feel worried or afraid, please remind me to pray this promise back to You: "Nothing can separate me from Your Love, Jesus. Nothing!"

I think my saddest times—and maybe everybody's saddest times—come from feeling unloved. On those days when everything seems to be going wrong around me, I sometimes feel like You've taken Your Love away from me and forgotten me. *That* feeling is even worse than whatever problem I'm struggling with! So I'm grateful that You've promised You will *never* stop loving me—or any of Your children—not even for a second. You tell me in the Bible: *I will not leave you or forget you. I have written your name on My hand.* These promises give me hope and encouragement.

Lord, I feel safe, secure, and loved when I remember that You're always *watching over me*. Thank You!

In Your loving Name, Jesus, *Amen*

READ ON YOUR OWN

ROMANS 8:38–39; DEUTERONOMY 31:6; ISAIAH 49:15–16; PSALM 121:3 NLT

THE GOOD SHEPHERD

"I am the good shepherd. I know my sheep, and my sheep know me."
—John 10:14

Dear Jesus,

The Bible tells me that You are *a shield to those who trust You*. So I'm coming to You today, Lord, and asking You to shield me with Your Presence—like an umbrella that keeps me dry when it's raining hard. You are the One who keeps me safe.

Sometimes I feel like I'm *not* safe and protected. That's how I feel when I crawl out from under the "umbrella" of Your Presence and I try to face the world without Your help. I don't do this on purpose. I just do it without even thinking. I forget how much I need You every moment. When I start to feel afraid, please use those feelings to help me see that I've wandered away from You. And remind me to run back to You—to the safety of Your Presence.

I'm so grateful that *You are my Shepherd*! You're always on the look-out for danger. Plus, You know exactly what's going to happen in the future, so You're able to prepare me for it perfectly. Because You are the *Good Shepherd*, You can shield me from danger so well that I never even know it was there! Jesus, help me follow You and live the way You want me to live. Thank You for protecting me from both danger and fear.

In Your protecting Name, Jesus, *Amen*

READ ON YOUR OWN

2 SAMUEL 22:31; PSALM 23:1, 4; JOHN 10:11, 14

TRUST ISN'T EASY

*L*ORD *All-Powerful,*
happy are the people who trust you!
—Psalm 84:12 NCV

Dear Jesus,

Please teach me to trust You one day at a time. This will keep me close to You and ready to do all the things You want me to do.

In my mind, I know that I can trust You completely. I have to admit, though, that I struggle to trust You with my heart. In fact, sometimes it's really hard to do that. But no matter how I'm feeling, I know I can always count on You to help me. I'm so thankful that You sent Your Holy Spirit to live inside me! He teaches me lessons that are tough for me to learn, and He does it with such a gentle touch. I want to become more and more "tuned in" to Your Spirit so that I can hear everything He whispers in my heart.

Lord, teach me to trust You with everything that's going on in my life. The truth is, I want to understand what's happening, but that isn't always possible. Please don't let my wanting-to-understand get in the way of remembering that You are here with me. As I go through this day, help me be cheerful and keep trusting You each step of the way.

You tell me in Your Word: *Don't worry about tomorrow. Tomorrow will have its own worries.* So instead of letting my thoughts get tangled up in worries about what might happen tomorrow, I am going to trust You today—one moment at a time!

In Your guiding Name, Jesus, *Amen*

READ ON YOUR OWN

PSALM 84:12 NCV; 1 CORINTHIANS 6:19; JEREMIAH 17:7; MATTHEW 6:34

A MYSTERY TO ME

*This teaching is the secret truth that was hidden since
the beginning of time. It was hidden from everyone,
but now it is made known to God's holy people.*

—Colossians 1:26

Dear Jesus,

No one can understand Your ways. So please help me come close to You and simply rest in Your Presence. I'm sorry for sometimes demanding to understand everything You're doing in my life. Some things are just too big for me to know. You are endlessly wise, and I am only human. Because my mind just can't understand everything that You do, many of the things in my life and in this world don't make sense to me. Please teach me to be okay with these mysteries.

And thank You for showing me so many things that used to be mysteries—*secret truths that were hidden since the beginning of time.* The New Testament is full of these truths about how You came to live on earth, how You died to save me, and how You rose to life again. Your plan to rescue those who love You isn't a mystery anymore! I'm hugely blessed to have these priceless "jewels" of knowledge that You've placed in the Bible!

When I don't understand how You are working, I have a choice to make: I can question Your ways. Or I can worship You in wonder. Lord, I choose worship and wonder! Because I am amazed by *the riches of Your wisdom and knowledge.*

In Your wise Name, Jesus, *Amen*

READ ON YOUR OWN

ROMANS 11:33; PROVERBS 3:5; COLOSSIANS 1:26

THE ONE WHO SEES ME

He knows how weak we are;
he remembers we are only dust.
—Psalm 103:14 NLT

Dear Jesus,

You are the Living One who sees me. You are more amazing and glorious than I could ever imagine. When I see You *face to Face* in all Your Glory someday, I know I'll be completely in awe of You! On that day, I'll totally understand what the word "awesome" really means, because that's how great You are! You are so much greater than anyone or anything in this world. For now, though, *I see only a dim likeness* of You. My sinful condition keeps me from seeing You clearly.

At least I know that *You* see *me* clearly and perfectly. You know everything about me—even my most secret thoughts and feelings. Honestly, Lord, that's a little scary. At least until I remember that You also understand how weak I am. *You remember that I am dust*—I'm only human. Even though I mess up a lot, You still love me with a Love that will never, ever end.

Help me remember that You paid a huge, horrible price for that love. You suffered and died on the cross to save me from my sins. *You became sin* for me *so that I could become right with God.* I love to think about this wonderful truth: Your perfect goodness has been given to me, and it's mine forever! This priceless gift has been mine ever since I asked You to be my Savior. I'm so thankful that *the Living One who sees me* is also the One who loves me forever!

In Your saving Name, Jesus, *Amen*

READ ON YOUR OWN
GENESIS 16:14 AMPC; 1 CORINTHIANS 13:12 NIRV;
PSALM 103:14; 2 CORINTHIANS 5:21

WORSHIP IS THE WAY TO WIN

Thanks be to God for his gift that is too wonderful to explain.
—2 Corinthians 9:15

Dear Jesus,

I've been discovering something new lately. I've been discovering how thanking You often wakes up my heart to the truth that You are with me. Thanking You also sharpens my mind and helps me see my life more clearly.

When I'm feeling like You're far away, that's exactly the time I need to thank You for *something*. There are always things to thank You for: Your Love, plus the gifts of forgiveness, salvation, and faith, are blessings that last forever. And then there are the everyday blessings that You pour into my life—like family, friends, a home, and food.

You've been training me to look back over the past twenty-four hours and see all the good things You brought my way. I like to write them in a notebook or diary so I won't forget. Writing down these blessings cheers me up and shows me how much You're doing in my life.

The Bible teaches me that *the devil, my enemy, goes around like a roaring lion looking for someone to eat.* So it's important for me to *control myself and be careful.* It's easier for the devil to attack if I let my thoughts drift away from You. Whenever that happens, please warn me that I'm in danger. Help me drive away the enemy by thanking and praising You. Worship is the way to win this war!

In Your amazing Name, Jesus, *Amen*

READ ON YOUR OWN
EPHESIANS 2:8–9; 1 PETER 5:8 NCV; 2 CORINTHIANS 9:15

LIVING *SUPER*NATURALLY

Enjoy the Lord.
—Psalm 37:4 CEB

Dear Jesus,

I will give an offering of praise to show thanks to You. I don't want to take any of Your good gifts for granted—not even the sun rising every morning. I admit that thanking You doesn't always come naturally to me, but You are teaching me to live *super*naturally.

The Bible says it's important to have a grateful attitude. Before that sneaky devil slithered in and tempted Eve in the garden of Eden, being grateful was the natural thing for people to do. They always felt thankful for Your blessings without having to remind themselves. But then one day, the devil pointed out the one fruit that Eve wasn't allowed to eat. And even though the garden was full of other fruit she *could* eat, all she could think about was the one she couldn't have. Her thoughts grew darker, and she gave in—she ate some of the fruit that God had told her and Adam *not* to eat, and then Adam ate some also.

When *I* spend time thinking about things I can't have, my thoughts get darker too. I forget about blessings like sunshine and moonlight, my family and friends, and my church. Instead, I just keep focusing on the things I don't have. But as soon as I come to You with a thankful heart, the Light of Your Presence pours into me and changes me. Help me to *live in the Light* with You, Lord. I want to *enjoy You* and learn to thank You more and more!

In Your wonderful Name, Jesus, *Amen*

READ ON YOUR OWN

PSALM 116:17; GENESIS 3:6; 1 JOHN 1:7; PSALM 37:4 CEB

CLOSER TO YOU

Come close to God, and God will come close to you.
—James 4:8 NLT

Dear Jesus,

I'm learning that thankfulness and trust are like best friends that are always ready to help me. I need to depend on these friends, especially when I'm having a rough day or when the world seems scary. Lord, You're teaching me to stop during those times and look around—to search for things like the beauty of the sky and the blessings of people who love me. When I think about the good things in my life and I thank You for them, I'm able to connect with You in a wonderful way. No matter how I've been feeling, if I keep on thanking You for my blessings, I begin to feel better and better.

I'm grateful that You're totally trustworthy—I can always count on You! All I have to do is say, "I trust You, Lord," and I remember that You are with me, taking care of me. I know I don't always trust You like I should. Please teach me to see troubles and tough days as a chance to "exercise" my trust-muscles and grow stronger. Help me learn to *live by what I believe*—on good days *and* hard days. Instead of worrying and struggling through tough times, I want to use them to *come closer to You*, Jesus. You always welcome me with open arms, and that is something I can really be thankful about!

In Your loving Name, Jesus, *Amen*

READ ON YOUR OWN

PSALM 92:1–2; PSALM 118:28; 2 CORINTHIANS 5:7; JAMES 4:8 NLT

THE MORE I LOOK, THE MORE I FIND

The Lord God took dust from the ground and formed man from it. The Lord breathed the breath of life into the man's nose. And the man became a living person.
—Genesis 2:7

Dear Jesus,

Thank You for all Your blessings! Everything I have is a gift from You, including each breath I breathe. I hardly ever think about the wonder of constantly breathing Your Life into my life. But it was only when You *breathed the breath of life* into Adam that *he became a living person.*

Sometimes I like to just sit quietly in Your Presence and thank You for every blessing I can think of—even the ones I usually forget. Like all the colors You've made. And food to eat. And warm water for my bath or shower. And having a coat to wear on cold days. And having an umbrella to keep me dry on rainy days. The list could go on and on and on! The more I look for good things in my life, the more I find. Lord, help me remember to look for Your blessings every day!

Of course, what I'm the *most* grateful for is *eternal Life*—being able to live with You forever! That's Your amazing gift to me simply because I *believe in You.* This gift is a priceless treasure that blesses me and *fills me with joy*!

In Your precious Name, Jesus, *Amen*

READ ON YOUR OWN

GENESIS 2:7; JOHN 3:16; PSALM 16:11

A THANKFUL HEART

Always be joyful.
—1 Thessalonians 5:16 NCV

Dear Jesus,

Would You show me how to be more thankful? I'm learning that being thankful not only brightens my day, but it also opens up my heart to You more and more. I want to enjoy Your Presence with me in the middle of every situation I face. So I'm going to be on the lookout for signs of Your Presence as I walk along *the path of life* with You.

A thankful attitude opens both my heart and my eyes. Then I can see You in the tiniest details of my life as well as in the big things. Help me slow down and see all Your blessings. I want to be sure to thank You for the many gifts You give me. There are so many, I can't count them all!

Please teach me to trust You more too. A strong, solid faith helps me walk through even my toughest times without stumbling. The more difficult my day is, the more I need to tell You: "Lord, *I trust in Your faithful Love*." This short prayer reminds me that You're with me, You're taking care of me, and You love me forever!

Jesus, You're the One I can trust completely. You're also the One who gives me so many blessings to be thankful for. And those are two reasons I can *always be joyful*!

In Your great Name, Jesus, *Amen*

READ ON YOUR OWN

1 THESSALONIANS 5:16–18 NCV; COLOSSIANS 4:2;
PSALM 16:11 NIV; PSALM 52:8 HCSB

HOLD ON TO THANKFULNESS

But we thank God! He gives us the victory
through our Lord Jesus Christ.
—1 Corinthians 15:57

Dear Jesus,

Please fill my mind with thankful thoughts—and then help me spend time thinking about those thoughts without being in a hurry. Sitting with You when my heart is full of gratefulness is the most wonderful place to be. The joy of Your Presence shines on me and warms me, inside and out.

A lot of times I pray so hard for something, hoping I'll get what I want. If You give me what I've asked for, I'll take a minute to praise and thank You. But then I usually move on to asking for the next thing I want—forgetting about what You've just given me. I'm sorry for that, God. Instead of always asking for more things, I want to hold on to an attitude of thankful joy. I need to think about how You've just answered my prayer . . . and keep thinking about it today and tomorrow—and even for days after that! One way is to tell others about the blessing You've given me. Another way is to write Your answer in a journal or diary. Then I'll always be able to look back and see how You've taken care of me.

Lord, teach me to remember *the wonderful things You have done* and to be thankful for them. Being grateful blesses me twice: once when I joyfully thank You and then again when I think back over my memories of how You answered my prayers.

In Your joyful Name, Jesus, *Amen*

READ ON YOUR OWN

PSALM 95:2; 1 CORINTHIANS 15:57; 1 CHRONICLES 16:12

TRUSTING AND THANKING

Always be willing to listen.

—James 1:19

Dear Jesus,

I want to live close to You so I can see everything You'd like to show me. I pray that You'll open my heart, mind, and spirit to Your Love and Presence. I don't want to miss anything that You have waiting for me!

Please help me stay aware of You as I follow my path through this day. It helps to know that You're with me every moment, at each and every step. And You aren't just *with* me. You're watching over me. That fact gives me so much comfort! I want to be alert and listen carefully to You and to the people You bring into my life. I'm learning that paying close attention to others and listening to everything they say blesses them *and* me. I'm also learning that I can listen the best when I pray and ask Your Holy Spirit to help me.

The Bible tells me over and over again that I need to trust You and thank You—no matter what's happening in my life. Trusting You and believing Your promises helps me stand strong and steady in this world. I'm thankful that You understand my weakness, and You *help my weak faith to grow stronger.*

You've been teaching me how important it is to thank You all through the day. A thankful heart blesses me by filling me with joy and keeping me close to You!

In Your caring Name, Jesus, *Amen*

READ ON YOUR OWN

REVELATION 1:18; JAMES 1:19; MARK 9:24 NLT; PSALM 28:7

ONE HUNDRED PERCENT GOOD

Jesus answered, "I tell you the truth. Before Abraham was born, I am!"
—John 8:58

Dear Jesus,

I want to take time to think about all the different blessings You give me. So I'm stopping right now to say: *"Thank You, Lord, because You are good. Your Love continues forever."* Thank You for the gift of life—every breath I breathe is a blessing from You. I'm also thankful for Your everyday blessings, like food and water, a home, clothes, and people who love me. But the greatest gift of all is the one You give me because I trust You as my Savior. That gift is Life forever with You!

As I think about how much You do for me, I find joy in knowing who You are—the great *I Am!* You are one hundred percent good. There isn't even a tiny speck of darkness in You. You are *the Light of the world.* And Your Love never ends—it goes on and on forever!

Because I belong to You, I know that I'm never separated from Your Love and Presence. But sometimes I *feel* like I'm far away from You, Jesus. Instead of thinking too much about those feelings and worrying about *if* You are near, help me simply trust that You *are* right here with me. Thank You for Your faithful Presence and for *Your Love that never fails.*

In Your blessed Name, Jesus, *Amen*

READ ON YOUR OWN

PSALM 107:1; JOHN 8:58; JOHN 8:12; PSALM 107:8

TAKING THE STING OUT OF TROUBLES

In your name they rejoice all the time.
They praise your goodness.
—Psalm 89:16

Dear Jesus,

Troubles are no fun—they can hurt like the sting of a bee. But You are teaching me that thankfulness can take the "sting" out of my troubles. In fact, the Bible tells me to *give thanks for everything*. It sounds a little crazy to me, especially when I'm feeling really upset about something. But I'm learning that when I give You thanks no matter how I'm feeling, then You give me joy. Even in the tough times.

It's kind of like a trade, though it doesn't really make sense to me. It's such a mystery that I can't even begin to understand how it works. But when I obey You by thanking You in the middle of my hardest times, I am blessed—even if I still have my problems.

Being thankful opens up my heart to Your Presence and opens up my mind to Your thoughts. I may still be in the same place, facing all the same old problems, but it's like a light has been switched on in a dark room. I begin to see things the way You see them. *The Light of Your Presence* helps me see more clearly—and it takes the sting out of my troubles. Help me, Lord, to *live in the Light* with You more and more!

In Your bright and shining Name, Jesus, *Amen*

READ ON YOUR OWN

EPHESIANS 5:20; PSALM 118:1; PSALM 89:15–16

357

THE ONLY REAL AND TRUE GOD

"Don't worship any other god. . . . [I] am a jealous God."
—Exodus 34:14

Dear Jesus,

Help me to worship *only* You! I want You to be more important than anything else in my life. The Bible says that You are *a jealous God*. You are the *only* real and true God. Your Word also teaches that worshiping other, fake gods has always been a big problem for Your people.

Those fake gods—those idols—can be all sorts of things. They can be other people, like the ones I see on my favorite TV shows or a kid at school who's really good at sports. An idol can be money, nice clothes, being popular, or anything that becomes more important than You, Jesus. I don't want to worship any of those things, so I need to *be careful and control myself*.

You've been helping me to see that these fake gods will never make me happy. They just make me want more and more. When I search for You, I find something that is *so* much better: Your *Joy and Peace*. I can't see or touch these gifts, but they're more precious than gold—they're priceless! That's because they fill up the empty places in my heart and soul.

The shiny things of this world don't last, but the Light of Your Presence goes on shining forever. It can't be turned off, no matter how hard people try. I want to walk through my whole life *in that Light* with You. Help me to shine with Your Light so others will want to find You too!

In Your priceless Name, Jesus, *Amen*

READ ON YOUR OWN

EXODUS 34:14; 1 PETER 5:8; ROMANS 15:13; 1 JOHN 1:7

I'M BLESSED TO NEED YOU

Search for the LORD and for his strength;
continually seek him.
—1 Chronicles 16:11 NLT

Dear Jesus,

This day of life is a precious gift from You, and I thank You for it. Please guide me to treat it as a great treasure by *searching for You* in every moment. As I look out at my day, I ask You to show me what's most important. I'm trusting You to help me make good choices about how to use my time and energy. Then, when I get to the end of the day, I can have peace about the things I have done—and also peace about the things I have *not* done.

I'm learning that even the quickest little prayer invites You into whatever I'm doing. Just saying Your Name can be a way of telling You that I love You, Jesus. And praying about everything reminds me that I *need* You all the time—every second of every day. I'm even learning to be happy about needing You, because that need is like a super-strong chain that connects me to *Your glorious Presence.*

This world likes to say that I shouldn't need anyone, but I'm discovering that needing *You* is the best way to live. I find so much joy and peace in the way You always take care of me. Thank You, Lord, for *Your Love that never fails* and never ends!

In Your wonderful Name, Jesus, *Amen*

READ ON YOUR OWN

PSALM 118:24; 1 CHRONICLES 16:10–11 NLT;
JUDE 24 NLT; PSALM 33:22 NLT

DECEMBER

The angel said to them, "Don't be afraid, because I am bringing you some good news. It will be a joy to all the people."

—Luke 2:10

WHAT THE SHEPHERDS SAW

That night, some shepherds were in the
fields nearby watching their sheep.
—Luke 2:8

Dear Jesus,

Christmas is coming, Lord, and I want to be ready. Please prepare my heart for this celebration of Your birth and the miracle of Your life here on earth. You are *the Word*—You are God—and You *became a human and lived among us*. You left heaven and made Your home on this planet, just like I do! You are the Gift that's greater than any other gift, and when I really think about it, I'm *full of joy* because of You.

At this time of year though, I hear the Bible's Christmas story so often that it's easy to forget what a miracle it is. A wonderful way to open up my heart to You is to think about the night when You were born. I like to imagine what the *shepherds* saw when they *were out in the fields* near Bethlehem, *watching over their sheep that night*. First, one angel appeared, and then *a very large group of angels from heaven* lit up the sky. *All the angels were praising God, saying: "Give glory to God in heaven, and on earth let there be peace to the people who please God."*

Help me to spend time thinking about the glory of Your birth, seeing it just as those shepherds did. And help me to worship You in wonder!

In Your marvelous Name, Jesus, *Amen*

READ ON YOUR OWN

MARK 1:3; JOHN 1:14 NCV; PHILIPPIANS 4:4; LUKE 2:8, 13–14

YOUR PRESENCE IS IN THE PRESENT

God our Savior helps us.
—Psalm 68:19

Dear Jesus,

I'm trying so hard to keep my eyes on You, but waves of trouble are washing over me like those giant waves at the ocean. I'm tempted to give up, Lord. These troubles keep taking up more and more of my time and attention. I'm afraid that, after a while, I won't be able to see You at all! Then, just in time, You remind me of Your promises: *You are always with me. You are holding my hand.* You know everything that's happening, and *You will not let me be tempted more than I can stand.*

In all of this, You're teaching me that worrying about tomorrow is *not* what You want me to do. But I admit that this is exactly what I've been doing. I've been trying to carry tomorrow's troubles today—and that load of problems is just too heavy for me! If I keep going like this, I'll end up falling flat on my face. I'm so thankful that You are *God my Savior who helps me.* You carry my heavy loads for me. All I have to do is give them to You.

Help me to live in *today*, not tomorrow—paying attention to Your Presence in the present moment. Please keep reminding me that *the present* is where I can walk close to You. I can lean on Your strength and trust You to guide me—today and every day.

In Your strong, guiding Name, Jesus, *Amen*

READ ON YOUR OWN

PSALM 73:23; 1 CORINTHIANS 10:13; PSALM 68:19; HEBREWS 3:13

363

SORT OUT MY THOUGHTS

Guide me in your truth.
Teach me, my God, my Savior.
I trust you all day long.
—Psalm 25:5

Dear Jesus,

I don't want to be weighed down by all the things I have to do. There are so many chores waiting for me—I don't even know where to begin. Maybe not right now, but *sometime* very soon, I need to clean my room and empty the dishwasher and take out the trash. And I promised that I would help decorate for Christmas this weekend.

No matter when all these things need to get done, they're taking up a lot of room in my brain. And this list of chores doesn't even count my homework and my practices! Lord, please help me figure out what I should do *today*. Then I can let the rest of the things on my list slip out of my thoughts until tomorrow—when You'll help me decide *again* what I need to do. Without all these extra thoughts clogging up my mind, it should be easier for me to keep *You* in the center of my thoughts.

That's my biggest and best goal, Jesus: to live close to You and be ready to do whatever You ask. It's easiest to talk to You and to know Your will when my mind isn't filled up with a bunch of other things. As I look to You and *seek Your Face* today, I ask that You open my heart to Your Presence. Please sort out my thoughts and fill me with Your Peace.

In Your saving Name, Jesus, *Amen*

READ ON YOUR OWN

PROVERBS 16:3; PSALM 25:5; PSALM 27:8 NKJV; ISAIAH 26:3

A WIDE-OPEN HEART

You keep your loving promise.
You lead the people you have saved.
—Exodus 15:13

Dear Jesus,

I get so much joy out of hearing You say to me, *"I love you with a Love that will last forever."* Honestly, I don't really understand that kind of love. That's because my mind and thoughts are so human. My feelings change again and again as I go through the ups and downs of my day. It's even easy for me to let my feelings about *You* change sometimes too. And then I miss out on the blessings of *Your Love and kindness.*

Please teach me to look past what's happening right now and keep my eyes on You instead. Help me to "see" the wonderful way You look at me: You always look at me with so much Love in Your heart. Knowing that You're with me every day—caring for me that much—gives me strength. *And* it helps me accept Your Love like a great big hug and then give my love back to You.

Thank You that You never change, Jesus. *You are the same yesterday, today, and forever.* I want my heart to be wide open to You—with Your Love pouring into me every minute of my life. My need for You is endless, Lord. I'm so grateful that Your Love for me is endless too!

In Your always-loving Name, Jesus, *Amen*

READ ON YOUR OWN

JEREMIAH 31:3; EXODUS 15:13; HEBREWS 13:8

THE RICHES OF YOUR JOY

Jesus Christ is the same yesterday, today, and forever.
—Hebrews 13:8

Dear Jesus,

You are *the Joy that no can take away from me.* As I rest in Your Presence, I get to experience all the wonders of this gift. You and Your Joy are mine forever!

That word "forever" is a big deal to me. There are lots of things in this world that make me happy for a little while, but none of them lasts as long as forever. I'm grateful that *You,* Jesus, are my never-ending Joy and my priceless Treasure. Everything else changes, but You never change—You're *the same yesterday, today, and forever.*

Whenever I feel like I've lost my joy, I know the problem isn't You . . . it's me. You never stop offering me Your Joy—I'm just not receiving it. Sometimes it's because I get caught up in other things: I'm thinking too much about the problems in my life right now. Or I'm looking too far ahead at the exciting plans in my future. I forget to spend time with You and talk to You. Help me remember to put You first every day.

I want to *love You like I did when I first started loving You.* Please keep reminding me that You're always close beside me, Lord. And when I *find my delight in You,* that's when I'm *really* able to receive all the wonders of Your Joy!

In Your joyful Name, Jesus, *Amen*

READ ON YOUR OWN

JOHN 16:22; HEBREWS 13:8; REVELATION 2:4 NIRV; PSALM 37:4 NIRV

LIGHT FROM HEAVEN

Because of God's tender mercy,
the morning light from heaven is about to break upon us,
to give light to those who sit in darkness.

—Luke 1:78–79 NLT

Dear Jesus,

You are *the Light from heaven* that shines on us. *You give Light to those who sit in darkness.* Sometimes I get into situations that are so hard and so confusing that I feel like there's darkness all around me. My mind comes up with all these different ways to get rid of the problems. But when none of my ideas seem to work, I get upset and wonder what to do next. Anytime I'm feeling powerless and frustrated, I need to look up and see Your Light shining on me. As soon as I remember that You're with me, I can find hope and rest in Your Presence.

The Bible teaches me to *be still and know that You are God.* Please help me to stop trying so hard to fix everything by myself. I need to relax with You and remember that You are *the Prince of Peace.* While I'm resting in Your Presence, I sometimes like to spend a few minutes taking deep breaths—breathing in Your Peace and breathing out my worries. This comforts me and helps me relax even more. The longer I sit quietly with You, the calmer I become. After a while, I'm ready *to tell You all my problems.*

Lord, I trust You to show me the way I should go. Please *guide me to the path of peace.*

In Your worthy Name, Jesus, *Amen*

READ ON YOUR OWN

LUKE 1:78–79 NLT; PSALM 46:10; ISAIAH 9:6; PSALM 62:8

A HOLY WHISPER

"The Father gives me the people who are mine. Every one of them will come to me, and I will always accept them."
—John 6:37

Dear Jesus,

When my mind and heart are quiet, I can hear You inviting me to come closer. I love this precious invitation from You. It's like I'm hearing a holy whisper: *"Come to Me. Come to Me. Come to Me."* Coming closer to You isn't a hard thing for me to do. It's not like work at all. It's more like opening my heart and my hands to You—letting go of fear and worries, letting them drift away like helium-filled balloons. As my worries float away, I can feel Your Love pulling me close to You, Lord.

Please help me, through *Your Holy Spirit,* to really open up my heart to Your Love and Presence. I want to *be filled with more and more of You.* Please give me *the power to understand how wide and how long and how high and how deep Your Love is,* Jesus. I want to feel this love that's so much *greater than I can understand.* Your Love is like the biggest, most beautiful ocean: it's too huge to be measured or explained. But I can know what it's like to have that kind of love in my life—because that's how You love me!

In Your amazing Name, Jesus, *Amen*

READ ON YOUR OWN

JAMES 4:8 NLT; MATTHEW 11:28; JOHN 6:37; EPHESIANS 3:16–19

YOU SHINE THROUGH THE DARKNESS

Before the world was made, God decided to make us his own children through Jesus Christ.

—Ephesians 1:5

Dear Jesus,

You are the Light of the world. And Advent is the time that we celebrate Your coming into this world as a baby. One way I like to celebrate Your birth is by looking at the lights on a Christmas tree. Those lights remind me to think about why You came into this world, Jesus. You are the Light that shines forever—breaking through the darkness and opening up the way to heaven for everyone who loves You.

Thank You, Lord, that nothing can change Your plan to save Your people. You promise that everyone who trusts You to be their Savior is adopted into Your royal family. We will live with You forever!

The Bible says that *Your Light shines in the darkness. And the darkness has not overpowered the Light*—Your Light is *so* much more powerful than the darkness! No matter how much evil there is in this world, and no matter how many people refuse to believe in You, Your Light still shines brightly. That's why I need to *keep my eyes on You*, Jesus. You give me the help and hope I need. Please teach me to keep thinking about You, no matter what's happening in my life. You comfort me with this wonderful promise: *"The person who follows me will never live in darkness. He will have the Light that gives Life."*

In Your shining Name, Jesus, *Amen*

READ ON YOUR OWN

JOHN 8:12; EPHESIANS 1:5; JOHN 1:5; HEBREWS 12:2 NLT

WATCHING WHAT I THINK

I praise you because you made me in an amazing and wonderful way.

—Psalm 139:14

Dear Jesus,

The Bible tells me that *You made me in an amazing and wonderful way.* One of those amazing, wonderful ways is that You've built my brain so that I can think about my own thoughts. So it's possible for me to "watch" the thoughts that run through my mind—almost as if they're on TV—and choose the thoughts I want to keep thinking about.

I'm learning that worry often comes from thinking about things at the wrong time. If I think about my problems when I'm lying in my bed, it's easy for me to start worrying. But when I'm careful about watching my thoughts, I can stop them as soon as they slip into my mind, *before* I start worrying.

Teach me how to train my mind to focus more on worshiping You and less on worrying. And please alert me when I'm paying attention to something at the wrong time—like thinking about a problem at a time when I can't do anything about it. Help me steer my thoughts *away* from that worry and steer them *toward* You, Jesus.

I feel happy when I pray verses from the Psalms back to You—worshiping You by telling You that I love You and I trust You. Some of my favorite verses are: "*I love You, Lord. You are my Strength. I trust You, Lord. You are my God.*" I feel a lot closer to You when I worship You like this.

In Your powerful Name, Jesus, *Amen*

READ ON YOUR OWN

PSALM 139:14; LUKE 12:22, 25–26; PSALM 18:1; PSALM 31:14

THE ONE THING

"Don't store treasures for yourselves here on earth."
—Matthew 6:19

Dear Jesus,

You are my Treasure! You're so much more valuable than anything I could ever see, hear, or touch in this world. *Knowing You* is *the Prize* that is greater than every other prize. Even winning a gold medal in the Olympics can't be compared with this awesome gift!

The treasures of this earth are often locked away in banks or hidden away to keep them safe from thieves. But the riches I have in You can never be lost or stolen. Your riches are things like love, peace, and joy. And I'm learning that the more I share these treasures with others, the more of them You put into my heart.

In this busy world, I often feel like I'm being pulled in ten different directions—all at the same time! My family wants this, friends say that, homework needs doing, the dog needs walking—so many things are demanding my attention. If I'm not careful, all that busyness can get in the way of spending time with You. I admit that, like Martha in the Bible, I do *get worried and upset about too many things.* But You've said that *only one thing is important.* When I make You that *one thing,* I choose *the right thing, and it will never be taken away from me.*

Jesus, You are the Treasure that can make all my moments shine!

In Your priceless Name, Jesus, *Amen*

READ ON YOUR OWN

PHILIPPIANS 3:14; MATTHEW 6:19; LUKE 10:41–42

371

EVERYTHING THAT COMES MY WAY

"Remain in me, and I will remain in you."
—John 15:4

Dear Jesus,

You make me powerful by *giving me Your strength*. With Your help I can handle anything that comes my way—all because I'm connected to You like a branch is connected to a tree. When I depend on You like that, You promise to give me the strength I need. As I keep my attention on You, Jesus, You strengthen me at just the right time. Your promise is a powerful weapon against my fear. Especially my fear of possible problems that might be lurking out there in the future. No matter how dark, or difficult, or scary things may look, I can trust You to make sure I'm ready for anything that You bring into my life.

Lord, I'm thankful for how carefully You control everything that happens to me. You constantly protect me from dangers. Some of them I know about, but many I don't. You're also helping me see that a lot of the future things I worry about will never actually happen. And when tough times come, I can trust that You'll be right there to guide me through the trouble—giving me everything I need. So the next time worry attacks, the smart thing for me to do is to pray to You and remind myself: *"I can do everything through Christ, who gives me strength."*

In Your strong Name, Jesus, *Amen*

READ ON YOUR OWN

PHILIPPIANS 4:13 NLT; JOHN 15:4; MATTHEW 6:34

WHO YOU MADE ME TO BE

You saw my bones being formed
as I took shape in my mother's body.
—Psalm 139:15–16

Dear Jesus,

You created me to live a life that's connected to You. I'm glad that living this way doesn't mean I have to stop being myself. In fact, being connected to You is what makes me *more* like myself! Living so close to You helps me become the person You meant for me to be when You created me.

On those days when I wander away from You, even for a little while, I've noticed that I start to feel empty and unhappy inside. But when I *walk in the Light of Your Presence*, You bless me with the greatest joy ever! My heart overflows with so much happiness that I can't help praising You—celebrating *Your goodness*!

Help me find more and more joy in living this close to You, Jesus. And teach me to want the things You want. Sometimes it feels like You're leading me to strange places and situations. That's when I need to hold even tighter to Your hand and trust that You know what You're doing. When I follow You, trusting You with all my heart, I learn that I can do things I never thought I could do!

Lord, You know me inside and out—much better than I know myself. And You always do what's best for me. I'm happy that living close to You is changing me more and more into the person You created me to be.

In Your beautiful Name, Jesus, *Amen*

READ ON YOUR OWN

PSALM 89:15–16; PSALM 139:15–16; 2 CORINTHIANS 3:18

EVEN IN THE NOISIEST PLACES

"You will call my name. You will come to me and
pray to me. And I will listen to you."
—Jeremiah 29:12

Dear Jesus,

I love to hear You whisper this promise again and again: *"I am with you. I am with you. I am with you."* It's sad that some people never hear Your whispers. Their thoughts get too filled up with the things of this world, and their hearts are closed to You. Other people may hear You only once or twice in their whole lives. That's because they hardly ever *search for You with their whole heart*. But I know that You are the *Good Shepherd* who is always near, constantly watching over me. And I want to be a sheep who is always paying attention to You, *listening to Your voice*.

Anytime I want to hear Your voice, I need to find a quiet place where I can spend time focusing on You—a place where I won't be pulled away by other voices. That quiet place is my "classroom." That's where I'm learning to hear You better, Lord. Someday, with lots of practice and with Your help, I'll know how to carry that quiet place in my heart. Then I can take it with me wherever I go, even into the noisiest places.

Even though I'm still new at listening to You, I can sometimes hear You whisper Your promise as I walk through my noisy day: "I am with you. I am with you. I am with you."

In Your wonderful Name, Jesus, *Amen*

READ ON YOUR OWN

ISAIAH 41:10; JEREMIAH 29:12–13; JOHN 10:14, 27–28

YOUR AMAZING LOVE

I go to bed and sleep in peace.
Lord, only you keep me safe.
—Psalm 4:8

Dear Jesus,

It is good to tell of Your Love in the morning and Your faithfulness at night.

As I praise You for the wonders of Your loving Presence in my life, You give me strength. You encourage me to keep trying to do what's good and what's right. And when I praise You out loud, You pour even more blessings into me! As I'm thanking and praising You for Your Love, please fill me with joy from head to toe. The Bible tells me You *fill me with a joy that cannot be explained—a joy that is full of glory.*

Because of Your amazing Love, You gave up everything to save me. Your Love will never fail. It's priceless and has no limits—*it reaches to the heavens.* It shines so brightly that it can get me through even my toughest days.

When I lie down to sleep at night, I like to look back over my day and see how carefully You guided me. I can see how You opened up the way for me. The more troubles I ran into, the more help and strength You gave me. Thank You for giving me everything I need to get through each day.

It's good to praise You for Your faithful help, especially at night. Then *I can go to bed and sleep in peace.*

In Your peaceful Name, Jesus, *Amen*

READ ON YOUR OWN

PSALM 92:1–2 NIV; 1 PETER 1:8; PSALM 36:5; PSALM 4:8

THE MOST WONDERFUL TREASURE!

God . . . made the world through the Son.
—Hebrews 1:2

Dear Jesus,

Before the world began, there was the Word. That was *You,* Jesus. *The Word was with God, and the Word was God.* That means You have always been, and You will always be. You have no beginning and no end. As I celebrate Your birth this Christmas, help me remember that You are God.

The Bible also says You are *the Word that became a man and lived with us.* You are the Savior, who is God Almighty! If You were only a man, Your life and death would not have been enough to save me from my sins. But because You are also God, You have the power to save me. What a great truth to celebrate! It's so amazing that You—the One who was born into the world as a helpless baby—are the very same One who created this whole world!

Even though You were rich, You became poor to help me. You became poor so that I could become rich. No Christmas present in the whole world could ever be as wonderful as the treasure I have in You, Jesus. Because of You, my sins can be *taken away as far as the east is from the west.* You have given me glorious Life that will never end—which is so much better than anything I could ever imagine! Thank You, Lord, for this awesome gift!

In Your amazing Name, Jesus, *Amen*

READ ON YOUR OWN

JOHN 1:1, 14; HEBREWS 1:2; 2 CORINTHIANS 8:9 NLT; PSALM 103:12

YOU KNOW WHAT YOU'RE DOING

Be strong and brave and wait for the Lord's help.
—Psalm 27:14

Dear Jesus,

I need You so much, Lord. And I'm asking You to light up my life with Your Love. I know I shouldn't whine or misbehave when things get difficult. Instead, I want to be able to thank You during my tough times. So I'm coming to You and asking You to give me courage and strength to get through the hard times. You've promised to take care of me and help me do what I need to do. I'm counting on You, Jesus!

I really want to stay close to You and feel Your Peace, but my attention keeps getting pulled away. I wonder whether I can do everything I'm supposed to do today. My mind starts rehearsing all the things I need to do—going over and over the same things in my thoughts. It's almost like I'm practicing for a part in a play. Help me instead to keep my mind on You as You show me the next step to take. The tougher my day is, the more I need to lean on You and trust You to make me strong.

Teach me to see this difficult time as a blessing. Tough times wake me up and remind me that I can't do everything on my own. I need You, Jesus! I want to be ready to follow where You lead me—trusting that You know what You're doing. Thank You for Your wonderful promise to *give me strength and bless me with Your Peace*.

In Your powerful Name, Jesus, *Amen*

READ ON YOUR OWN

EPHESIANS 5:20; DEUTERONOMY 33:25; PSALM 27:14; PSALM 29:11

MY WORDS MATTER

My heart has heard you say, "Come and talk with me."
And my heart responds, "LORD, I am coming."
—Psalm 27:8 NLT

Dear Jesus,

Help me *hold firmly to the hope that I claim to have* and to keep trusting that *You are faithful—You will do what You promise.*

Sometimes all I can do is hold on to You. Especially when lots of things are going wrong at the same time. I wish I could figure out the answers to my problems by myself, but that's often impossible. When I don't know what to do, what I really need is to *come and talk with You* and *tell You that You are my hope.* That means trusting You and believing that You're the answer to everything.

I'm learning that my words matter a lot—not just to the people around me but also to me. I've noticed that when I whine and complain, I start to feel worse and worse. And the people who hear me complaining get discouraged too. But when I keep on saying that I trust You, I begin to feel more confident, trusting that You'll show me what to do about my problems.

I can be full of hope because I know You keep Your promises. And one of my favorite promises is that *You will not let me be tempted more than I can stand.* You'll give me *a way to escape.* Sometimes that escape comes through my own words of faith. Words like, "I trust You, Jesus. You are my hope." Using my words this way helps me keep holding on to You. Help me, Lord, to never let go of You!

In Your hope-filled Name, Jesus, *Amen*

READ ON YOUR OWN

HEBREWS 10:23 NIRV; PSALM 27:7–8 NLT; 1 CORINTHIANS 10:13

YOU ARE THE LORD OF PEACE

We pray that the Lord of peace will give you peace at all times and in every way. May the Lord be with all of you.
—2 Thessalonians 3:16

Dear Jesus,

Sometimes I wish I could understand everything. But You've been teaching me that even if I could read all the books in the world, I'd still never find peace. The only way to have peace is *to trust You with all my heart instead of depending on my own understanding.*

But that's not so easy for me to do! I love figuring things out. It makes me feel like I'm in control of my life. The trouble is, this world keeps throwing problems at me—like one of those machines that keeps shooting out tennis balls. As soon as I figure out one problem, another one comes flying at me. Soon my mind is racing again, trying to figure out the answer to this new problem. But what I really need to be doing is looking for *You*, the One who understands everything and is always in control. Please forgive me, Lord. Help me *search for You with all my heart—and find You.*

I'm thankful that Your Peace is really *not* hard to find. And neither are You! Because I belong to You, You wrap me up in the blanket of peace that comes from living close to You. I'm so thankful that I always have You with me, Jesus. And the more I trust You, the more of Your precious Peace You give me!

In Your perfect Name, Jesus, *Amen*

READ ON YOUR OWN

PROVERBS 3:5; JEREMIAH 29:13; ROMANS 5:1; 2 THESSALONIANS 3:16

WITH YOUR HELP

He makes me like a deer, which does not stumble.
He leads me safely on the steep mountains.
—Habakkuk 3:19

Dear Jesus,

I love walking with You! I'm learning, though, that the path we're following goes up sometimes and drops down at other times. If I look into the distance, it seems like I can almost see heaven shining up ahead in the sunlight. But I know that, for now, my job is to *follow You* and trust You to guide my steps here on earth. While we're walking, I'll keep thinking about heaven, and I'll try to stay close to You, Jesus.

One of the hardest times for me to trust You is when lots of things go wrong. If my day gets all mixed up and messed up, I start feeling really stressed-out. But You've been showing me that problems are actually good for me. I've noticed that every time I trust You to see me through the hard times, You're waiting there with blessings that are *much greater than the troubles*! As I walk along my path, holding on to Your hand, I also hold on to the truth that You have carefully and lovingly planned every step of the way.

When the path goes up steep and rocky hills, please keep my faith strong. Help me hold tight to Your hand and breathe deeply, knowing that I'm safe in Your Presence. If I listen carefully, sometimes I hear Your comforting words: "Don't be afraid. With My help, you can do it!"

In Your comforting Name, Jesus, *Amen*

READ ON YOUR OWN

JOHN 21:22; 2 CORINTHIANS 4:17; HABAKKUK 3:19

NEW STRENGTH

They will soar high on wings like eagles.
They will run and not grow weary.
They will walk and not faint.
—Isaiah 40:31 NLT

Dear Jesus,

The Bible promises that *those who trust in You will find new strength.* I love spending time with You and just sitting in Your Presence. In this world, people stay so busy. And during the Christmas season, there are even *more* things to do than usual: special school and church activities, shopping for gifts, baking, decorating the house, traveling to visit family. In this busy, busy time, please help me remember to make time for You. That way, as I *seek You* and talk with You and enjoy Your Presence, I won't forget that Christmas is really all about *You*, Jesus.

Spending time with You and waiting for You to answer my prayers shows that my faith in You is real. It means I'm trusting that prayer really does make a difference. So I *come to You—tired and carrying a heavy load.* As I rest in Your Presence and tell you all my troubles, You lift the heavy load off my shoulders. I'm grateful that *You can do much, much more than anything I could ask or imagine.*

I love hearing You whisper, "I am with you," during our quiet times together. And I praise You for the way You give me *new strength* whenever I spend time with You. Thank You, Lord!

In Your strong Name, Jesus, *Amen*

READ ON YOUR OWN

ISAIAH 40:31 NLT; PSALM 105:4 NLT;
MATTHEW 11:28; EPHESIANS 3:20 NCV

381

LITTLE TASTES OF HEAVEN

He gave up his place with God and made himself nothing.
He was born as a man and became like a servant.

—Philippians 2:7

Dear Jesus,

When I sit in Your Presence, *You shine Your Light into my heart, letting me know a little of Your Glory.* Even that little bit is too great for me to understand, but it changes me in lots of ways. My mind works better, my heart feels cleaner, and my body feels stronger. Please help me open myself up even more to the glory of Your wonderful Presence!

I can't imagine how much You gave up when You left heaven and came to earth as a helpless baby. No other king would ever give up his castle! But You did that so You could understand what it's like to be human—what it's like to be *me*. Jesus, *You became poor to help me, so that I can become rich.* You died on the cross to give me the riches of heaven.

And if that wasn't enough, You chose to be born in a stable with a feeding trough for Your crib, even though You are God. There was nothing glorious or beautiful about that! Still, the angels lit up the skies as they announced "Glory!" to the amazed shepherds who were out in the fields.

Jesus, You left heaven to come to earth. And when I sit with You, I get to experience just a tiny bit of heaven. The closer I get to You, the more You bless me with little tastes of how wonderful heaven will be! Lord, I praise Your holy Name!

In Your holy Name, Jesus, *Amen*

READ ON YOUR OWN

2 CORINTHIANS 4:6; PHILIPPIANS 2:6–7;
LUKE 2:13–14; 2 CORINTHIANS 8:9 NIRV

LIGHT SHINING IN MY HEART

You are all children of the light and of the day;
we don't belong to darkness and night.
—1 Thessalonians 5:5 NLT

Dear Jesus,

You came as Light into the world so that whoever believes in You would not stay in darkness. You didn't just *bring* Light into the world. You *are* the *Light that shines in the darkness. And the darkness has not overpowered the Light.* Nothing can put out Your Light because You are all-powerful!

When I believed in You, Jesus, I became a *child of Light.* Your brightness soaks deep down inside me. It helps me see things the way You see them—things in the world *and* things in my heart. Every time Your Spirit lights up what's inside of me, He shows me what pleases You and what doesn't please You. Help me get rid of the things You don't like, Lord. I really want to do the things that make You smile instead.

I'm thankful for Your Light that fills me with joy and helps me see everything more clearly. *The devil who rules this world has blinded the minds of those who do not believe. They cannot see the light of the Good News—the good news about Your Glory.* But because I belong to You, I have *Your Light shining in my heart*! Thank You, Jesus!

In Your bright Name, Jesus, *Amen*

READ ON YOUR OWN

JOHN 12:46 NCV; JOHN 1:5; 1 THESSALONIANS 5:5; 2 CORINTHIANS 4:4, 6

YOU ARE IMMANUEL

God has said, "I will never leave you; I will never abandon you."
—Hebrews 13:5

Dear Jesus,

You were given the name *Immanuel.* That *means "God is with us"*—and it's a perfect name for You because You are always with me. This incredible promise from the Bible gives me something to be happy about every single day.

Sometimes I try to find my happiness in the things of this world. That's silly, I know—because none of that stuff lasts. Your Presence, though, is a blessing that will go on and on, giving me joy forever. I'm so happy You've promised that *You will never leave me.*

It might sound a little strange, but even on days when everything seems just about perfect, I don't always enjoy my life as much as I could. I think it's because I know things won't *always* be so perfect. Even the very best day—or the very best vacation—has to end. Sometimes I wish I could just "stop the clock" and keep things as they are, but I can't.

Help me remember that Your best blessings are the kind that never end. I know that You also give me gifts of this world—like my friends and clothes and fun things to do. I'm really thankful for these blessings, but they're not the ones I need most. If I want the kind of joy that never goes away, I need to stay close to You, Jesus. Because it's *being with You that fills me with Your forever kind of joy.*

In Your joy-filled Name, Jesus, *Amen*

READ ON YOUR OWN

MATTHEW 1:23; HEBREWS 13:5; PSALM 16:11

LIKE THE WISE MEN

*When the wise men saw the star, they were filled with joy. They
went to the house where the child was and saw him with his
mother, Mary. They bowed down and worshiped the child.*
—Matthew 2:10–11

Dear Jesus,

You are *the King of all kings and the Lord of all lords*. You live in a
Light that's so bright, no one can go near it. I'm happy that You're also my
Shepherd and Friend—the One who never lets go of my hand. I worship
You for how great and glorious You are! And I come close to You, finding
rest in Your loving Presence.

You are both God and Man—the only person who ever lived in this
world without sinning. I really need You, Jesus! Because only Your birth
on that first, long-ago Christmas could save me from my sins.

Instead of trying to understand how You—God—could be born as a
human baby, I want to learn from the wise men in the Bible. They followed
that shining star for a long time. They followed it all the way to *You*. And
then *they bowed down and worshiped You*. Like those wise men, I want to
bow down in worship as I think about the amazing miracle of Your birth!

Please help me grow in my worship of You—learning to praise You more
and more. You are my Savior, my Lord, and my King. You gave *everything*
to take care of me. I praise You for all that You are—and all You have done!

Lord, You are *the Light that shines from heaven and guides me to the
path of peace*.

In Your great and majestic Name, Jesus, *Amen*

READ ON YOUR OWN

1 TIMOTHY 6:15–16; MATTHEW 2:10–11; LUKE 1:78–79 NLT

THE ANGEL'S MESSAGE

The angel said to them, "Do not be afraid. I am bringing you
good news that will be a great joy to all the people."
—Luke 2:10 NCV

Dear Jesus,

When an angel appeared to the *shepherds who were in the fields* near Bethlehem, he told them about Your birth. He said, *"Do not be afraid. I am bringing you good news that will be a great joy to all the people."*

The Bible says "Don't be afraid!" over and over again. Thank You, Jesus, for this comforting command. You know I still get scared. *A lot.* But You don't judge me or punish me for being afraid. Instead, You offer me the joy of Your Presence.

I'm learning that joy is a powerful cure for fear. The bigger and greater the joy is, the more it can push away my fear. The angel's announcement to the shepherds was one of *great* joy! Help me to never forget how amazing the good news of the Christmas story is!

The moment I trusted You as my Savior, You forgave all my sins. Thank You, Jesus, for forgiving my sins from the past, the ones from today, and even the ones I haven't done yet! This priceless gift of grace means that heaven will be my home someday. Until then, I have the gift of Your Presence—the gift of *Yourself*—and that's the greatest present of all! You pour out Your Love on me and promise to be with me forever. As I think about the angel's wonderful message to the shepherds, my heart is *full of joy*—all because of You, my Savior!

In Your wonderful Name, Jesus, *Amen*

READ ON YOUR OWN

LUKE 2:8–10 NCV; EPHESIANS 2:8; PHILIPPIANS 4:4

I'M IN YOU AND YOU'RE IN ME

Christ's love is greater than any person can ever know. But I pray that you will be able to know that love. Then you can be filled with the fullness of God.
—Ephesians 3:19

Dear Jesus,

You tell me in Your Word that *I am in You and You are in me*. This is an amazing mystery to me! I mean, I'm just a kid, and I make a lot of mistakes. But You are the Creator of the universe! You keep the earth spinning and the sun shining and all the stars in the right place—without ever making a single mistake. Yet because I trust in You, Jesus, You and I don't just live *with* each other; we also live *in* each other. The Bible teaches that I'm *filled with Your fullness*. How wonderful it is to learn that I'm filled up with *You*! I can only understand a little bit of this teaching, but it's enough to make me want to dance for joy!

I live and move and exist in You, Lord. This means that every step I take, every word I speak, every breath I breathe—*everything* is done in Your Presence. You're always watching over me, taking care of me. My whole life is soaked in Your invisible but very real Presence! You know everything about me, from my most secret thoughts and feelings to what I had for lunch today. I can't be as close to anyone else as I am to You.

The more I realize that You're with me, the more alive I feel. I never have to be lonely again! Please keep me aware of Your loving Presence as I walk step by step through this day.

In Your loving Name, Jesus, *Amen*

READ ON YOUR OWN

JOHN 14:20; COLOSSIANS 1:27; EPHESIANS 3:19; ACTS 17:28 NLT

CONNECTED TO YOU

"No branch can bear fruit by itself. It must remain joined to the vine. In the same way, you can't bear fruit unless you remain joined to me."

—John 15:4 NIRV

Dear Jesus,

Please help me find joy even on my toughest days. It's hardest for me to be joyful when I'm juggling a bunch of problems all at once. Sometimes I'm still working on one problem when another one shows up. And then another! And another! My mind spins round and round, trying to fix all the problems. I get so tired and confused. *When I have many kinds of troubles,* please remind me that You are with me and You're already working them out. And because You are God, You can even bring good things out of all these troubles.

Anytime I'm struggling with lots of problems, help me to look for *You*—remembering that You are right here with me. I need to stop thinking about all the worry and frustration I'm feeling. Instead, I need to reach out and connect with You in prayer. It's kind of like "unplugging" my thoughts and feelings from my troubles and then "plugging" them into Your Presence. When I do that, my dark mood gets lighter and brighter. And as I *remain joined to You* like this, You help me see my problems the way You see them.

I can be joyful even in the middle of my problems by staying connected—"plugged in"—to You, Lord. *Being with You fills me with joy!*

In Your joyful Name, Jesus, *Amen*

READ ON YOUR OWN

JAMES 1:2–3; ROMANS 11:33; JOHN 15:4 NIRV; PSALM 16:11 NCV

LISTENING TO YOU

*A voice came from the cloud and said, "This is my Son, whom
I love, and I am very pleased with him. Listen to him!"*
—Matthew 17:5 NCV

Dear Jesus,

I love listening to the songs You always sing to me as I read my Bible: *"I
am happy with you. You can rest in My Love. I will sing and be joyful about you."*

The voices of this world sing a very different song—and it doesn't
sound good at all! They tell me so many different things, and many of
them are lies. Help me not to listen to those voices. Teach me how to
fight against the lies with the truth of Your Word. Remind me to step away
from the noise of the world and find a place to be still and quiet with You.
Because it's in the still and quiet places that I can hear Your voice the best.

When I listen to You, I discover all kinds of wonderful treasures! I love
it when You show me something new about Yourself—through Your Word,
or Your people, or the wonders of this world You created. But if I want to
find Your brightest, richest treasures, I have to search for them. The Bible
tells me just how You want me to search for You and Your blessings: *"Keep
on asking, and you will receive what you ask for. Keep on seeking, and you will
find. Keep on knocking, and the door will be opened to you."*

In Your blessed Name, Jesus, *Amen*

READ ON YOUR OWN

ZEPHANIAH 3:17; MATTHEW 17:5 NCV; MATTHEW 7:7 NLT

YOU'RE THINKING ABOUT ME

How precious it is, Lord, to realize that you
are thinking about me constantly!
—Psalm 139:17 TLB

Dear Jesus,

I come to You, feeling tired and worn-out and just wanting to rest in Your Presence. It comforts me *to realize that You are thinking about me constantly*! That's so amazing and wonderful, Lord! Please help me learn to think about *You* more and more. Even when I'm very busy, just remembering You're with me *gives me rest*—rest from worry and fear and stress. Your Peace pours into me as I think about Your promise that *You are with me always.*

I admit that sometimes I get really tangled up in all my problems. I worry about things that are happening now and about future problems that *might* happen sooner or later. If I keep on worrying, my joy goes flat like a tire with a hole in it. All that worry and fear pulls the joy right out of me. When this happens, please remind me to bring those scary thoughts to You. I need to talk to You about each one, ask for Your help, and trust You to guide me. As I spend time talking with You, Jesus, You fill me back up with Your Joy.

Anytime I give my troubles to You, I begin to feel so much better. Instead of feeling tired and worn-out, I start to feel happy and full of energy. I'm learning that one of the best ways to keep Your Joy strong in my life is to sing praises to You—*the King of glory*!

In Your precious Name, Jesus, *Amen*

READ ON YOUR OWN

MATTHEW 11:28; PSALM 139:17 TLB; MATTHEW 28:20; PSALM 24:7 NLT

THE GREATEST COMMANDMENT

*Jesus replied, "'You must love the L*ORD *your God with all your heart, all your soul, and all your mind.' This is the first and greatest commandment."*
—Matthew 22:37–38 NLT

Dear Jesus,

You know my heart—I want to think about You more and more. But that's not always what I do. Too often, I'm thinking about what I need, how I look, what people think of me, and on and on. That's not how I want to be thinking. And I know that's not how You want me to be thinking either! I need Your help to change the things my brain pays the most attention to.

I've noticed that the more I love somebody, the more time I spend thinking about that person. So learning to love *You* completely—*with all my heart, all my soul, and all my mind*—is the best way to get control of my thoughts and stay focused on You. The Bible calls this *the greatest commandment*, and it's the greatest goal I could ever have for my life! The more I learn about Your wonderful Love and how it *never fails* me, the more I'm able to love You, Lord.

Help me open up my heart so I can receive more of Your Love—believing that it's as high and deep and wide and long as You've promised. And teach me how to love You more and more, Jesus. This will *set me free* from my selfishness and give me the power to keep thinking about You—even when I'm really tired or super-busy. Then *I will be truly free*!

In Your amazing Name, Jesus, *Amen*

READ ON YOUR OWN

MATTHEW 22:37–38 NLT; PSALM 52:8 NLT; 1 JOHN 4:19; JOHN 8:36 NLT

BACKWARD AND FORWARD

[Jesus said,] "The person who follows me will never live in darkness. He will have the light that gives life."
—John 8:12

Dear Jesus,

As this year comes to an end, I need to take some time to look backward. And I need to look forward too. Please guide my thoughts as I think back over this last year. Remind me of the good times as well as the hard times. Help me to see the ways You worked in each of these memories. Because I know You've been right beside me every step of the way.

When I was in the middle of my tough times—holding tight to Your hand for help—You comforted me with Your Love and Presence. When things were going well in my life, You were there too, filling me with Your Joy. You were with me on the mountain tops—my happiest times—and in the dark valleys when I was feeling sad. And You were with me every moment in between!

My future stretches out in front of me—all the way to heaven. Jesus, You are my Friend who is always by my side. You're also my Guide who is carefully leading me. You know every step of the way, and You're walking with me step by step. The joy that waits for me in heaven is *a joy that cannot be explained, and it is full of Your Glory*! As I get ready to step into a new year, please shine Your Light on me and light up the path You want me to follow.

In Your glorious Name, Jesus, *Amen*

READ ON YOUR OWN

ISAIAH 41:13; PSALM 48:14; 1 PETER 1:8-9; JOHN 8:12

ABOUT THE AUTHOR

Sarah Young, author of the bestselling 365-day devotionals *Jesus Calling* and *Jesus Always*, has sold more than 35 million books worldwide. *Jesus Calling* has appeared on all major bestseller lists. Sarah's writings include *Jesus Calling*, *Jesus Listens*, *Jesus Always*, *Jesus Today*, *Jesus Lives*, *Dear Jesus*, *Jesus Calling for Little Ones*, *Jesus Calling Bible Storybook*, *Jesus Calling: 365 Devotions for Kids*, *Peace in His Presence*, and more, each encouraging readers in their journeys toward intimacy with Christ. Sarah and her husband were missionaries in Japan and Australia for many years. They currently live in the United States.

CONNECT WITH SARAH AT:

Facebook.com/JesusCalling

Instagram.com/JesusCalling

YouTube.com/jesuscallingbook

Pinterest.com/Jesus_Calling

Twitter.com/Jesus_Calling

IF YOU ENJOYED THIS BOOK, YOU MAY ENJOY THESE DEVOTIONALS BY SARAH YOUNG

Jesus Today Devotions for Kids

Jesus Always: 365 Devotions for Kids

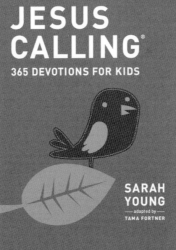

Jesus Calling: 365 Devotions for Kids

You Can Find Peace and Hope in Jesus

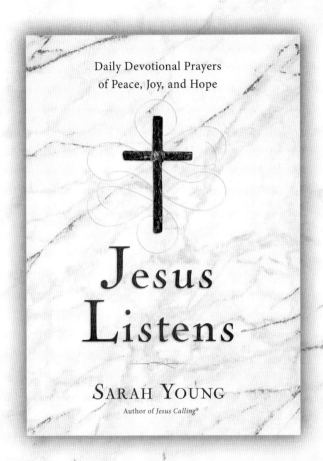

Daily Devotional Prayers
of Peace, Joy, and Hope

Jesus
Listens

SARAH YOUNG
Author of *Jesus Calling®*

In this 365-day devotional prayer book from the author of *Jesus Calling*, you'll find confidence to come to God in all circumstances with short, heartfelt prayers based on Scripture.

OTHER BOOKS FOR KIDS
by Sarah Young

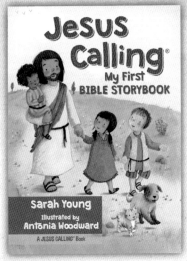

Jesus Calling® My First Bible Storybook

Jesus Calling® for Little Ones

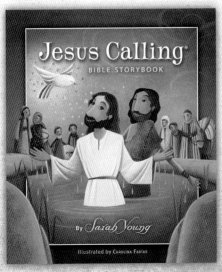

Jesus Calling® Bible Storybook